DAYS OF REVIVAL

being the

History
of
Methodism in Ireland

Vol 2

(1771-1790)

C. H. Crookshank, M.A.

*Author of "A Methodist Pioneer," and "Memorable Women of
Irish Methodism in the Last Century."*

TENTMAKER PUBLICATIONS
1994

TENTMAKER PUBLICATIONS
2 Anne Street, Clonmel, Co. Tipperary, Ireland

ISBN 1 899003 02 9

*

HISTORY OF METHODISM
First Published in 1885
in 3 volumes.

This Edition, retypeset and
published in 6 volumes.
Printed by Genesis Print, Clonmel.

3

CONTENTS

CONTENTS

CHAPTER 17 (1787)

CHAPTER 18 (1788)

CHAPTER 19 (1789)

CHAPTER 20 (1789)

CHAPTER 21 (1790)

CHAPTER 1

1771

AT Glenarm John Smith found an opening to proclaim the glad tidings of salvation, and that under remarkable circumstances. It being deeply impressed on his mind that he should go and preach there, although he knew no one in the town he at once followed what he believed to be the guidance of the Holy Spirit. Near Glenarm he overtook a young lady riding, with her servant, and on entering into conversation with her, she told him that the town was a very wicked one. He enquired if there were any good men there, and she said: "Yes, there is one, William Hunter." The evangelist rode on, enquired for the house of the one pious townsman, and when he reached it, a respectable young woman came to the door. He asked her name, and being told "Betty Hunter," he alighted, and said: "Betty, take in my saddle-bags, take my horse down to the inn, and tell every one you meet that a visitor at your house has good news to tell at seven o'clock." She did so, not knowing why. At the appointed hour the house was well filled; John Smith preached, and did so twice each day for nine days. So deep and general was the interest excited in the services, that even some members of Lord Antrim's family were present, and would allow none to molest the servant of God, saying they believed him to be "an honest and good man." When about to leave, he asked the landlady of the inn how much he was to pay for his horse. "Nothing, sir," she replied; "a gentleman has paid all, and will do so if you stay a month."

On March the 24th Mr. Wesley arrived in Dublin, accompanied by Mr. John Pritchard, a native of Meath, who, through a sermon of Mr. Jaco's in London about five years previously, had found redemption in Christ Jesus. He entered the itinerancy at the Conference this year, and proved to be a most devoted and useful preacher.

Wesley was aware that the Society in the metropolis was in an unsatisfactory state, there having been a continual jar for at least two years, "which had stumbled the people, weakened the hands of the preachers, and greatly hindered the work of God." He therefore determined to enquire fully into the case, and spoke, first to the preachers privately, then to the leaders, and afterwards met and conversed with them all together. The main point in dispute evidently was the authority of the preachers and leaders respectively."

In the Methodist discipline," writes Wesley, "the wheels regularly stand thus: the Assistant, the preachers, the stewards, the leaders, the people. But here the leaders, who are the lowest wheel but one, were quite got out of their place. They were got at the top of all, above the stewards, the preachers; yea, and above the Assistant himself." To this chiefly he ascribed the gradual decay of the work in Dublin, and thought the whole evil might be removed as all parties appeared desirous of peace. He therefore drew up a paper in which he carefully defined the position of the leaders:— they had no right to restrain the Assistant if they thought he acted improperly, but might mildly speak to him, and then refer the matter to Mr. Wesley to be decided. They had no authority to hinder a person from preaching, to displace a leader, to expel a member, to regulate the spiritual affairs of the Society, to make any public collection, or to receive the yearly subscriptions. All this was the work of the Assistant. Neither had the leaders any authority to regulate even the temporal affairs of the Society; this belonged to the Society stewards. The power of the leader consisted simply in authority to meet the members of his class, to receive their contributions, and to visit those that were sick; and the power of all the leaders united was authority to show their class-papers to the Assistant, to deliver the money they had received to the stewards, and to bring in the names of the sick. Such was the constitution of Methodism in 1771, as plainly laid down by its venerated founder. What the result would have been if it had been more liberal, is a question that it is impossible now to decide; but as a matter of fact, there can be no doubt it was not satisfactory to all parties in Dublin, and there were subsequent years of contention.

While Mr. Wesley was in the city he preached at least twice in the new chapel in Gravel walk, where many attended who could not, and some who would not, go to the other side of the city, so that he was fully satisfied that the services there would be for the glory of God. He was also agreeably surprised to find that the congregations in Dublin continued to increase during his visit, instead of gradually declining, after the first three or four days, as on former occasions, which he accepted as a token of good.

On April the 8th he started for the provinces, where on account of the extreme coldness of the weather he was obliged for some time to keep within doors. At Tyrrell's Pass the service was held in the shell of a new chapel: at Mullingar there was "a serious and decent congregation," which seemed completely unconcerned: but at Longford the people were quite of another spirit, and listened with eagerness to every word. For twenty years no place in the kingdom seemed so barren as this, but now the seed so long scattered sprang up, and there was promise of a plentiful harvest. Having preached at Loughan, Athlone and Aughrim, he returned to Athlone where he found the people dwelling at ease, because there was no opposition. In Tullamore also he lamented the want of zeal, the Society being no larger than two years previously.

Birr, Coolalough, where Mr. Pritchard joined him, Mountmellick and Portarlington having been visited, Wesley reached Kilkenny, where the new preaching house, "a neat and commodious building," had just been finished, and before he entered it in the evening it was filled from end to end. At Enniscorthy, there being then no chapel, he took his stand, protected in some measure from a bitter wind by the side of a house, and the people standing close together sheltered one another. Two of the brethren from Wexford having earnestly requested him to go thither, he preached in the market-house to a large and respectable congregation, which was as well conducted as any in the kingdom.

At Waterford he endeavoured to calm the minds of some that had separated from their brethren, but it was labour lost. He also states that on Sunday he went to the cathedral, where a young gentleman most valiantly encountered the "grievous wolves," as he termed the Methodists. Wesley says he "never heard a man strike more wide of the mark. However the shallow discourse did good, for it sent abundance of people, rich and poor, to hear and judge for themselves." This young gentleman was the Rev. George L. Fleury, who two years afterwards was appointed Archdeacon of Waterford. Two years previously, as well as on this occasion, he took advantage of Mr. Wesley's presence in the city to attack Methodism; and the two sermons, which were published anonymously, "were made up of the stale objections and invectives that had been used, by his superiors and seniors, times without number." Mr. Wesley wrote a pointed and pungent reply, which was published in Dublin a short time afterwards, entitled; "A letter to the Rev. Mr. Fleury." It is only justice to the memory of this clergyman to add that he lived to acknowledge his folly. In after years, referring to this controversy, he said, with more candour than elegance: "I was but a novice and a greenhorn then."

At Clonmel Wesley preached in the market-place to a large audience, some of whom seemed inclined to make disturbance, but were kept in awe by the soldiers who were present. At Bandon he laboured to gather those who had been scattered, and to unite all in following after holiness. At Cork, on examining the Society, which was reduced from one hundred and ninety members two years previously to one hundred and seventy, he found many growing in grace, many rejoicing in the perfect love of God, and many more who were earnestly seeking the "mind that was in Christ Jesus." At Kilfinnane there was a large and attentive congregation in the room above the court-house, in which the Church service was held. At Limerick the audiences continued to increase both morning and evening during the fortnight he remained in the city and neighbourhood, and at its close he says he "found no Society in Ireland, member for member, so rooted and ground in love." Having preached at Ballingarrane, and visited Askeaton, after a few days he pushed on through violent wind and rain to Galway. Here the congregations included a large number of soldiers, and not a few townspeople. On the following day the Mayor and several others of influence in the city were present.

At Ballinrobe Wesley preached to about forty or fifty hearers. At Cappivicar every one appeared to be exceedingly serious, and some six-and-twenty seemed resolved to work out their own salvation and help others to do the same. Observing many fashionable people in the court-house at Castlebar, he spoke to them with much closeness and power. At Rahans, "one of the pleasantest seats in the country," he was the guest of Mr. Brown and his kind and amiable family. At Sligo he found a marked improvement in the Society, for he preached to an exceedingly earnest congregation, such as he had not seen there for years: and the prosperity of the work through the circuit was such as rendered necessary the appointment at the ensuing Conference of a third preacher.

At Ballyshannon, where Wesley was acquainted with some of the leading persons in the town, he preached in the assembly room; but these quondam friends were ashamed to own him. At this time Methodism had no existence in the neighbourhood, and the inhabitants in general were exceedingly immoral. At Manorhamilton he preached in a pleasant meadow to a very large congregation; but found little life in the Society. It was, however, very different on the Enniskillen circuit, where he rejoiced greatly at the evident tokens of spiritual prosperity. Thus, at Swanlinbar "the people were full of faith and love, and panting after the whole image of God." At Lisbellaw, where the good man had no intention of preaching, he found a congregation waiting in the streets to hear him, and the sermon was listened to with the deepest attention; and at Sidaire there was a large number who thirsted for the water of life. Having preached at Mrs. Whitley's in Roosky, he came to Augher, where he found the people very cold, presenting a striking contrast not only to what they themselves had been, but also to the earnest Christians whom he had just left. Knowing that few would come to the house, he stood in the open air, and had about forty or fifty hearers, who seemed to be unconcerned enough. A gentleman at Drumquin having requested him to preach there, he began without delay, and it being the fair day, there was a numerous congregation, but not so many as at Magheralough. Amongst those present at the latter service were Mrs. Brown, a respectable widow who lived at Creevy, and her son George, who stood outside the congregation not understanding what was said, yet deeply impressed by the appearance of the venerable preacher. Soon after attending this service the strong prejudices of Mrs. Brown against Methodism having been removed, she invited the preachers to her house, which proved with the Divine blessing a means of much good to herself and family. Her two sons, George and Hugh, were thus led to decide for God and enter heartily into His work.[1] Through the influence of this now godly and zealous woman, Mrs. Margaret Johnstone — a member of the noble family of Annadale — who resided at Lisleen, was brought to religious decision; and no sooner had the Gospel proved to be to her the power of God unto salvation, than she at once opened her house for the worship of God and the entertainment of His servants. From that period her growth in grace was marked and rapid; her path being indeed as "the shining light, that shineth more and more unto the perfect day;" while she herself was truly a "mother in Israel."

Mr. Wesley remained at Londonderry for about a week, preaching to large congregations that included several clergymen, and found much more life in the Society than he had expected. He met the members of a choir that he had formed two years previously — the first there is any record of in Irish Methodism; but as the preachers had not taken care or thought about them, they scattered, "and no wonder," he says, "for nothing will stand in the Methodist plan unless the preacher has his heart and his hand in it. Every preacher therefore should consider it not his business to mind this or that thing only, but everything."

Wesley arrived at Cookstown on Tuesday, June 18th: the house at which he alighted was filled with whisky drinkers, and the whole town was all

---

(1) *Arminian Magazine*, 1784, p. 520.

business and confusion, it being the fair day. However, a tent made by the Society at Terryhoogan, two years previously, was set up; the people flocked from all quarters to attend the service; and, although many of them were far from sober, behaved tolerably well. On Wednesday he preached at five a.m., and at noon to a lifeless company; and then, accompanied by Francis Wrigley and John Smith, rode to Stewartstown, where the service was held in the courthouse, and a large number of people assembled, most of whom listened with attention, though very few of them appeared to understand anything about religion. On Thursday the itinerants went to Castlecaulfield, where Wesley preached on the green before the castle to a numerous and attentive congregation. On Friday at eleven there was a still larger audience in the same place, whom he exhorted to be "not slothful in business," but "fervent in spirit, serving the Lord." In the evening he preached at Armagh in Mr. M'Geough's avenue. The congregation was in an arbour, with the widespread branches of the trees quite overshadowing them.

On Saturday Mr. Wesley rode to Caledon, where two years previously the Rev. C. W. Congreve, Archdeacon of Armagh, had received him with the most cordial affection, and invited him to preach in his new church; but now, his love having grown cold, Mr. Wesley was left to preach in the street to a quiet congregation. On Sunday evening at Armagh such a multitude of people assembled, and were so closely packed, that, though in the open air, the heat was almost unbearable.

On Monday at noon Wesley preached at Blackwatertown, and in the evening at Clonmain, where the congregation was very dull. At Cockhill he found many of the people alive to God. At Grange there was a larger and still more earnest congregation; but the most encouraging Society was at Derryanvil, several of the members of which continued to rejoice in the perfect love of God. At Portadown the people were attentive, and at Kilmoriarty there was the largest audience he had seen during the week. At Tanderagee the people flocked together from all sides, and at the closing service there was "a London congregation, both for number and seriousness." He also preached at Kilwarlin, near Lisburn, where in 1765 an opening had been obtained, and where, a few weeks previously, one of the preachers, Thomas Motte, had died in peace, having travelled only two years.

At Lisburn there was a numerous audience; at Newtownards, the people had not the same spirit as those at Lisburn; and at Belfast Wesley "never saw so large a congregation there before, nor one so remarkably stupid and ill-mannered." Having conducted a service at Carrickfergus, he preached at Larne to a very attentive people; at Glenarm to a large number of respectable hearers; and to a much larger audience at Ballymena. At Ballinderry a great multitude received the word with readiness of mind; the people were earnest and simple-hearted; and the Society consisted of about fifty members. In the house where he dined, the father and mother, with one son and five daughters, were all walking in the light of God's countenance. During his visit a touching incident occurred. As he prayed with an old woman, a little girl, her grandchild, said with tears, "Oh! grandmother, have you no sins to cry for, as well as me?"

Having spent two hours very pleasantly at the Earl of Moira's, Wesley rode on to Drumbanagher, and preached to a serious congregation. That at Newry on each of the two following evenings was much larger, yet all heard and many seemed much affected. At Carlow he discoursed to a numerous and wild assembly, and also endeavoured to remove the differences in the poor shattered Society. Having preached at Baltinglass, and to a "lovely congregation" at Donard, he returned to Dublin on July the 12th, well satisfied with his excursion.

On May the 7th, Mrs. Bennis wrote to Mr. Wesley from Waterford as follows:- "I just now received a satisfactory letter from brother Swindells. He says the Lord has begun a great revival in Dublin, and trusts He will carry it on. O that He would do so here also! Since you left this, brother Christian has preached regularly: his heart seems earnest for the work and the people of God. The day that you left town I met the women's bands: the Lord did wonderfully bless us together, and I find my heart closely united to them."[2] And again on July the 7th, "There has been no material alteration here since my last. Mr. Newall paid one visit to the city and Mr. Bredin three; in the interims brother Christian acts as usual, and I think whilst they have him, they can feel no lack. I have had some opportunities of conversing with him, for which I have reason to be thankful; the cause and people of God are very dear to him, and he loves you as his father. I have heard some object to his opinions, but I think his manner of managing them is such that they do no hurt to him or the people."[3]

On examining the classes in the metropolis, Wesley found that the number

---

(2) *Christian Correspondence*, p. 33.
(3) Ibid., p. 36.

of members had in two years decreased from upwards of five hundred to less than four hundred, but he had hope of an improvement, as offences appeared to be removed, and brotherly love restored.

The Conference assembled in Dublin on July the 18th and 19th, and was "a solemn and useful meeting." The net increase in the number of members during the year was upwards of five hundred. On the evening of the 22nd Wesley embarked for England, having spent nearly four months in this country.

John Smith was again appointed to Enniskillen, with Robert Wilkinson, Richard Whatcoat, and James Perfect. Although the circuit was not nearly so extensive as it had been a few years previously, yet it was still very large, numerous fresh openings having been found. The preachers had to bear many discomforts. The round took them eight weeks; and during this time each slept in nearly fifty different places, some of them damp, and others not very clean. They generally preached two or three times each day, besides meeting the Societies and visiting the sick; and often their only fare was potatoes and a little salt meat. It was, however, most encouraging to those appointed to labour here, to see tokens of continuous and increasing spiritual prosperity in every part of the circuit.

Of those converted to God at Old Cleens, the most noteworthy was Mrs. Blair. One of her sons, Andrew, then a thoughtful, studious young man, was brought to a saving knowledge of God, joined the Society, and became one of its brightest ornaments and most acceptable preachers. His talents were of a high order, his mind was well stored with Scripture truth, and he was greatly beloved. George Dice, who entered the itinerancy in 1780, was converted about this period; and also Gustavus Armstrong, then a lad twelve years of age, and so uniformly upright and consistent was his conduct, that a very shrewd woman, who had known him from infancy, said "Gustavus Armstrong was a saint from his birth." Other young men also were converted, and joined the Society, who became zealous leaders and local preachers. Amongst these were Matthew Dice and George M'Donald, who lived at Old Cleens, and John Maguire, son of the farmer who first received Mr. Dillon at Aughrim. It was a cause of devout thanksgiving that those who were appointed leaders, and the families by whom the preachers were entertained, continued without exception to retain an unabated attachment to Methodism, and to give evidence of growing spiritual life.

The gospel message reached various places in the neighbourhood of

Sidaire. At Currin, Wm. Henderson and his family embraced the truth, a society was formed, and several persons were converted to God.

The most distinguished of those who at this time joined the Society in the circuit, was James M'Donald, then but a boy. More than half a century later he used to refer to this period with holy delight. He possessed a clear apprehension, lively imagination, and great readiness of speech, and was brought under the notice of Mr. Wesley, who appointed him to a circuit in 1784. He travelled in the Connexion forty-nine years, with great acceptance and success; and was for a short time editor of the *Wesleyan Methodist Magazine.*[4]

At this time the Gospel was first preached at Ballyreagh. Mr. William Graham, one of the first who received the preachers, was converted to God, and became a member of a class which met near his residence. Not only were many led to a saving knowledge of the truth, but of these several became most acceptable and useful ministers. In connection with this Society Thomas Barber, Joseph Armstrong, and John Darragh learned the first principles of religion, and sustained the offices of leader and local preacher until they were called into the ministry.

In the neighbourhood of Aghalun[5] a gracious work of awakening commenced, during which societies were formed at Leitrim, Grogey, Lisadearny, and other places, and many were able to testify that the Son of man had power upon earth to forgive sins. Several young men here began to call sinners to repentance, three of whom at least, Samuel Mitchell, James Jordan, and James Rennick, afterwards entered the itinerancy. At Grogey the preachers were entertained by Mr. Joseph Foster.[6]

About this year Mrs. Frances Russell, of Drumbadmore, was made the happy partaker of the pardoning love of God, and pressed forward to a high state of spiritual life, which she maintained through the vicissitudes of nearly sixty years. She heartily invited the preachers to her house, and it was favoured with many times of refreshing coming from the presence of the Lord.

Mr. Alexander M'Nab, a Scotchman, was appointed Assistant on the Newry round. He was a man of considerable note, his intellectual gifts were

(4) He was father of the late eloquent Rev. G. B. Macdonald, and grandfather of the Rev. F. W. Macdonald.

(5) Now called Brookeborough.

(6) Grandfather of the Revs. John and Thomas Foster.

of a high order, and his style fluent and attractive; but the consciousness of his power and popularity made him somewhat impatient of contradiction and ecclesiastical restraints. Of his circuit he says, though the people were naturally of a friendly disposition, and kind to the utmost of their power, yet he suffered greater privations than his constitution could bear, and he had many painful exercises of mind. The earlier part of the year was therefore spent very uncomfortably; but the latter made amends for former trials, as he saw fruit to his labours, and his own soul was blessed with an uncommon degree of peace and love. Through grace he obtained a deeper acquaintance with religion, and enjoyed more of the presence of God than he had ever experienced before.

On October the 15th, Mrs. Bennis wrote from Limerick — "Brother Hern and family leave town to-morrow; he was much blessed here, and has left an increase of sixteen in the Society. He is indeed a good, upright, faithful labourer. His wife, finding the affairs of the Society much embarrassed, refused the usual subsistence, and supported herself and children by working at her trade, though her youngest child was an infant. Mr. Collins has arrived. We do not doubt his abilities and good qualities; but are rather cast down by having another married preacher, with a young family sent to us, before we can recruit our finances. We now owe a heavy debt, and the weekly collections are not equal to the weekly expenses. The bulk of the Society are poor, so that the weight lies on a few, who are willing, and do contribute to answer the present expenses; but the debt still lies. Could we not have a single preacher at least every other year, till we are out of debt."[7] Of this request Mr. Wesley takes no notice in his reply.

At the latter end of the year Mr. Johnson, owing to the enfeebled state of his health, having felt compelled to withdraw from the itinerancy, settled in Lisburn, where he continued to work for Christ, and his labours were much acknowledged. But his usefulness was not confined to the pulpit; he longed for the happiness of the afflicted and those who were literally bound with misery and iron. Thus when some of the Hearts of Steel were under sentence of death at Carrickfergus, he visited them, and the Lord so blessed his plain, earnest words, that four were deeply convinced of sin, and cried for mercy, until the Lord spoke peace to their souls, and they with their latest breath professed faith in Christ.

---

(7) *Christian Correspondence*, pp. 41-42.

CHAPTER 2

1772

IN Dublin Mr. Freeman, who took such a deep and active interest in the services in Gravel walk chapel, did not long enjoy them. In November, 1771, when visiting a member of his class who was ill of fever, he took the infection, and died in a few days. Soon after his removal the cause at the new chapel became so low that it was thought desirable by the trustees to sell the premises. This so grieved Mrs. Freeman that as a compromise it was resolved to seek Mr. Wesley's advice and to abide by it. He replied that if no conversions took place in the following quarter they might then sell, but not otherwise. At the close of the three months, at the love-feast a soldier unexpectedly stood up and testified to having received the pardon of his sins during the quarter, and thus the chapel which has proved the birthplace of many souls was saved to the Society.

At about this period a remarkable conversion took place which had an important bearing on the subsequent history of Methodism. Mrs. Mary Smyth, born in 1742, was the daughter of Mr. Samuel Grattan, a wealthy goldsmith of the city of Dublin, who died in 1768. Her husband, Mr. William Smyth, was highly connected, being related to a number of distinguished dignitaries of the Established Church. His father, the Rev. John Smyth, was Chancellor of Conner; his grandfather, the Rev. Thomas Smyth, was Bishop of Limerick (1695-1725); and Dr. F. A. Smyth, one of his uncles, was Archbishop of Dublin (1766-71).

The circumstances connected with the conversion of Mrs. Smyth are replete with interest. Shortly after her marriage, it was announced in the public papers that Garrick was about to take a final leave of the stage — an event frequently intimated, but one which did not actually take place until some years later. Mrs. Smyth, who was a passionate admirer of theatricals, expressed her determination to witness the last acting of this celebrated man. Her husband endeavoured to dissuade her, but in vain; and as it was inconvenient for him to leave Ireland at that time, he requested his brother, Colonel Smyth, to accompany his wife to London. On their arrival they made immediate application for tickets, but none could be obtained. Colonel Smyth then, taking advantage of a former acquaintance with the Duchess of Leeds, sought her assistance, which was willingly given, and Mrs. Smyth accompánied her Grace to the theatre. Not only was her wish thus gratified, but Mrs. Smyth became the guest of the Duchess during the remainder of her sojourn in London.

The Rev. William Romaine was at this period in the zenith of his popularity, and had charge of the parish of St. Anne's, Blackfriars, where his services were accompanied with marvellous spiritual power. Hearing of the immense crowds that attended his ministry, and the astonishing effects produced, Mrs. Smyth expressed a strong desire to hear him, though her new friends were unanimous in their reprobation of the man and of the doctrines he preached. In vain it was urged that he was a Methodist — an enthusiast — one whom it was improper for her to hear; and that to procure admittance to a place so crowded was utterly impracticable. The more Romaine was reprobated, and the greater the difficulty seemed of obtaining admission to the church, the more urgent was Mrs. Smyth in her wish to hear him; nothing could deter her, for go she would, in defiance of every remonstrance. Romaine preached from the words: "Who knoweth the power of Thine anger? Even according to Thy fear, so is Thy wrath." The word preached was applied by the Holy Spirit with power, leading her in humble penitence to the foot of the Cross, so thus she was enabled to lay hold on Christ as her Saviour.

Mr. Smyth's state of mind, when he heard of his wife's conversion, was little short of derangement; and with the utmost anxiety he hastened to London. There he learned from herself more fully what the Lord had done for her, and the great change that had taken place in her heart and life. He was overwhelmed with surprise and mortification, yet reluctantly consented to accompany her to hear Romaine, and judge for himself. In answer, no doubt, to the earnest believing prayer of Mrs. Smyth, the gospel message reached the heart of her husband, and he also was led to realize "the overwhelming power of saving grace." Mrs. Smyth's cup of blessing was then full, the Lord having granted what was doubtless the great desire of her heart; both she and her husband being united in love to Christ, and in the full determination henceforth to live for the glory of God.

Mr. and Mrs. Smyth, on their return home, not finding in the Established Church that sympathy and help which they desired, became members of the Methodist Society. Occupying a high social position, they took a leading part in all that concerned the advancement of Divine truth, and their residence became the resort of earnest and devoted Christians. Being the centre of a large and influential circle of friends they diffused through it a powerful influence for good.

However party feeling may have subsided in the metropolitan Society, difference of opinion as to doctrine and discipline evidently still continued. The action of the British Conference of 1770, in drawing up and publishing certain strongly-worded minutes in regard to Antinomianism, proved the signal of a keen and bitter religious controversy, which continued for five years, and which extended to Dublin. Some of the members of Society wrote to the Rev. J. Fletcher, as the champion of evangelical Arminianism, expressing their thanks for his able vindication of Divine truth; while others wrote expressing their disapproval of his views. Fletcher, with characteristic Christian courtesy, replied to both parties in one letter, sending his grateful acknowledgments to each — to one for their thanks, and to the other for the manner in which they had withheld theirs, while he himself rejoiced that both had "agreed to disagree."[1]

The breach, however, widened, and feeling became stronger, as five months later Wesley wrote to Mr. Alexander Clark, one of the leaders, saying that when he appointed him steward of the Society in Dublin, he both loved and esteemed the preachers; but that now he solemnly warned him of his danger, as he drank in the whole spirit of Patrick Geoghegan.[2]

At Limerick the Society in general, and the select bands in particular, were much quickened by the appointment of Mr. Collins to the city. He arranged for several days of fasting and prayer for the revival of the work of God, and these were much blessed; the class meetings were lively; the cottage prayer meetings revived; the public congregations much larger, and a deeper seriousness and spirit of inquiry were observable in the hearers. This was followed up by his successor, Mr. Glassbrook. whose Christ-like character won the hearts of all, and whose manner of enforcing holiness made it attractive, even to its opposers. Several were added to the Society; others in goodly numbers were converted; and some made perfect in love.

At Clones, James Boyle, to whom allusion has already been made, having realized peace and joy in believing, began at once to work for Christ. He was called upon to assist in prayer meetings, and possessing unmistakable ability, was encouraged both by preachers and people to exercise his talents,

---

(1) *Some Genuine Letters of the Rev. Mr. Fletcher*, Dublin, 1788, pp. 36-38.
(2) *Irish Evangelist*, 1864, p. 39.

and many souls were brought to the Saviour through his instrumentality.[3] During this year a somewhat remarkable incident occurred in the town. A grave and respectably-dressed person one day called on James Boyle, and told him he was a Methodist preacher, and that if the people were apprized of it, he would hold a service in the evening. The congregation assembled, and the preacher came. He gave out one of Wesley's hymns, raised the tune, prayed, and then announced as his text, "For I determined not to know anything among you save Jesus Christ, and Him crucified." Having preached an orthodox sermon, until he proposed to describe the blessings that grew from union with Christ, he made a pause, and said — "I can go no further. I know nothing of it, I will only say, live in peace and love one another, and the God of love and peace will be with you and bless you." At the next market day he appeared on a stage as a mountebank doctor, and what further became of him is not known.

Soon after this James Boyle removed to Aghalun, where he welcomed the preachers to his house, and exerted himself zealously in the cause of his Master. Although he had not the satisfaction of seeing a society formed immediately in the town, yet good was done, and seed sown which subsequently brought forth fruit in the neighbourhood.

A very gracious awakening attended the labours of the preachers in the county of Monaghan in 1771-72. Numerous Societies were formed, and amongst the rest one at Gola, where the itinerants were entertained by Mr. John Whitley,[4] who, at one time intended to enter the ministry, and in 1774 received an appointment, but owing to domestic circumstances was prevented from filling it. He was a man of acute mind and sound judgment, and truly humble in his religious views and feelings. He was also much esteemed as a class leader and local preacher, and for many years exerted a most beneficial influence on the Societies of the Clones circuit.

John Smith arrived at a part of the country about seven miles from the town of Clones, and the word preached by him there was accompanied with mighty power. Large numbers were convinced of sin; and so deep was their distress, that it was said of him that he sent the people mad. This, together with the novelty of his doctrines, and intense earnestness, brought many to hear him, and amongst the rest, a young woman named Catherine Stuart.

(3) *Methodist Magazine*, Dublin, 1812, pp. 130-1.
(4) Grandfather of the Messrs. Whitley, of Enniskillen, and Messrs. Grayden, of New York.

She went on one occasion with some friends to the appointed place of meeting, and was greatly disappointed on hearing that Mr. Smith had been unable to attend, having sent John Price from Tonyloman as his substitute. They arrived a little before the service, and found the local preacher sitting with an open Bible in his hand, speaking to those present, and frequently appealing to the Book. Amongst other things, he said, "Before my conversion I used to dispute with John Smith, but never found myself at such a loss as when he read these words — 'Behold, what manner of love,'" etc.; and on saying this, the young evangelist surveyed his audience with such tenderness and earnestness that even the look reached Catherine's heart, but she slighted the feeling of conviction that arose in her mind. During the sermon such was her mental conflict that, unable to restrain her feelings, she cried aloud in bitter anguish, and then sank insensible on the floor. On returning home, her mother was annoyed, corrected her severely, forbade her going to the Methodist meetings, and confined her to the house. At length Catherine having heard that a love-feast was about to be held at Clones — the first meeting of the kind held there — she determined to go, and with a friend set out the night previous. Her mother pursued her, and arrived in town before the service began; but in compliance with the earnest appeal of her daughter, consented to go with her. The meeting was held in the market-house, and at its close mother and daughter were invited to partake of the refreshments provided by the Society for those who had come from a distance. The opportunity was seized by the preachers of speaking faithfully to Mrs. Stuart, who at length consented to allow her daughter liberty of conscience, and soon after, being justified by faith, Catherine obtained peace with God. She was spared for more than half a century, during which she maintained her confidence, although called upon to suffer, on account of her religious profession, persecution of a peculiarly painful as well as protracted nature.

When John Smith preached on one occasion in Clones, amongst his hearers was William M'Cornock, a native of the county of Donegal, then about twenty-six years of age. He had received a liberal education, and at one time taught a school, and at another acted as a surveyor. He, however, fell into intemperance and other sins, and lived in rebellion against God for several years. Such was his character when he heard John Smith preach. He was greatly surprised when told of the very defective education which the preacher had received, and led to desire a personal acquaintance with him. Soon after an opportunity offered, when the devoted evangelist narrated to the sinner what manner of life he himself had lived, and what God had done for his sóul. William M'Cornock listened to the marvellous story till deep conviction of his own sinfulness and folly was followed by an earnest desire for salvation. At length God manifested Himself in mercy to his soul, and he at once engaged in the Lord's work. Returning home he went to Pettigo, and called at a friend's house. While here the servant girl mocked him; but when he prayed with the family, she was convinced of sin and soon after converted to God. He was thus the means of introducing Methodism into this little town. Notwithstanding persecution, and the strenuous efforts of his friends to lead him back into his former course, he could not be moved. He became valiant for the truth, and proved instrumental in turning many from the error of their ways, including some of the most ignorant and wicked in the part of the country in which he lived. In 1779 he was called into the itinerancy, and God abundantly blessed his labours both in his native land and in the West Indies.

Laborious as was the work on the Enniskillen circuit during this year, the servants of God received ample compensation in seeing the good cause prosper; two hundred and sixty-eight members were added to the Society.

On the list of stations for 1772 the name of John Smith does not appear, it being arranged that he should be set free from circuit work to travel through the country as a missionary. His duty was to conduct open-air services, avail himself of new openings to preach the Gospel, and engage in revival work as he had opportunity. He was thus the first preacher appointed as a general missionary in Ireland, after Methodism had been in some measure consolidated. The work was just that for which he was specially adapted, and was most needed in this country; but it was of such a nature that it is impossible now to trace its course. He went as a pioneer to the moral deserts of the province of Ulster, and many were brought to Christ, who, in all probability, would otherwise never have been reached.

After the close of the British Conference, as Mr. Swindells with one or two other preachers crossed the Channel, a circumstance occurred which indicated his fidelity in his Master's work, and was crowned with the Divine blessing. There was on board the vessel in which he sailed a gentleman of property, George Pigott, Esq., of Chetwynd, near Cork, who was returning from Bath, where he had gone in the vain hope of recruiting his health. Mr. Swindells, earnestly desiring his spiritual welfare, succeeded in awakening his interest in religious conversation, and then seized the opportunity of impressing on his mind the necessity of a change of heart in order to enter the kingdom of heaven. So deeply was Mr. Pigott affected that at the end of the voyage he invited the devoted evangelist to his house, and soon after was led in penitence of spirit to the foot of the Cross. He had an only son, at that time a colonel, and subsequently a major-general in the army, who had so displeased him that he disinherited him. Mr. Swindells having heard this, ventured to expostulate on the subject, which led him to add a codicil to his will, bequeathing to his son the property previously left to others. For some time Mr. Pigott was greatly tempted with doubts and fears, probably owing to the feelings he had cherished with regard to his son; but at last, having made a full surrender of himself to the will of God, he obtained a complete victory. Thus, on one occasion, after Mr. Swindells had been conversing with him, and before engaging in prayer, they united in singing the beautiful and appropriate hymn beginning — "My God, the spring of all my joys." When they came to the third verse, and were about to sing the line — "*If* Jesus shows His mercy mine," Mr. Pigott exclaimed — "Stop! stop! leave out that *if*; there is no need of it now. Jesus does show His mercy mine. He does whisper I am His." The last words he uttered were addressed to the honoured instrument of his salvation. "Follow me," he said, "and we will praise God and the Lamb to all eternity. I am near my rest; and when I arrive there Jesus will say, 'This is a brand which I have plucked out of the fire.'" Colonel Pigott, having ascertained how deeply he was indebted to Mr. Swindells, settled on him a handsome annuity, which the good man thenceforward punctually received.

Another conversion at this period, of deep interest and fruitful of much good, was that of Mrs. Gayer, who was daughter of Valentine Jones, Esq., of Lisburn, and had married in 1758 Edward Gayer, Esq., clerk of the Irish House of Lords. He resided in a beautiful mansion delightfully situated at Derryaghy, described by Mr. Wesley as "one of the pleasantest spots in the kingdom." She was remarkably attractive in her appearance and manner, a charming singer, and highly accomplished. Passionately fond of dancing and other worldly amusements, the life and soul of a highly respectable and fashionable circle of friends, she entered into the gaieties and frivolities of the times with all the enthusiasm of an ardent temperament.

But some time after her marriage she became very deeply concerned about the salvation of her soul. In her anxiety she consulted a clergyman concerning her state, and what she should do to obtain relief of conscience. He said that her spirits had become depressed, and that she should travel, go more into society, and engage more frequently in fashionable amusements. She followed his advice, and not finding rest of soul, then endeavoured at once to raise her spirits and satisfy conscience by a strange compromise — entering heartily into the world, yet faithfully attending to her religious duties. This she carried so far that on one occasion, when she went to a ball at Dublin Castle, she took her prayer-book with her, and after each dance retired and read a portion of it. But, being still unhappy, she went about to establish her own righteousness as the ground of her acceptance with God, being ignorant of "the righteousness which is of God by faith." She attended every service of the church, engaged in works of mercy, fasted and prayed; but all failed to bring the longed-for blessing. Instead of realizing holiness, the Spirit gave her a deeper insight into the depravity of her heart; and her sense of condemnation so increased that she was in danger of giving up, in utter despair, all hope of salvation, when the Lord in mercy interposed on her behalf.

Mr. Crommelin,[5] who was surgeon of a regiment of dragoons then stationed in the neighbourhood, and was a hearty Methodist, having occasion to visit Mr. Gayer on business, embraced the opportunity of introducing religious conversation. Mrs. Gayer was surprised to hear a gentleman, and especially an officer in the army, speak on such subjects; and, being favourably impressed with his spirit and views, told him of her "restless wandering after rest." He then showed her the "new and living way," whereby we have access unto God, even by Christ Jesus; and urged a present acceptance of the Saviour. As he thus told "the old, old story of Jesus and His love," Mrs. Gayer believed, and the Spirit itself witnessed with her spirit that she was a child of God. Mr. Crommelin strongly recommended her to become a member of the Society; but this she hesitated to do, being unwilling to act contrary to the prejudices of her husband against Methodists and Methodism.

Not long after having thus been brought into living union with Christ, Mrs. Gayer having occasion to call on Mrs. Cumberland, at Lisburn, that good woman inquired whether she had ever heard the preachers, told her how different their sermons were from those they were in the habit of hearing, and related some of the wonderful results which had followed their labours. Mrs. Gayer inquired when a service would be held. Mrs. Cumberland replied

---

(5) Apparently a grand-nephew of the celebrated Louis Crommelin, the founder of the linen trade in Ulster.

that a meeting would take place in her house on the following day, and invited Mrs. Gayer to be present; an invitation which she accepted, and took with her her only daughter, a girl of thirteen. The word which Mary Gayer then heard came with power to her heart, and having thus been deeply convinced of sin, her prayer was soon after answered, and she was enabled to rest on Jesus as her Saviour, to the unspeakable joy of both herself and her mother. The blessing then received she retained until she passed triumphant home, sixty years subsequently. In connection with the above meeting both Mrs. and Miss Gayer were led to become members of the Society.

At Charlemont the congregations became so large that the room used for the service did not afford sufficient accommodation; but a malt-kiln was taken, and fitted up for the use of the Society and congregation. One of those who attended the services was Mrs. Dickson, who, on account of her age, was unable to walk to the parish church at Loughgall, about four miles distant. Her son James, with whom she lived, was annoyed at her having any connection with the Methodists; but at length went to hear for himself, although determined never to get identified with such a people. Having slipped into the malt-kiln, and secured a position unobserved, his mind was most favourably impressed with what he heard, which subsequently led to his conversion to God, and his official connection with Methodism, which continued for upwards of half a century.

In August Mrs. Bennis visited Waterford, and her report to Mr. Wesley is — "This Society is increased in number and grace since I was last here: I meet a band and a class; we all speak with freedom. I love the people and I believe they love me. There are three preachers on the circuit, and they all have work enough." And again on October the 18th she writes, "I left the Waterford Society in a prosperous situation." To this success there can be no doubt Mrs. Bennis herself contributed much by her holy example and zealous efforts, a fact which is thus acknowledged by Mr. Wesley in a letter to her, dated November 3rd — "Your time was well bestowed at Waterford; many, I doubt not, will remember it with thankfulness. But why this want of discipline in Limerick? Whenever this is dropped all is confusion: see that it be immediately restored. Captain Webb is now in Dublin, invite him to visit Limerick: he is a man of fire, and the power of God constantly accompanies his word."

Reference is here made to Captain Thomas Webb, a retired military officer, who was wounded in the eye at the siege of Louisberg, and was one of the brave army under Wolfe that scaled the heights of Mount Abraham. In 1765 he found peace with God while conversing in Bristol with a Moravian minister; and soon after became a Methodist, entered heartily into work for Christ as a local preacher, and was one of the principal agents in planting Methodism in America. He was brave, hearty and generous, highly esteemed by Wesley, and remarkable for his deep piety and fervent zeal. The invitation to Limerick was given and accepted, and blessed results followed. The chapel was not large enough to accommodate the congregations; many were awakened, and the members of the Society quickened, so that estrangements were removed, and all seemed united in Christian love and zeal.

In the parish of Ardstraw George and Hugh Brown made themselves exceedingly useful. Not satisfied with labouring in those places already visited by the itinerants, their desire was "to preach the Gospel in the regions beyond," and facilities for doing so were not lacking. A member of the Society having removed to one of these districts of country, George seized the opportunity of conducting a service there; many flocked to hear, some of whom received the word with meekness, were led to the Saviour, and became members of the Society. Opposition soon arose, the local clergy endeavoured in vain to prevent their people from attending the services; the Presbyterian minister read a paper to his hearers excluding from the Lord's table all who were identified with Methodism; and when this failed recourse was made to violence. A number of men, well armed, were despatched to a meeting conducted by Hugh Brown, to take his life: and on arriving they first "sent in a black-a-moor to pull the fellow down." But he returned saying, "I will not, for he is a fine fellow, and is preaching the word of God." They then rushed in, the lights were extinguished, and the young preacher escaped through a window, much to the chagrin of his would-be assassins. Some of the most violent opposers, however, were eventually won for Christ. Thus a woman who went to one of the services determined by cursing, swearing, and singing songs to create disturbance, became affected in such a manner that she was obliged to withdraw without saying a word. She then came to hear, and God was glorified in her conversion.

CHAPTER 3

1773

JANUARY the 1st, 1773, was set apart by the Society at Limerick as a day of fasting and prayer for the revival of God's work; and during the whole day, as well as at the covenant service in the evening, the Lord heard the supplications of His people, and wonderfully manifested His presence in their midst. The blessed results were most apparent, old prayer-meetings were re-established, the congregations increased, and valuable additions were made to the Society.

The Countess of Huntingdon felt a deep interest in Ireland, and was instrumental in establishing several congregations in the country. On Mr. Shirley representing to her ladyship the deplorable moral and religious state of the metropolis, she gave instructions for the erection of a commodious building for the celebration of Divine worship according to the forms of the Established Church; and meantime, at the suggestion of Mrs. Paul, wife of the Dean of Cashel, the Merchant Tailors' hall was secured and set apart for this purpose. Several ministers were sent from England at the expense of the venerable Countess, and their preaching was attended with considerable success. At length the plan of erecting a chapel was abandoned, and early in this year the old Presbyterian meeting-house in Plunket street was rented instead. Earnest and successful services were conducted here by several students from Trevecca, by Mr. Shirley, and by the Rev. C. Stewart Eccles, who, when a student at Trinity College, had been led to decision for God through the sermon preached by Mr. De Courcy in St. Andrew's church-yard, and was now actively and zealously engaged in evangelistic work.

Meanwhile the work continued to extend and prosper in the north. On one occasion J. Smith went to Knockmanoul much weighed down in spirit, having heard that the Society there had not retained its fervour. On arriving at Molly Gregg's[1] he immediately inquired for his room, into which he entered without delay, shut the door, and spread his case before the Lord. It seemed to him for some time as if he pleaded in vain; but he persevered, and so absorbed was he in prayer that he was deaf to repeated calls to dinner.

(1) Mrs. Graham's.

The day drew to a close, and his door remained unopened. At length Molly Gregg, whose kind heart could not brook the idea of the preacher fasting for such a length of time, opened the door, and found him so earnestly pleading with God as to be unconscious of her presence. Shortly after she again entered, and said: "The house is filled with people, and many are outside unable to get in." Whereon he leaped to his feet in exultation, saying: "O! Molly Gregg, I have got it, and will now go and deliver my message." During the subsequent service the Spirit of God descended in mighty power: sixteen souls were converted, and a gracious work commenced, which is said to have been "the most extensive revival in the north of Ireland."

Most likely in connection with this blessed work a persecution arose, which for its virulence, duration and fatal results, has perhaps no parallel in the history of Methodism in Ireland. Men professing to be zealous sons of the Church, proclaimed the doctrines of the forgiveness of sins and the witness of the Spirit to be deadly errors. Abusive language, dirt, stones and clubs were the arguments they employed. A man might swear, tell lies, get drunk, indulge in all manner of licentiousness, and yet, if he went to church occasionally, be deemed by priest and people a good Christian; but if he began to read his Bible regularly, pray in his family or with his neighbours, reprove sin, or listen to the preaching of the Methodists, he became an object of reproach and hatred, was set up as a mark to be shot at, and treated as the filth and offscouring of the earth. Almost every hand was uplifted against the Methodists. The aristocracy opposed them; the clergy, both in and out of the pulpit, railed at them; and the magistrates, in general, not only denied them a hearing, but in some instances were amongst their most bitter persecutors. The bonds of friendship were severed, family ties broken, and young men and women driven from the homes of their fathers to seek shelter elsewhere. The preachers especially were the objects of hatred and malignity. In some instances brave men armed with guns and bayonets, and carrying a supply of provisions, escorted the servants of God, travelling by by-roads in order to escape attacks from lawless mobs. Mr. G. Irvine, of Magheralough, and others, often thus acted as a bodyguard to the itinerants.

In Belturbet one fellow resolved to stand inside a door at the end of the market-house, and to slam it in the face of the preacher as soon as he approached; but just as the servant of God drew near, a sudden gust of wind drove the door so violently against the man, that he himself was thrown down on his back, and so bruised that he was a long time in recovering. Two members of the Society at Tonyloman were so beaten that they died from the effects. This attracted public attention, and the perpetrators of the outrage were arrested at the instance of a local magistrate.

Thomas Halliday was seized by order of Mr. Carleton, of Markethill, near Enniskillen, a magistrate of great influence in that part of the country. When Mr. Halliday was brought before him he found the justice of the peace accompanied by a gentleman, who at once proceeded to examine him, and who, in the course of conversation, made such objections to Scriptural truth that Mr. Halliday, looking him full in the face, said: "I wish, sir, I knew who your minister is; for I would go directly and tell him what an infidel he has in his parish, and show him that it is his duty solemnly to warn you of your awful state." He being himself the rector of the parish, became confused, Mr. Carleton burst into laughter, and the preacher was dismissed.

God in His providence sometimes interposed in a most solemn and impressive manner on behalf of His servants. For instance, a constable having in his pocket a warrant issued by a clerical magistrate for the arrest of a local preacher, arrived at the place of meeting as the text was announced, but before he could execute his unjust commission was himself arrested by death. A profound impression was thus made on the minds of those who instigated the persecution in this immediate neighbourhood, which thus terminated.

Warnings of danger sometimes came from unlikely quarters. Thus John Smith was on his way to preach at a hamlet a little distance from Swanlinbar; in going to which it was needful to cross a large bog, and also a river, which was much swollen, but spanned by a bridge. He was met by a woman, who told him a mob was waiting at the bridge to ill-treat him. At first he disregarded the warning, because she had been accustomed previously to make use of abusive language to him. The woman, however, called to him a second time, and this made him hesitate to proceed. The place where he intended to preach was about a mile further on, and instead of going by the bridge, he spurred his horse, leaped a hedge, swam the river, crossed a part of the bog, which even in summer was dangerous, and reached his destination in safety. He preached to the people, and having ascertained that his persecutors, thinking he would be compelled to return by the bridge at night, waited there to accomplish their malicious purpose, he returned in safety by the same perilous way as that by which he had gone.

On one occasion, when John Smith was riding within two or three miles of Killashandra, he was met by a minister, who, in a most insulting manner, said to him: "How dare you go about preaching, frightening the whole country out of their senses, and thinning my congregation?" To which the evangelist replied, that instead of turning the brains of the people, he only endeavoured to turn their hearts to the Lord, thus teaching them true wisdom. The minister, in a rage, called him a scoundrel and a canting rascal, and horsewhipped him unmercifully. John Smith, like his blessed Master, "when He was reviled, reviled not again; when He suffered, He threatened not; but committed Himself to Him that judgeth righteously." The minister rode away foaming with rage. Before eight days had expired, his house at Killygowan took fire during the night, and it was with the utmost difficulty that he and his household escaped, destitute of everything except the clothes they wore.

One evening as John Smith was conducting a service in a house near Swanlinbar two young men, who should have been gentlemen, conspired to pull down the preacher, and cast lots as to which should take the initiative. The lot fell on the more audacious of the two; but the moment he entered the room all his strength and resolution forsook him, and he fell on the floor with such violence that blood gushed out of his mouth and nose. His companion pulled him out, and they staggered home frightened almost out of their senses. In order to excuse their failure they spread the silly story that whosoever the preacher looked at through his large eye-glass was at once struck into fits.

The greatest enemy to the work of God in this country was a gentleman who held the commission of the peace. He formed a gang of the worst characters in the neighbourhood, of which he was the ringleader, who, on all possible occasions, assaulted "Swaddler John and his followers," as the Methodists were termed, did not hesitate to make false accusations against them, and succeeded in getting some imprisoned. More than once John Smith was thus unjustly deprived of liberty. On one occasion he was locked up in a house in Swanlinbar by this magistrate, who, pistol in hand, threatened death to any one who should come near the prisoner. Yet these threats did not prevent the people from gathering at the window of the room, where the servant of God was confined, to converse with and cheer their friend. Some time after this the magistrate passed through a series of terrible calamities. He was forsaken by his wife; one of his sons, a promising young man, was torn to pieces by a wild beast; his estate was frittered away; and, having lost his social position and been superseded in the magistracy, he wandered about as a vagabond, and died blaspheming God.

The junior preacher on the Enniskillen circuit, John M'Burney, who had just entered the ministry, preached one day in the market-place at Clones. Many attended, and a gracious influence was realized; but some ungodly men, chiefly Roman Catholics, assembled and greatly disturbed and annoyed the congregation; so that it was thought the place must be given up, as no magistrate would interfere. Just when the dread of this was at its highest a very unexpected and strange occurrence took place. An old military pensioner, a Presbyterian, surprised the preacher and congregation. by taking his stand beside a tree in the centre of the market-place, with musket in hand, and swore that he would shoot the first man that would pass that tree to disturb the preacher. Not one of the rioters, although they shouted at a distance, attempted to pass the prescribed limit. The rough old soldier mounted guard regularly every Sabbath afternoon for some weeks, until all opposition ceased in the town. The young preacher, however, soon after fell a victim to the cruelty of his persecutors elsewhere.

On the evening of March 4th he conducted a service at Mr. Perry's, near Aghalun, and while singing a hymn a large mob surrounded the house, and six ruffians, armed with clubs, rushed in and fell upon the people; but they were thrust out, and the door fastened. On this, the rioters smashed the windows, broke into the house, and hauling out both men and women, beat them without mercy. Mr. M'Burney was dragged out, and when he attempted to rise, knocked down. The villains continued beating him on the head and breast as he lay senseless on the ground; yet after awhile, coming to himself, he got up, but being too weak to stand, staggered and fell. Then one of the mob set his foot on the preacher's face, swearing he would "tread the Holy Ghost out of him," and another thrust a stick into his mouth. From the effects of this ill-treatment he never recovered.

Mr. Mitchell, who lived about a mile from the town, was also one of those who were basely maltreated, and his house was attacked on the following Saturday by a riotous mob, who threw large stones at the windows and broke the door. Mr. Perry and Mr. Mitchell then obtained warrants for the apprehension of some of the rioters, but the constable would not execute them. At the following assizes in Enniskillen, the grand jury threw out all the bills. Such was the administration of justice in Fermanagh, which tended only to encourage a spirit of persecution. A Methodist preacher could not pass through the Protestant town of Enniskillen without endangering his life.

The Methodists were thus, in certain instances, for their own protection, constrained to repel force by force. On one occasion, during the time of service at Mr. Foster's, Grogey, the house was attacked by a riotous mob, and several of the congregation having seized guns, fired over the heads of their assailants to frighten them. Not prepared for such a reception, the ruffians were about to retreat, when their leader recalled them, exclaiming, "Come on, boys; it's only turf mowl they're firing." Then one of the congregation took deliberate aim and fired. A man was wounded, and gave a jump, swearing it was "quare turf mowl " he had got, while his companions took to flight. By a marked Providence the injury thus inflicted proved a means of lasting good: for the poor fellow was led to see his folly and sin, gave his heart to God, and joined the Society.[2]

On March the 26th Mr. Wesley landed at Dunleary, and having been forbidden by his physician to ride, brought with him for the first time his chaise, which, however, he was deprived of the opportunity of using, as the commissioners of customs would not permit it to be landed. This was overruled for good, as had it come on shore it would have been utterly spoiled. Wesley was obliged to hire another vehicle, which had its own misadventures. At Ballyhack ferry it went overboard, and was with difficulty recovered; at another place it took five hours to drag it less than a dozen miles; and in a third it was disabled by the breaking of one of the axletrees; while more than once it was in danger of being dashed to pieces by furious mobs.

In Dublin Wesley examined the Society, and found it somewhat lessened in numbers; but well united together in truth and love. Having preached at Tyrrell's Pass, Mullingar, and Longford, he came to Athlone, where a whole army of soldiers, with their officers, were present at the service. He then proceeded to Ballinasloe and Aughrim, and thence to Eyrecourt, where the crowd gave him a loud huzza as he passed into the market-place to preach, and during the service all were civil and many serious. A great awakening had taken place in the town, and many of the most notorious and profligate sinners had obtained the great salvation. At Clara he preached in the church, "the neatest in the kingdom," that he had seen. At Tullamore all the soldiers in the town were present, none of whom were more affected than one who had been most notorious for his wickedness, but now seemed fully resolved to forsake his sinful ways. At Mountmellick there was "an artless, earnest,

(2) *Irish Christian Advocate*, 1885, p. 5.

serious people." At Mountrath the Lord was present, both to wound and to heal. At Kilkenny there was "a numerous congregation, about as genteel, and full as unawakened, as that at Portarlington." The next day it was considerably larger, and many seemed to be deeply affected. At Enniscorthy, as no public building was available, Wesley stood at Hugh M'Laughlin's door, so that both those within and without could hear.

At Waterford there was cheering evidence of spiritual prosperity, the number and seriousness of the congregations being very satisfactory; but with the tokens of success persecution arose. Word having been brought that Mr. William Hobbs, the Mayor, was willing that Mr. Wesley should preach in the bowling green, he went thither, and a large multitude quickly assembled, some of whom attempted to raise a disturbance, the majority of the congregation being deeply attentive. At that time the windows of a house, occupied by wealthy merchants named Farrell, looked out on the green. Messrs. Farrell and family, together with a priest, stood at the window, and encouraged a Catholic mob to attack Mr. Wesley. These rowdies knocked down John Christian, with two or three more, who endeavoured to quiet them. Some gentlemen then rushed into their midst, and having inflicted some heavy blows, seized the ringleader, and delivered him into custody: while another, Sir John Alcock, conducted the venerable preacher in safety home. The rioters, who were workmen in the employment of Messrs. Farrell, were subsequently brought to trial; but as the chief delinquent, upon whom the whole guilt was thrown, had escaped, and the jury was packed, the other traversers were acquitted. But though they eluded earthly justice, they did not escape the hand of an overruling Providence. The priest, who encouraged the mob, fell down dead at the altar on the following Sunday; and Messrs. Farrell, from being the most extensive and opulent merchants in the city, were shortly reduced to extreme poverty. So sudden was the change in their affairs that the case was frequently referred to by their own people, to show the danger of religious persecution.

To return to Mr. Wesley. At Cork he held a solemn watch-night service, and left the city with much satisfaction, having seen some fruit of his labours. At Bandon the congregations were such as he had not seen in the town for twenty years. This success he attributed to the labours of William Collins, "who is," he says, "another proof that at present a prophet is not without honour even in his own country." During this year a youth of sixteen was converted in Bandon, and joined the Methodists, amongst whom he

subsequently occupied a prominent position. Thomas Bennett was certainly
a pillar in the Church. For seventy-two years he walked with God, and amidst
the business and other duties of life, uniformly exhibited the Christian
character. With fidelity and acceptance he sustained the offices of steward,
leader, and trustee. His attachment to Methodism was unwavering, and his
contributions to support the cause liberal.[3] He is still remembered by a few
in the town, who in their youth thought him somewhat uncouth in speech,
and very strict in discipline, yet withal genial and generous.

At Limerick Wesley found a settled, serious people, but in danger of
sinking into formality. All the members of the select Society once experienced
salvation from sin, some continued to enjoy the blessing, but the greater part
were more or less shorn of their strength. Here William Myles, a young man
of seventeen, one of Wesley's hearers, was strongly impressed with what he
heard, and led earnestly to seek the pardon of his sins. Soon after he was
received into the Society, and five years subsequently entered the itinerancy.

At Newmarket Romanists and Protestants flocked together from every
side, and for the time appeared to be greatly affected. At Clare where there
was no Society, and next to no congregation until the soldiers came, Wesley
was glad to accept a bed in the barracks. At Galway he preached in the
courthouse to a large and well-conducted congregation. At Castlebar, on
finding the charter school a picture of slothfulness, nastiness and desolation,
and all the children dirty, untidy, and neglected, he reported the facts to the
trustees, with the hope of effecting a reformation. At Sligo the congregations,
rich and poor, were so large and so remarkably serious, that he had "a faint
hope of seeing some fruit even in this cold and barren town." At
Manorhamilton the audience was numerous and attentive.

At Swanlinbar there was a large number of hearers, mostly experienced
Christians, and still more on the following morning; but the grand concourse
was on that evening, when the hearts of the people were as wax melting
before the fire. The curate in the town then was the Rev. James Creighton,
A.B., who in 1765 had been ordained by Dr. Cradock, Bishop of Kilmore,
whose first counsel to him to "say nothing at all about faith in his sermons,"
was by no means calculated to advance his holiness or promote his success.
He had been meditating a sermon against the Methodists, but very wisely
before executing his purpose, sought light on the subject, by sending a series

(3) *Wesleyan Methodist Magazine*, 1845, p. 1232.

of questions to Mr. Wesley, to which concise answers were sent, together with a copy of the "Appeal to Men of Reason." These eventually proved the means in the hand of God of leading Mr. Creighton to seek and find the blessings of salvation, and to his becoming thoroughly identified with Methodism.

On May 24th Mr. Wesley, having preached at Tonyloman, set out for Sidaire, accompanied by the circuit ministers, Jas. Hudson, John Watson, and Michael M'Donald. One of his horses having a shoe loose, he borrowed Mr. Watson's steed, and left him with his chaise. Having to pass through Enniskillen, when the itinerants came near the town, some masons at work at the west bridge gave them some coarse words. The vituperation increased as they proceeded, but many soldiers being in the street, who received the preachers with respect, the mob shrunk back. An hour later Mr. Watson followed in the carriage; but before he arrived at the bridge, which had been blocked up with large stones, many ran together and began to pelt him with whatever came to hand, but an old man cried out: "Is this the way you treat strangers?" and rolled away the stones. The mob quickly rewarded him by plastering him over with mortar from head to foot. They then fell upon the chaise, which was cut with stones in several places, and well-nigh covered with dirt and mortar. From one end of the town to the other, the stones flew thick about the coachman's head, some of which were two or three pounds weight.

Next day the preachers returned from Sidaire *en route* to Roosky, and as they passed the eastern end of Enniskillen, both men and women greeted them with abusive language, together with dirt and stones; but the steeds of the itinerants soon left their persecutors far behind. John Smith came to the town about an hour later. The masons at the west bridge having seen him approaching, prepared at once for an onslaught. He was afraid that his horse would leap into the river, and therefore having alighted, made his way through the midst of them as best he could, much wounded.

At Derg-bridge Wesley found the minister and people waiting for him; but the church could not near contain them, so he preached to a mixed multitude of rich and poor — Episcopalians, Presbyterians and Romanists — in the open-air. He then rode to Mrs. Johnstone's, Lisleen, where, after tea, he was told another congregation was waiting, to whom he preached, without further delay, warning them "of the madness which was spreading among them" in desiring to leave the Church. At Londonderry no less than five of the local clergy attended the service each evening. "One would have imagined," he says, "from this friendliness of the clergy, joined with the good-will of the Bishop and the Dean, the Society would increase swiftly; but in fact it does not increase at all; it stands just as it was two years ago; so little does the favour of man advance the work of God." At Fahan he preached "to a serious, artless congregation." Here he was the guest of a widow lady, whose son, the Rev. John Abraham, chaplain to the Chapel-of-Ease, Londonderry, was after some time brought to the saving knowledge of Christ, and then stood forth valiantly for the truth, preaching it with great force, earnestness and fidelity.

At New Buildings Wesley found the Society "as lively as ever, and more exactly regular than any other Society in these parts." At Castlecaulfield he preached to a numerous congregation on the green, and again in the evening near the barracks at Charlemont. At Armagh the audiences in the avenue were very large and exceedingly serious, rich and poor kneeling down together on the grass while he engaged in prayer. Here he wrote his invaluable sermon on "Predestination," which he had preached at the request of several of the clergy. Having discoursed at Clonmain and other places in this neighbourhood, he came to Derryanvil, where were some of the liveliest Christians he had seen in the kingdom, eight of whom testified that they had never lost the evidence, nor felt any declension since the time they were perfected in love. At Tanderagee the congregation was exceedingly numerous, the day concluded with a meeting of the Societies, assembled from all the surrounding country, and great was their rejoicing, many were filled with consolation, and not a few feeble hands were strengthened.

At Lisburn Mrs. Gayer, for the first time after her conversion, had an opportunity of hearing Mr. Wesley preach, which she greatly enjoyed. At the close of the service she was introduced to him, and he, having obtained her address, said that he would call and see her. Knowing the strong feeling Mr. Gayer had against Methodism, and fearing the reception Mr. Wesley would receive from him, she, with her daughter, made it a subject of special prayer during most of that night, that the Lord would dispose the heart of her husband to receive the servant of God graciously. On the following day Mr. Wesley walked out to Derryaghy from Lisburn, and met Mr. Gayer in the avenue leading to his residence. The former inquired if Mrs. Gayer lived in that house, the latter replied, "Yes, she is my wife," and entered into conversation with Mr. Wesley, not knowing who he was. Mr. Gayer was much impressed with the culture and gentlemanly deportment of the stranger, felt drawn towards him at once, and invited him to dinner. Thus prejudices were completely removed, and arrangements made for regular preaching at Derryaghy; which, commenced by Mr. Wesley before a large congregation on that very day, was subsequently continued in a place fitted up for the purpose by Mr. Gayer at his own expense. Not only was a room set apart in the house for the preachers, called "the Prophet's Chamber," but they were also kindly and hospitably entertained, at regular intervals, for many years.

At Newtownards the hearers in the new market-house were most attentive, especially the backsliders, several of whom determined to return to their heavenly Father. In Belfast the audience was numerous, but trifling enough; yet by degrees became serious. At Carrickfergus there was a lovely congregation in the shire hall, very large and earnest, several were added to the Society, and Wesley was not without hope that there was seed sown here that would never be rooted up. At Ballymena he was kindly offered the use of the meeting-house, where all that could get in were closely stowed together. He declared "the grace of our Lord Jesus Christ" to a loving people at Ballinderry, many of whom experienced this blessing, and many more felt their need of it. In Dublin he had left three hundred and seventy-eight members, and now found four hundred and twelve, many of whom were truly alive to God. On July the 5th he embarked for England, having spent a little more than three months in this country.

The good cause continued to prosper much, especially in the north. Many souls were saved, the spiritual life of the Societies was deepened, and the net addition to the member ship in the province of Ulster alone, during the twelve months, was nine hundred and forty-one. These statistics, as well as others already given, are not, however, to be regarded as presenting anything like an adequate idea of the results of the labours of the itinerants. It was computed that in this and five preceding years, the north of Ireland was drained of one fourth of its population by emigration to the American settlements. These emigrants were chiefly from the agricultural districts, where Methodism had proved most successful.

During the remainder of the year a few brief glimpses are given of the itinerants earnestly and successfully at work in leading sinners to the Saviour, and in opening new and important fields of Christian usefulness. Thus at Limerick, several days in the autumn were set apart for fasting and prayer, which not only proved solemn and refreshing seasons to all, and especially the young men who were greatly stirred up, but also led to several being added to the membership; some converted, and others renewed in love.

Once when John Smith went to Gortnaleg, he was so hoarse that he could not speak above a whisper. He knew not what to do when he saw Peter Taylor's large barn filled with people hungering for the Bread of Life, and he groaned within himself. At length he said with intense earnestness: "Lord, be Thou wisdom and utterance to Thy poor, weary, and afflicted servant, and speak by Thy Spirit to this people." Immediately all the people fell on their knees and pleaded for a present blessing. Meanwhile, John Smith continued wrestling with God, until nineteen souls were led to the Saviour.

Thomas Payne, a brave soldier of the Cross, who was appointed to labour on the Armagh circuit, says that the damp, dirty, smoky cabins of Ulster were a great trial to him; but what made amends for all these inconveniences was, that the people in general were the most zealous, lively and affectionate Christians in the kingdom.

An inroad was made into the neighbourhood of Stranorlar. That part of the country seemed to be in the peaceable possession of the god of this world, with none to dispute his authority, until visited by the preachers. Rumours began to circulate that the Methodists were about to come to the district, and everything that is evil was stated of them. Some asserted that they were the false prophets and false Christs, foretold by the Saviour; while others began to examine their Bibles to see if these things were so, and a few thought the Methodists were right; but the majority affirmed that it was not fit that such fellows should live. One of the earliest to preach here was Geo. Brown from Creevy, and a great congregation assembled. As they returned home the curate of the parish met them, and reproached the people in strong terms for going to hear "illiterate, designing impostors, who had no end in view but corrupting and debasing men's minds." Notwithstanding this opposition, several were converted and became members of the Society.

It was also about this period we discover the first trace of a footing gained by Methodism in Portadown. A member of the Society at Kilmoriarty, named Samuel Lisk, removed into the town, and opened his house to receive the preachers; but it does not appear that any society was formed for some time, and he therefore maintained his connection with the class at his previous home. In his house Mr. J. M'Neese, Mr. T. Payne, and other devoted men declared the truth as it is in Jesus, and not a little opposition was stirred up, which does not seem, however, to have gone further than the infliction of petty annoyances. After some time Lisk removed to a distant part of the country, and a stable, kindly lent by an innkeeper named Gardiner, was the only place which could be procured for religious services.

In Charlemont the Society and congregation so increased that a larger house was felt to be indispensable. So just at the right time, an all-wise Providence enabled Mr. Bates to secure a suitable site, and obtain financial help, so that a chapel was completed before Christmas, and opened by Barnabas Thomas, one of the circuit preachers.

CHAPTER 4

1774

AT this period a lady was brought into connection with Methodism, who subsequently did a glorious work for Christ. Mrs. Agnes Smyth was the daughter of William Higginson, Esq., of Lisburn; and thus was one of a family which, for more than a century-and-a-half, has occupied a leading position in that town and neighbourhood. Brought up in circumstances of affluence, and surrounded by those whose lives were strictly moral, she was from earliest years the subject of the gracious influences of the Holy Spirit. Even when a little child she felt that God loved her and she loved Him, and was wont with unquestioning confidence to look to Him in prayer for relief in every trouble, and not in vain. She became most careful to do what appeared her duty; read at least two chapters of the Bible every day; and attended the services of the parish church with the utmost regularity. As, however, she grew older, and entered into the fashionable amusements of the world, these good impressions passed away, and she became gay, vain and thoughtless.

In 1770 Miss Higginson, being then but a girl of fifteen, was married to the Rev. Edward Smyth, a clergyman who had many wealthy and influential relatives, through whose assistance the young couple expected to succeed in life, but were sadly disappointed. One of those from whom they had expected much, Dr. F. A. Smyth, Archbishop of Dublin, died in December, 1771, without having either given his nephew a benefice, or left him a bequest. This disappointment led Mr. Smyth to look out for a curacy, in quest of which he, with his wife, went to Dublin, where, in the house of his brother, Wm. Smyth, Esq., Mrs. Smyth first met some members of the Methodist Society. The religious views and practices of these people were utterly opposed to all her previous ideas. The profession of a conscious sense of sins forgiven seemed to her "proud and presumptuous;" and preaching without episcopal ordination, "strange and unlawful." However she was led to search the Scriptures to see "whether these things were so." Through conversation with these servants of God her mind was awakened to a sense of her fallen state by nature, and the consequent necessity of a change of heart; but she did not venture to attend any of the services of the sect then almost "everywhere spoken against." Meantime her husband did not succeed in getting a suitable position as soon as was anticipated; and her mother, to whom she was very fondly attached, died. Thus one trouble followed another; but these disappointments and trials were greatly sanctified and blessed. At length, in December, 1773, Mr. Smyth obtained the curacy of Ballyculter, in the county of Down, and removed thither in the following year. Their house not being ready for their reception, they were kindly invited by Lord Bangor to Castle Ward; but the fashionable and frivolous amusements of their temporary home were so utterly distasteful, that neither Mrs. Smyth nor her husband could be prevailed upon to join in them. The Lord was thus preparing them for Christian work, of which we shall hear more again.

The persecution on the Enniskillen circuit, to which reference has been made, at length grew so violent that its malignity compelled the reluctant authorities to take active measures for the preservation of life and property, but not until they had found that their own persons and possessions were in danger. Then the magistrates began to manifest some sympathy with the persecuted Christians, and severe punishment was inflicted on the violators of the law. Many of those who had taken a leading part in the persecution sought to escape the consequences of their misdeeds by emigration or by enlisting in the army, while others, to veil their former conduct, became zealous in running with the altered tide of popular feeling.

But this fierce and terrible persecution did not end until after John Smith had fallen a victim to its violence. In 1774, as the devoted evangelist rode to Charlemont to attend the March quarterly meeting, a man named Nixon, a bailiff to a gentleman at Aghintain, near Clogher, waylaid and struck him on the back of the head with a pitchfork, knocking him down, and then so maltreated him as to leave him apparently dead. But so intent was he on doing his Master's work that, weak and suffering as he was, he managed to get to Charlemont for the service, and there became so exhausted that he was obliged to retire to the house of a kind widow, a Mrs. Richardson, where he lingered for a few days. For some time he was in great distress of mind; but soon the clouds were dispelled, and his soul was filled with joy unspeakable. His pain of body was great, but the love of Christ so overflowed his heart as at times to render him almost insensible to bodily sufferings. For about twelve hours he scarcely ceased praising and glorifying God, until his room was a very heaven on earth. At length, as nature gradually sank, Samuel Bates repeated the words: "Lord, now lettest Thou Thy servant depart in peace, according to Thy word: for mine eyes have seen Thy salvation;" and the spirit of the saint passed hence to join the glorious company "which came out of great tribulation, and have washed their robes, and made them white in the blood of the Lamb." Many who heard the dying testimony of this devoted Christian were led thereby to religious decision, and thus in death as in life he glorified God. John Smith "fell in the heat of the battle vanquished, and yet a conqueror." The body of this earnest worker was carried to the new chapel. Solemn and impressive services were held, at which many were "baptized for the dead." The remains were then interred in the old graveyard at Leger hill: in what precise part cannot now be determined, as there is not even a stone to mark the place. But his "record is on high;" and his memorial is found in the many who have been led to the Saviour as the result of his devoted life.

Although open opposition thus ceased, the Society began to suffer from what proved to be much more injurious to its well-being, internal discord. The celebrated Calvinistic controversy now extended to Ireland, and its pernicious effects were increased by a misapprehension of the Arminian doctrines as stated by some of the preachers. In Dublin discontent arose. "I have been credibly informed," says Mrs. Paul, wife of the Dean of Cashel, in writing to the Countess of Huntingdon, "that great dissatisfaction prevails among Mr. Wesley's people, owing chiefly to the influence which Mr. Fletcher's book has on the preaching of the ministers of the Society. Of this book I know nothing but from report. It appears, however, to have unsettled the minds of many, from what I can learn; and a few have left the Society in consequence of it." The opportunity was considered favourable by Calvinistic Methodists for disseminating their opinions in this country. "I am at my wit's end," writes the zealous Countess, to Mr. Hawkesworth, her preacher in the metropolis, "to find help for the people of Ireland. A student from the College shall go immediately, you will then be able to visit some of the large towns, whilst he remains with the people in Dublin; but I am in great hopes of sending some who may get admittance to the churches, perhaps Mr. Venn, Mr. Madan, or Mr. Talbot. I shall write to them without delay, and inform them of this opening."[1]

Accordingly the Rev. Thomas Jones was sent over. Soon after his arrival Mr. Hawkesworth visited Limerick and Waterford; and at the latter place met with considerable encouragement, which induced him to prolong his stay. Mrs. Bennis happened to be in the city at the time, and gave Mr. Wesley a sad account of the state of the Society there. By the frequent neglect of preaching, and the almost total neglect of discipline, the people were scattered; and of the few that remained some were grieved, and some offended with the new doctrine of salvation by works that they considered was preached. Then Mr. Hawkesworth held his services at the same hours as those of the Methodists, and they were largely attended by many, including not a few of the Society, though warned not to go and hear him. When Mrs. Bennis called on him, and charged him with taking advantage of the disturbed state of the Society, to widen the breach, and gather all to himself, he indirectly acknowledged that this was his motive in coming.

Mr. Wesley in reply said: "I enclose James Perfect's letter to you, on purpose that you may talk with him; he has both an honest heart and a good understanding; but you entirely mistake his doctrine. He preaches salvation by faith in the same manner that my brother and I have done; and as Mr. Fletcher has beautifully explained it. None of us talk of being accepted for our works: that is the Calvinist slander. But we all maintain, we are not saved without works; that works are a condition (though not the meritorious cause) of final salvation. It is by faith in the righteousness and blood of Christ that we are enabled to do all good works; and it is for the sake of these, that all who fear God and work righteousness are accepted of Him. It is far better for our people not to hear Mr. Hawkesworth. Calvinism will do them no good; as to the rest I refer to my enclosure to Mr. M'Donald, with whom I wish you to have some conversation. Be not discouraged, I really believe God will visit poor Waterford in love; do you go on; bear up the hands that hang down;

---

(1) *Life and Times of the Countess of Huntingdon*, II., p. 165.

by faith and prayer support the tottering knee; reprove, encourage. Storm the throne of grace, and persevere therein, and mercy will come down."[2]

This clear, seasonable and earnest epistle, together with its enclosures, no doubt exercised an influence for good on both preachers and hearers in the city; but the evil done could not be completely undone. Among those lost to the Society through this controversy was one whose name deserves more than a passing notice, Mr. William Scroder. His parents were respectable, and when a youth, his careless, reckless spirit was a source of great pain and anxiety to them. About the year 1760 a privateer was fitted out at Waterford, and he, being then eighteen years of age, with others entered on board her. They had not left the port many days when, after a sharp action, a French vessel was captured, with which they were returning, when a violent storm arose in which both privateer and prize were lost; but the lives of the crew saved, almost miraculously. This providential deliverance had a salutary effect on William's mind, and from it resulted those religious impressions which led to his conversion. He became a member of the Society, and an active and acceptable leader and local preacher. His talents were not brilliant; but his spirit was earnest, his style quaint, and his life in harmony with the principles he inculcated. At this period he embraced Calvinistic opinions, withdrew from the Society, and continued for many years to preach in rooms in the city to a few followers who were warmly attached to himself and his religious views.

How long Mr. Hawkesworth remained at Waterford is uncertain; but he was succeeded by Mr. Jones, and others in Lady Huntingdon's Connexion. They likewise visited other places, and were instrumental in laying the foundation of congregations at Cork and Sligo. At the latter, not only were the views of Mr. Maiben, the leading member of the Society, Calvinistic, but also those of the Assistant, Mr. Christian; and through their influence the town was visited by Mr. Hawkesworth. Thus a separate body was formed, from which eventually arose the present Congregationalist church. So powerful was the influence of the Calvinists, that even Charles Graham was led for a time to embrace the doctrine of a limited atonement; but soon came back to the people of his early choice.

When Mrs. Bennis returned to Limerick in April, she found the Society there also rent and torn, "for the most trifling matters that can be conceived."

---

(2) *Christian Correspondence*, pp. 69-71.

Mr. Wrigley, who had been in Cork, and exchanged with Mr. Hern, was now Assistant of Limerick. He was abrupt and imperious in his manner, a strict disciplinarian, rather inclined to stand on his official dignity, and of unbending integrity; yet withal having a kind heart. He had evidently come into collision with the young men of the Society, written a vehement letter to Mr. Wesley, and expressed his determination to put them out if they did not acknowledge their fault. Mr. Wesley quietly replied, "I never put any out of our Society for anything they say of me."

Mr. Wrigley, however, was succeeded by Mr. G. Snowden, who soon gained the love and esteem of all the people, and peace and harmony prevailed. The select bands set apart some days to wrestle with God for a revival, and not in vain. On July 21st Mrs. Bennis writes: "By a letter from Mr. M'Donald I learn the work of God is prospering in the county of Wexford; but in Waterford they are still lifeless. We have proposed to them, and all the country Societies on this and that round, to set apart the first of next month as a day of fasting and prayer, solely on their behalf. Perhaps the Lord will be entreated and cause the dry bones to live." Five months later she writes again from Limerick: "The work of God goes on blessedly here under Mr. Snowden and Mr. M'Donald; we have indeed happy meetings both in public and in private. The Lord is also at work in Waterford, and in most of our country Societies; but as you have got an account of these I need not recapitulate."[3]

There were in Dublin at this period two young men, Matthias Joyce and Bennett Dugdale, fellow apprentices in Mr. Exshaw's printing establishment. Joyce had been a Roman Catholic, but influenced by curiosity had gone to hear Mr. Wesley preach, and was so impressed that he returned to the services. This, together with the reading of a tract which an all-wise Providence had placed in his hands, led him to renounce Popery. Both he and Dugdale were brought under deep conviction of sin, and went to Mr. Jaco, the Assistant in the city, who spoke to them faithfully and lovingly, and gave them notes of admission into the Society, saying: "The Lord write your names in the Lamb's book of life." Joyce subsequently entered the itinerancy, and Dugdale became a most acceptable and useful leader and local preacher for many years.

At this time Mr. Pritchard had charge of the Newry round, where, he says, they gathered in some hundreds from the barren mountains. He received

(3) *Christian Correspondence*, pp. 76-77.

efficient help from Mrs. Gayer, who engaged heartily in work for her Redeemer. One of her first cares was to secure the erection of a chapel in Lisburn, where there was none, the services being. conducted in private houses. This was accomplished in the course of twelve months, chiefly through her assistance; and during the year no less than seventy persons were added to the Society in the town and neighbourhood.

Mr. M'Nab was the Assistant on the Londonderry circuit, where the Lord was pleased to bless him in increasing and strengthening the Society. An opportunity having been obtained for preaching at Newtownlimavady,[4] through the Divine blessing on his ministry, Mrs. Martha M'Gee was enabled to rejoice in a sin-pardoning God, and became a member of the Society. She was called the "Mother of Methodism in Newtownlimavady," being one of its first members, and for sixty years one of its most active and faithful supporters. So consistent was her conduct that even the enemies of the truth were constrained to acknowledge the genuineness of her piety.

Notwithstanding the serious losses in membership sustained during this year, in Dublin nearly one hundred by discord, and in Enniskillen upwards of two hundred by persecution, there was a net increase in Ireland of three hundred and twenty-eight, chiefly on the Armagh, Londonderry, and Newry circuits.

Of the many rescued from Popery, through the Divine blessing on the labours of Methodism in Ireland, the name of Anne Devlin should have more than a passing notice. Born in the county of Fermanagh, she was in early years the subject of the gracious influences of the Holy Spirit, and in answer to earnest prayer obtained a sense of sins forgiven; but in an evil moment she yielded to the strong pressure brought to bear on her, again went to mass, and thus lost her confidence. The state of this young woman now became terrible. She fell into utter despair, more than once was on the verge of putting an end to her miserable life, and was at length taken to the priest, and afterwards to the bishop. The former said, that when these melancholy notions were out of her mind, all would be well; and advised her to take pleasure in the world, to keep jovial company, and to be sure to dance a great deal; adding, "A shilling to the priest, and a few days in purgatory, will do away with all." The bishop spoke much to the same effect, anointed her with oil, and then threw the tow that he had used into the fire, saying: "The witchcraft

---

(4) Now called Limavady.

is all over!" But the bitter anguish was still there: and the poor girl, having done wrong, instead of going back to the Source of peace, wandered further from God, plunged deeper in sin, and thus bound herself more firmly to Satan.

In this state Anne remained until she was twenty-one years of age, when she heard a sermon preached by Mr. James Perfect, who was then stationed on the Enniskillen circuit. Under the preaching of the word a gleam of hope once more entered her mind; she began again to pray, and her spiritual distress returned. On reaching home her friends offered to send for the priest, but she told them it was of no use, unless to tell him of her lost state. She continued thus in deep distress for about twelve months, when the Lord once more revealed Himself in tender compassion, set her soul at liberty, and gave her the assurance that He had healed all her backslidings.

Two years later (1774) she resolved publicly to renounce all connection with Popery; having heard which, the priest sent her word that he would "tear her out of the Church, and make hawk's meat of her." But she answered that God was above him, and through Divine grace she feared neither him nor the Pope. Mr. Skelton having removed from the parish, she applied to his successor to be received into the Church: and he, having heard her say that she knew her sins were pardoned, exclaimed, "Alas! alas! the poor widow's daughter is gone mad. Go home, my girl, to your mother." She then went to another clergyman — probably Mr. Skelton — who approved of her resolution, and having given proper directions and promised his protection in case of persecution, wrote to the minister of her own parish to comply with her request.

Numerous methods were employed to try to turn the young convert aside from the right way. The old priest was brought to see and reason with her. He said that none could be saved out of their Church, and that all heretics were on their way to hell; but she expressed her determination never to return to popery. On another occasion Anne's mother and some friends arranged to get her married by force, without acquainting her of their intention, and they had even fixed the time; but on the morning of the day decided on, a younger sister told Anne of the plot, and she fled for her life. The mental anxiety through which she then passed, together with the fatigue and exhaustion of her journey, brought on an attack of fever, which when the people in whose house she had sought refuge discovered, they would not permit her to remain. So she was obliged to return home. On coming back her mother refused to receive her unless she would yield. This, however, she declined to do, choosing rather the rude shelter of a poor cabin, where, with scarcely any attention or sustenance, through the Divine blessing she recovered.

Friendless and homeless Anne then wandered about from place to place, supporting herself by knitting and other kinds of work, until her health began to decline, in consequence of the privations and persecutions she had to endure. The Lord then raised up many friends amongst His people: more especially Mrs. Johnstone, of Lisleen, who, having heard of her circumstances, received her as a sister, and thus afforded her a holy and happy home.

Mr. James Dickson, of Charlemont, a man whose heart glowed with love to Christ, and yearned over sinners, in all the zeal and tenderness of his first love, went to Dungorman to the wake of some neighbour or friend, and there, amid many who, according to the then and still too prevalent practice, had met for worldly mirth, he stood up valiantly for God. The Holy Spirit accompanied the word faithfully spoken, and amongst those who "were pricked in their hearts" was a Mrs. Frizzell. From the deep seriousness apparent in many countenances, Mr. Dickson felt encouraged to follow up the good work. Accordingly, he and another man, named Verner, like-minded with himself, shortly after returned, to exhort and hold meetings for prayer. Many tokens for good followed, and they were led to attempt the formation of a class. They appear to have set about the work in the right spirit and in the right way. They went to all whom they thought desirous "to flee from the wrath to come;" spoke to them individually on the subject of their salvation, and, being very much in earnest, their words were attended with all the weight of felt truth. Amongst others, they visited Mrs. Frizzell, and told her their own experience of the knowledge of salvation, which then, though only a revived gospel truth, appeared to her, and to others generally, quite a new Methodistic doctrine. Their visit was not without some effect, for she was induced to attend the meeting of the class, though at the risk of being scorned and mocked by the ungodly. The service was rather protracted that morning; for the good men, being in the spirit of winning souls to Christ, took no note of time. But Mrs. Frizzell was a punctual woman, and as the hour of her usual Sabbath service drew near, remembering that she had a long walk to the meeting-house, she left before the class ended. After she had gone, it was painfully suggested to her mind that she had insulted the good men, and this temptation so haunted and harassed her the whole of the following week that she resolved not to return to class the next Sabbath morning. The devoted evangelists, however, who watched over her soul, on missing her, immediately went to visit her, and spoke so of the love of Christ to her as.a lost and wandering sheep, that, as she said, "they quite won her by love." This proved the turning-point in her life. She returned to the neglected service, and there she soon experienced the peace and gladness of all that believe. Her soul was thus made exultingly happy in God her Saviour, and from that hour she never for one day, during an unusually protracted life, lost her first love: her Sun never set, or withdrew His light from her soul. In her own limited and humble sphere, Mrs. Frizzell engaged in work for her Master. She met a class for many years, in the discharge of the duties of which she manifested that vigilance, tenderness, and zeal which nothing but close and constant communion with God can produce and sustain. Her wisdom and piety drew many around her for spiritual counsel, which was ever given with cordial promptitude and unaffected lowliness of spirit. She was also especially endeared to the young, whom, as the lambs of the flock, she carried to God in earnest, believing prayer; and many of them grew up to maturity, filled important positions in the Church, and gratefully embalmed her memory in their hearts.

In the Derg country the work prospered greatly, meetings were held in all directions, the young men especially labouring with much zeal and success. George Brown having recovered from a serious illness, resumed his happy toil, walking hundreds of miles to preach, and seeing much fruit to his labours. He refers amongst others to one meeting that he held, when there being no house large enough to contain the audience, he preached "by moonlight" to a great congregation near Strabane, and the Lord gave His enriching blessing. The most influential of those converted at this period was Alexander Boyle, Esq., of Kirlish Lodge, who did much by his godly example, Christian efforts, and generous liberality to extend the cause of vital religion. For a period of twenty years this district of country was indeed a "school of the prophets," giving to the Methodist ministry a host of devoted and gifted men. George and Hugh Brown, Hugh Moore, John and Thomas Kerr, Thomas Owens, John Harper, Matthew Stewart, A. Hamilton, sen., Robert and James Smith, Robert M'Coy, and Samuel Steele, were all men of this place and period.

John Price was on the Enniskillen circuit, and with characteristic zeal and enterprise he extended his labours beyond his appointed sphere. In the neighbourhood of Ballyshannon the people were irreligious and immoral, almost to a proverb, their principal amusements being hunting, horse-racing, gambling, and cock-fighting, which generally were accompanied by scenes of drunkenness and strife. The first place in this part of the country into which Methodism was introduced was Cloghore, near Belleek, and Mr. Price was the honoured instrument. Under his faithful ministrations of the word of life John Fitzpatrick and his wife and three others were led to give their hearts to God. The good work rapidly extended to the adjoining townland of Carricknahorna, where John Myles had the privilege of receiving the messenger of mercy. The first class consisted of seven persons, all of whom, having lived in the fear of the Lord, died leaving a blessed testimony of the power of Christ Jesus to forgive sins.

While one of the itinerants was preaching in the open-air at Aughnacloy, a young man of seventeen, Jackson Horner, brother of the preacher, was convinced of sin, and soon after obtained a sense of pardon. He became a member of the Society, provided a room for the preachers, and was thus the means of re-introducing Methodism into the town. He also sustained the office of a leader for sixty-seven years with fidelity and success.

Mr. Pritchard was stationed on the Armagh circuit, where he found that the labours of his predecessors had been greatly blessed; but he had much to discourage him. The brother appointed to labour with him was not able to fill his appointment, so he was left without help. Fearing lest the work should suffer he made it a subject of special prayer, and laboured to the utmost of his strength, and the Lord continued to vouchsafe His blessing, increasing the number and the holiness of the people; thus fulfilling the assurance, "As thy days, so shall thy strength be."

CHAPTER 5

1775

THE Rev. Edward Smyth of Ballyculter, now became more evangelical in his views and pointed in his preaching, which his brother clergy soon learned and objected to in a way that did not show much respect for the Word of God. Thus in a conversation between him and the Dean of Down, the former having quoted one or two texts of Scripture in support of his opinions, the Dean promptly replied, "Let us have no Scripture introduced, the less of that the better!"[1]

Early in the spring of 1775 Mrs. Smyth went on a visit to her father at Lisburn. Here she attended the parish church three Sundays in succession, longing to hear something of the death and merits of the Saviour; but in the three discourses she only heard His name mentioned once. Grieved at heart, she thought it was wrong for her to let fear keep her from the Methodist services, where she might hope for the needed instruction. The obstacles were great; her pride resented association with a despised people; her husband did not wish it; and her father forbade it, at the peril of forfeiting his favour. But a deep sense of duty impelled her onward. She determined to go: and went, blushing with shame, hiding herself when there, and then hurrying away at the close of the service, lest she might be recognised. Having informed Mr. Smyth of what she had done, and found to her joy that he not only withdrew his objection, but even gave his consent, she went again with more courage. Now she joined heartily in the service, which shame had prevented her from doing before; and heard Mr. Payne preach from Jeremiah 23:29, a sermon, every sentence of which seemed to go home with convincing power to her heart.

Having a strong impression that she should cast in her lot with this people, she was led to attend the services frequently. On one occasion Mrs. Gayer invited her to accompany her to Mrs. Cumberland's. "No," thought Mrs. Smyth, "or I shall be for ever called 'a Swaddler,'" and declined. But Mrs. Gayer would not be put off, and did not let her go until she consented. Here she met a few devoted servants of God in Christian fellowship, which was

---

(1) *The Religion of the Heart Delineated*, p. 47.

greatly blessed to her, and at once became a member of the Society.

Soon after this Mrs. Smyth, one Lord's day, was made unspeakably happy. The Lord by His Holy Spirit revealed to her so clearly the condition of salvation by faith in a crucified Saviour, that she was lost in amazement at His boundless love. So marked was the change, that on going downstairs her friends at once observed it. "Why, Nessy," said her sister, "I have not seen you look so well this great while;" and no wonder, for her soul was filled with joy. "All I knew," she says, "was, that I loved my Saviour above all things, and that He loved me; which conviction I thought I would not forego for all the world, as it seemed dearer to me than life itself." This heavenly joy continued, and Divine light shone into her soul, the Scriptures being wonderfully opened to her understanding and applied to her heart.

On April the 2nd Mr. Wesley landed at Dunleary, and proceeded at once to Dublin, where he was the guest of Mr. and Mrs. Wm. Smyth. On examining the Society he found the membership exactly the same in number — three hundred and seventy-six — as it had been two years previously; but there was more peace and love than there had been for many years. While in the metropolis he took the opportunity of waiting on the Countess of Moira, notwithstanding the long and bitter controversy which had just taken place, in which her venerable mother took so deep and practical an interest. At the request of "the good old Dean," he also assisted in administering the Lord's supper in St. Patrick's.

Wesley remained eight days in Dublin, and then began his tour through the provinces. He preached at Edenderry, and accompanied by Messrs. M'Nab and Bradford, came to Tyrrell's Pass, where he met Messrs. Wride, Hern, and Floyd, the circuit ministers, and where he preached to a large congregation with much power, met the Society, and administered the Lord's supper. At Longford a chapel had been built in the previous year, and a great number of the people attended the service; but he found very little of the spirit which had been there two years before. At Athlone on Sunday, the 16th, Mr. M'Nab preached at five in the morning, and Mr. Wesley at eight and at half-past five, and afterwards held a love-feast. Having visited Aughrim and Eyrecourt, he preached at Birr, with a good hope that God would at length revive His work in the town. At Clara, where he was the guest of A. Armstrong, Esq., J.P.,[2] he occupied the marketplace, the people attended

---

(2) Son-in law of S. S. Simpson, Esq., J.P., of Oatfield.

`5`

`4``4``4`

eagerly from the market, and there was no buying or selling during the service. At Coolalough he preached twice and met the Society; at Tullamore he had a large congregation; and at Portarlington, "still unstable as water," he preached and met the Society. At Mountmellick on Sunday, the 23rd, Mr. Bradford preached early in the morning; and Mr. Wesley at nine and at five, and afterwards met the Society and administered the Lord's supper. At Maryborough he read prayers in the church, and preached to a numerous audience, which seemed much affected. At Kilkenny he was shocked at the smallness and deadness of the congregation, which was a little revived on the next evening, but not much; so on going away he left Mr. Hern behind him to preach there, which he says he did with much freedom to large audiences.[3]

At Waterford the rain drove the people into the preaching house, "the most foul, horrid, miserable hole," says Wesley, "which I have seen since I left England!" But the next day he got out into the open air, and a large congregation attended. He had intended to leave on the following morning, but as he saw a good many Highlanders present, and thought he night not have such another opportunity of addressing them, he remained another day in the city.

By a singular coincidence, just eleven days after the death of his old but faithless friend, the Rev. R. Lloyd, Wesley arrived again at Rathcormack. He had a long drive of more than forty miles, and not being able to obtain accommodation in the inn, was obliged to proceed nearly twenty more to Cork. Here he was much pleased with the state of the cause, the congregations were large and deeply attentive, the singing such as he had seldom heard before, and the Society increased both spiritually and numerically. At Bandon he preached in the Main street, and found the Society here likewise much established in grace, and greatly increased in numbers. This he ascribed to God's blessing on the labours of John Bristol and George Snowden, "two plain men, who put forth all their strength in His work."

At Limerick, about six weeks previously, Mr. M'Donald, the preacher stationed on the circuit, having taken ill of fever, while delirious in the absence of his nurse, jumped out of the window of his room into the yard at the rear of the preaching house, and died in half-an-hour. In this city Wesley preached to a large congregation of Catholics and Protestants in the yard of

(3) Unpublished Diary of J. Hern.

the custom-house, where many could hear within as well as without. On examining the Society he found it to consist of one hundred and one persons, being seven less than two years previously. At Newmarket he had a deeply serious audience; at Galway a more civil and attentive congregation than he had ever seen there before; and at Ballinrobe an auditory that in number and seriousness surprised him.

When Mr. Wesley reached Sligo he saw the sad havoc the Calvinistic controversy had made; finding himself disowned by former friends, the Society but the wreck of what it had been, and the preaching room in the hands of others. Notwithstanding the smallness of their numbers, the prospects of this Society soon looked more hopeful: for the little company left were as much alive to God and more united than ever. A preaching house was soon after erected in Bridge street, a small and tumble-down structure, with a thatched roof, so low that some years subsequently when Mr. R. Banks was stationed on the circuit, being tall of stature, a hole had to be made in the earthen floor to enable him to stand erect!

At Swanlinbar, knowing that a large part of the congregation had tasted of the powers of the world to come, Wesley spoke on the glory that should be revealed, and they seemed deeply affected. At Belturbet he preached in the town hall, and the Lord opened the windows of heaven, and showered His blessing down. At Clones, where he was entertained by Richard Kelso, the service was held in the old Danish fort, and the largest audience he had seen in the kingdom assembled to hear. The Society had been strengthened by the accession of a few of the more respectable inhabitants, including a young gentleman named Armstrong, who left by will forty pounds, to assist in the erection of a chapel; a brother of his, who subsequently removed to Dublin, was also identified with the cause; and a young lady named Bradshaw, a relative of theirs, who became a leader. The congregations so increased under the preaching of the Word, that a piece of ground was taken in Carra street, where a neat chapel was erected this year; but for the sake of an ill-judged economy a large dwelling-house was built in front, leaving an inconvenient entrance to the chapel. This sacred edifice, however, proved to be the spiritual birth-place of hundreds of immortal souls.[4]

But to return to Wesley. Having preached at Roosky and Sidaire, he came to Derg-bridge, and found a large congregation waiting, who appeared one

(4) *Irish Evangelist*, 1861, p. 193.

and all to be deeply serious. "Indeed," he says, "there is a wonderful reformation spreading throughout this whole country for several miles round. Outward wickedness is gone, and many, young and old, witness that the kingdom of God is within them."At Londonderry he found the members growing in grace, and increased in numbers from fifty-two to nearly seventy. He accepted an invitation to dinner from the Bishop, the Hon. F. A. Hervey,[5] with whose preaching and manner of reading the service, as well as Christian courtesy, he was most favourably impressed. At Castlecaulfield his sleeping accommodation was far from comfortable, as the rain came in freely through the thatch; but he says he "found no present inconvenience, and was not careful for the morrow."

At Dungannon he preached in the market-place to a numerous congregation. This year the preachers were first invited to the town by Mary Rice, who had been a member of the Society at Castlecaulfield, and thenceforward Dungannon was regularly visited by the itinerants, although no Society was formed until some years subsequently. At Killyman and Armagh Wesley had large audiences, and at Clonmain many were much affected. On Tuesday, June the 13th, Wesley was seized with illness, which well nigh proved fatal, yet for four days subsequently, though in a burning fever, he continued travelling and working as usual. That evening he preached "with ease to a multitude of people" at Cockhill; but next day at Grange it was with no little difficulty he got through the service. So finding himself worse he drank copiously of treacle and water, and applied treacle to his feet. This having proved effectual in relieving, though not in removing the disorder, he proceeded to Derryanvil, and preached in the open air. On Friday he again conducted a service on the parade at Lurgan; and on the following day a skilful physician having given him some medicine he set off for Tanderagee, where he was kindly received by the rector, the Rev. H. Leslie, LL.D., and thence to Derryaghy, where his overworked system sank, both mind and body having completely failed. Here he received from the family the kindest attention. Serious apprehensions were entertained throughout the kingdom, and fervent prayer was offered for his recovery. One day Mr. Payne with a few friends at Derryaghy, earnestly prayed that God would graciously prolong the valuable life of His servant, and, as in the case of Hezekiah, add to his days fifteen years. Mrs. Gayer suddenly rose from her knees, and

(5) He was a brother of Lady Mary Fitzgerald, and subsequently became Earl of Bristol.

exclaimed: "The prayer is granted!" Soon after Mr. Wesley was restored to health, and, it is worthy of notice, survived from June, 1775, till March, 1791, a period of fifteen years and eight months.

The Rev. E. and Mrs. Smyth, who were in Lisburn at this time, and had been looking forward with no ordinary interest to meeting Mr. Wesley, were at length gratified. Mrs. Smyth wrote to her sister-in-law: "Mr. Smyth and I dined in company with Mr. Wesley at my uncle Gayer's yesterday. We spent a most happy day. The sweet old man seemed in good spirits. What a blessing is the communion of saints!"

Twelve days after Wesley arrived at Derryaghy, to the astonishment of his friends, he set out for Dublin, where he soon resumed his usual labours, preaching twice each day; and remained for more than three weeks. He makes no reference to holding a Conference this year in Ireland; but Mr. Hern writes that on Friday, July the 14th, he rode to Dublin with Mr. Clendinnen, and reached there that evening, when they had a watch-night service. He also says: "We had a very smart Conference, but concluded in peace and love." On Friday, the 21st, he left the metropolis, with Messrs. Slocomb, Snowden, and Halliday, and came in safety to Mountmellick.[6]

On the 23rd Wesley having again assisted in administering the Lord's supper at St. Patrick's, embarked for England, and thus ended this memorable visit to the Emerald Isle.

At the above Conference Messrs. John and Jeremiah Brettel and Hugh Brown were appointed to the Enniskillen circuit, where they found a poor but affectionate people. There were thirty-nine places to supply, and they had the satisfaction of seeing the work of God prosper. On one occasion Mr. Jeremiah Brettel preached the funeral sermon of a pious young woman, from the words, "Is not this a brand plucked out of the fire?" and soon after visited a new place in the neighbourhood, where he met an old man, who said to him, "I heard you preach at the funeral of my cousin; and I read the text over a hundred times afterwards. People greatly prejudiced me against your sort of people, but they told me lies of you: and now I am resolved, 'as for me and my house we will serve the Lord.'" The result of this decision was that his seven children soon after were all enabled to rejoice in the love of God. The old man also became so happy and active in the Divine service, as almost to think himself young again.

---

(6) Unpublished Diary.

A zealous local preacher on this circuit being deeply impressed that he ought to visit Fintona, which was then noted for its wickedness, rode there, and, calling at a house, told the family he would stay and preach if they would call in some of their neighbours. They received him hospitably, and invited all the people round. At the close of the service he announced that he would preach again on the next evening, in another house, if anyone desired it. Thus he was invited by several families, remained some days, and the Lord gave His blessing. Many were awakened to a sense of their state, and led earnestly to seek the kingdom of God. Some of the members of an adjoining Society then visited the town, and arranged for a watch-night service, which excited great interest. A violent woman, who lived a few yards from the place of meeting, protested against anyone belonging to her going thither. At length she yielded to the earnest entreaties of her daughter, who desired to attend, but prayed that she might never see her way back again. During the service an uncommon power descended on the people, many were deeply affected, and led to cry aloud for mercy; and not a few found the blessing they sought. The woman mentioned above heard the noise, and went to the door, but soon returned to her own house, and there cried earnestly for mercy. Some persons were sent for to pray with her, and the Lord heard and delivered her from all her fears. Meantime, her daughter had also obtained the pardoning love of God, and they rejoiced together. The Rev. Philip Skelton was then rector of the parish, and, desiring to see one of the preachers, Mr. Jeremiah Brettel called, whom he received kindly, and inquired particularly of him concerning his reasons for preaching, his doctrinal views, and his religious experience; and they parted in good terms.

There were four preachers appointed to the Athlone circuit, which then included Westmeath, King's County, Queen's County, Tipperary, Meath, Galway, Mayo, and Longford.

Amongst those on the Newry circuit who at this period joined the Society and were converted to God, were two young men, John and William Hamilton, who resided at Mullaghglass, and subsequently became laborious and successful preachers. William especially was remarkably quaint, terse and homely in his style, and seldom failed to arrest the attention of his hearers and leave a lasting impression on their minds and hearts.

During this year John Price, who was stationed on the Londonderry circuit, preached at Coleraine in the street. Mr. Stephen Douthett was one of his hearers, and was so deeply impressed with what he heard that at the close of the service, when the preacher expressed his intention to visit the town again if anyone was willing to entertain him, he gladly embraced the opportunity, and made the messenger of the Lord welcome to his house. Thus Methodism for the first time obtained a footing in this town, It is a noteworthy circumstance that about the same time that Mr. Price was thus led to visit Coleraine, the Methodists of Lisburn arranged with one of their preachers to make a similar effort in that town, and united in special prayer that the Divine blessing would rest on his labours.

CHAPTER 6

1776

SOON after the conversion of Mrs. Edward Smyth her husband was likewise brought to a saving knowledge of the truth, and began to evince fervent zeal, not confining his labours to the church, but holding services in private houses, both in his own parish and in the neighbouring one of Dunsfort. These meetings were greatly owned of the Lord in the salvation of many, most of whom were at once enroled in classes as members of the Methodist Society. Mrs. Smyth wrote in January, 1776: "I believe there has seldom been a greater revival of religion than in Dunsfort parish. The Lord hath confirmed it by signs and wonders. He seems truly to be pouring out His Spirit upon all flesh. Persons come five miles, and return home in the midst of the snow, to hear the word preached. Many young strong men have roared out through the anguish of their spirit. Some people were seized with fainting, trembling, contraction of their limbs, and violent crying. Mr. Smyth exhorted in a barn in that parish on Tuesday last, and it was thought he had six hundred hearers. Wonders are to be seen almost every time of our meeting."[1]

Margaret Davidson having met with the Rev. Edward Smyth and his excellent partner at Derryaghy, was invited to spend some time at their house. She had not been there very long when Mr. Smyth took her with him to a meeting at Dunsfort, and there insisted on her declaring to the people what

(1) *The Religion of the Heart Delineated*, pp. 76, 77.

the Lord had done for her soul. Such was the impression made by her address, that Mr. Smyth considered it advisable to leave her to work amongst the people. Meetings were arranged for each evening; large numbers flocked to hear the poor blind woman; some of these were brought into great distress about their souls, and persevered in prayer until they found rest in Jesus. The services were continued with signal success until, within a month, she could number one hundred who had been brought out of darkness into marvellous light.

Although there was much opposition to this work, a wonderful moral and religious change took place throughout the neighbourhood, which was most apparent. Amongst the many then brought into connection with Methodism, whose names were household words for more than half a century in that district of country, were David Thompson, of Ballyculter, a man of much piety, integrity and zeal, who was appointed to take charge of the first class formed, and was most acceptable as a leader and local preacher; Bernard Clinton, of Sheepland, who had been a zealous Roman Catholic; Thomas and Barbara Teer, of Killough, where a society of eleven members was formed; John and Jane Coates, of Slieveroe; Mr. and Mrs. Coulter, of Kilclief; and a host of others of like spirit.

The second Sunday school in Ireland of which there is any record, was one of the fruits of this gracious revival. It was opened by the Rev. Dr. Kennedy, incumbent of the parish of Bright. He was painfully impressed with the total disregard of the Lord's day amongst the young people in some villages through which he had to pass, and assisted by Thomas Teer, got the boys and girls together on Sundays to practise psalmody. This made a little stir. Soon to singing was added exercise in reading the Psalms and lessons for the day, which being rumoured abroad, excited great attention, and the numbers that attended increased considerably. Those who came were desired to bring what Bibles and testaments they could in order to being better instructed and examined in what they read, and children of other denominations were invited to share the advantages of the meeting. Thus in the year 1778 the gathering, which had begun as a singing class, had matured into a school, held regularly every Sunday for an hour and a half before the morning service. The good work went on and prospered until the latter part of 1785, when Dr. Kennedy having heard of the establishment of Sunday schools in England, thought that his plan should be more comprehensive and systematic, according to the English method. During the winter information

was circulated on the general subject, and funds obtai.
interested in the project. The necessary preliminaries havin,
the Bright Sunday school was re-opened on the first Sunday
well organized, with an efficient staff of teachers, includin,
Thomas Teer.

Under a sense of duty Mr. Smyth wrote a letter of admonition to the great man of the parish, who was living in open sin. This, instead of leading him to repentance, excited his hostility, so that he deprived the writer of his house, and ordered his tenants not to receive him. Thus the faithful minister and his family were compelled to seek shelter in a little thatched cabin, with only two rooms and no attendance; but this reverse of fortune did not give Mrs. Smyth an uneasy thought. She could write, "Glory be to God for such a shelter! It is more than the King of kings was always assured of." Animated by this spirit, she entered heartily into the duties of her new position, rising easy and late, taking little rest, and denying herself all but the mere necessaries of life.

The fearless testimony and faithful preaching of Mr. Smyth, accompanied by the saintly life of his devoted wife, made a deep and gracious impression on the mind of the Hon. Miss Sophia Ward, daughter of Lord Bangor, showing her the transitory and unsatisfactory nature of worldly pleasure, and leading her to see the necessity of a life devoted to God in order to happiness. So that during the dispute between Mr. Smyth and her father, not only were her sympathies with the faithful minister, and not the faithless parent, but she was enabled by Divine grace to lay hold for refuge on the hope set before her in the Gospel. She also formed a high estimate of Irish Methodism, which she retained during her subsequent protracted life, and generally manifested in the final disposal of her property.

At this period the Society in Dublin sustained a severe loss in the death of Mr. Garrett, one of its oldest and most consistent leaders, who for sixteen years had been an eminently holy and useful man, and his end was glorious. The Lord poured into his soul such a full tide of blessing as enabled him to rejoice in the prospect of the Paradise of God, and made even his face to shine. When his voice was almost lost in death, he exclaimed, "Glory, glory be to God! the Lord, the Saviour! O, He has conquered for me! He has conquered in me sin, death and hell. I come! I come. Come, Lord Jesus, come quickly!"

In Cork a soldier named Whitmore, a notorious blasphemer, who had murdered one of his comrades and was sentenced to death, was visited by Mr. John Watson, the Assistant on the circuit. Through the Divine blessing on the faithful and earnest efforts of this servant of God, the wretched criminal was led to see his awful guilt, and the great love of God in Christ to him, so that he went cheerfully to the place of execution, rejoiced in the prospect of soon being with his Saviour, and gave out and sang a hymn immediately before his spirit was hurried into the eternal world.[2]

The British Conference met this year on August the 6th, when the increase in membership reported from Ireland was five hundred and sixty-one; but two serious complaints were made with regard to this country. Of the upwards of £600 raised by the Yearly Collection, only thirty-five shillings had been contributed in the Emerald Isle, and that in one town only — Bandon. The brethren in the rest of the country affirmed that they were responsible only for the contingent and travelling expenses of their own preachers. But the Conference thought differently; and they were required to pay, in addition, the expenses of all English preachers going to and from Ireland, and of any sickness or unavoidable distress that might befall them or their wives in this country. It was also further reported that in Ireland, most likely in Dublin, part of the leaders met together on Sunday evenings, without any connection with or dependence on the Assistant, and therefore it was formally declared: "We have no such custom in the three kingdoms. It is overturning our discipline from the foundations. Either let them act under the direction of the Assistant, or let them meet no more. It is true they can contribute money to the poor; but we dare not sell our discipline for money."[3]

Jeremiah Brettel, who, with his brother and Robert Davis, was appointed to the Armagh circuit, says they had to preach at thirty-four different places, which included some considerable towns, such as Newry, Lurgan, Tanderagee and Charlemont. In this last place especially they had a good Society, and some very pious people.

Messrs. Pritchard, Hern, Mill and R. Armstrong were appointed to the Londonderry circuit. Mr. Pritchard says the circuit was large and laborious to travel, having to go to Coleraine on the one hand, and to the dreary county of Donegal on the other, and round by Lough Derg to Lisleen. Mr. Hern gives fuller details. The appointments included Londonderry, Kilrea, Coleraine, and Newtownlimavady, in Derry; Drumclamph, Lislap, Magheracolton, Whiskey

---

(2) Unpublished MS.

(3) *Minutes*, I., pp. 124-25.

hill, Kirlish Lodge, Creevy, Killeter, Lisleen, and Killeen, in Tyrone; and Castlefin, in Donegal. The September quarterly meeting was at Lisleen; having held which, Messrs. Pritchard and Hern, accompanied by Mr. A. Boyle, went to Charlemont, to attend the quarterly meeting there. The Rev. E. Smyth preached in the street at eleven o'clock, afterwards held the love-feast, and preached again in the evening. God was present. Then Mr. Hern preached "with great freedom." The next day a similar series of services was held at Lisburn.

The itinerants and Mr. Boyle then proceeded to the north, preaching at Ballymena and Ballymoney *en route* to Coleraine, where on the following Sunday, October the 6th, Mr. Hern preached. He could not sing; but this lack was supplied by the zeal and devotion of a young woman, afterwards Mrs. M'Kenny, and several other members of the Society at Ballymena, who walked the entire distance, nearly thirty miles, that they might thus assist at the service. Surrounded by this choir Mr. Hern took his stand in the Diamond when the several congregations were retiring from their respective places of worship: and soon had an attentive audience, "almost the whole town attended." Charles and John Galt, who had been at the Presbyterian meeting-house; Robert and Thomas Rice, who were returning from the parish church, and Thomas Bennett, were among the hearers, and afterwards attended the Methodist services, more or less frequently. The preachers and their kind friend remained in the town for the two following days, preaching each evening in the market-house "to a great multitude." With the financial assistance of Mr. Boyle, the wing of an old barrack which had been long unused and was falling into decay, was secured as a place of worship. By throwing several rooms into one, an apartment was fitted up for the services, capable of containing from three to four hundred persons. Another portion was prepared for the preachers to lodge in during their periodic visits, while they boarded with the people, being received with much attention and respect. A class was formed of which Robert Douthett was appointed the leader; and before the close of the year there were almost sixty members of Society, chiefly persons in very humble circumstances, called "the poor folk at the barrack." The moral improvement in the conduct of these, however, was so marked, that the Society gained the good will and confidence of those of more influence.

In Kilrea the Rev. J. Haughton, who had been in the itinerancy, and recently obtained this parish, received the preachers with much cordiality;

but did not long survive his appointment, as in about two years after he was taken to the home above.

Early in September Samuel Bradburn, "the Methodist Demosthenes," sailed for Ireland, having been appointed to Limerick, and a few days after his arrival on the circuit spent his last shilling. He entered upon his work with fear and trembling, but God gave him great favour in the eyes of the people, so that he was soon agreeably settled, and was cheered by the attendance of "amazing congregations." During the following month he preached fifty-seven times, and on the 29th conducted a watch-night service, and preached, prayed, and sang four hours without intermission. In the midst of this hard toil, he says, he was very happy; but it proved too much for him, and his health gave way.[4]

In the meantime, through the influence of Lord Bangor, a petition was sent to Dr. Trail, Bishop of the diocese, charging the Rev. E. Smyth with erroneous teaching and irregularity in conducting public worship. He was therefore cited to appear before his lordship at Knockbreda on October the 21st. The Rev. Wm. Bristow, the vicar-general, a clergyman of liberal Christian principles, who had been appointed vicar of Belfast in 1772, was summoned to appear for the prosecution; and when called on said he had heard Mr. Smyth conduct public worship, and pray and preach extempore, and that his prayers and sermons were highly instructive and scriptural, in accordance with the Articles, Homilies and Liturgies of the Church of England, and well fitted to promote the spiritual improvement of the people[5] Mr. Smyth also had an opportunity, which he improved, of giving a public testimony to the truth, proving that the doctrines he preached were in harmony with the Word of God, as well as the teaching of the Church. Although he completely refuted every accusation, he was deprived of his cure, through an illegal stretch of power. This circumstance, though most trying, was over-ruled for good, as Mr. Smyth resolved to accept no preferment in the Church, and give himself wholly to the work of God in connection with Methodism. Although living on a very small annuity, he never lacked either food or raiment; his sphere of usefulness was greatly enlarged, and many souls were converted through his instrumentality.

Meanwhile the good work prospered in Dunsfort and Ballyculter. Mrs. Smyth writes: "I can give you but a small notion how the Word of the Lord

---

(4) *Life of Bradburn*, pp. 57, 58.

(5) *Irish Evangelist*, 1868, p. 26.

runs and is glorified. All around, young and old, flock to the standard of Jesus, as the doves to their windows. I think the class in this town (Strangford) consists of thirty-six, almost all alive to God; and particularly some girls, who seem resolved to take the kingdom of heaven by violence."

The Rev. J. Abraham visited Mr. Smyth and was greatly quickened. Mrs. Smyth describes him as a most amiable young man, who, although his friends were greatly opposed to his identifying himself with Methodism, seemed resolved to follow Christ fully, be the consequences what they may.

In the neighbourhood of Cavan the word was received by Mr. Robert Creighton, of Kilmore. He writes as follows — "My two sisters and I some time ago joined Mr. Wesley's Society, and have ever since entertained the preachers. My brother, the Rev. J. Creighton, at first opposed us much, on account of our religious principles; but he is now, through grace, himself convinced of the truth."

In Dublin the spirit of contention appears to have arisen again. Mr. M'Nab who had been the Assistant of the circuit during the two previous years, says he had reason to believe that he was made a blessing to many souls, and that he was persuaded he would have been more abundantly so, had it not been for some discontented men in the Society, who strove to do him all the hurt they could: and they succeeded in restraining his usefulness, as they had done that of many of his brethren before him.[6]

In November Mr. Hopper paid a short visit of two weeks to the city, probably to try and allay this ferment. He only says, however, that he preached every evening to large audiences, and God blessed His word and gave him success. He visited a few backsliders also, who were glad to see the face of an old friend.

Mr. Slocomb, who had been appointed to the Clones circuit, and is described by Wesley as "an old labourer, worn out in the service," came to the house of Mr. Maguire at Mullalougher, ill of fever, the week before Christmas. Although he was tended with unremitting care and affection, on the last day of the year he sank under the virulence of the disease, and his spirit entered triumphantly into his Master's joy. When Mr. and Mrs. Maguire returned from the interment of this faithful old soldier of the cross, they found that two of their children had taken the infection, and soon after Mr. Maguire and two others of the family caught the disease; but the Lord supported and

(6) *Arminian Magazine*, 1779, p. 248.

healed them. Mr. Maguire then resolved to remove to Dublin, which he did as soon as practicable: and in the metropolis he and his family identified themselves heartily with Methodism.

CHAPTER 7

1777

EARLY in 1777 Mr. Bradburn was removed to Dublin, where the people in general manifested great love to him, and having less to do than in Limerick, his health gradually improved In preaching he felt "a heavenly sweetness," and souls were converted under the word.

The Rev. E. Smyth visited the metropolis at the same time, and preached frequently in the Methodist chapel. That an Episcopal clergyman, the nephew of an archbishop, and one whose family was so highly respectable, should pursue such a course excited much interest and curiosity, and multitudes flocked to hear.

Amongst those thus attracted by the fame of the preacher, was a young man named Henry Moore, who was under great concern for his soul. He was much impressed with what he saw and heard; but the sermon did not meet his case. However he determined to be a regular hearer, and had no doubt that the word preached would prove to him the savour of life. So he returned in a day or two with great expectations; but was much disappointed when he found the pulpit occupied by a layman in plain clothes, Mr. Bradburn, and was about promptly to leave the chapel when better thoughts prevailed, and he resumed his seat. The word came with power to his heart, and the service proved to be the turning point in the history of this young man, who in time became one of the foremost Methodist preachers of his day.

Soon he obtained peace and joy in believing, became a member of the Society, and thus got acquainted with Edward Gibson, Matthias Joyce, Bennett Dugdale, and others of the devoted band of godly young men then identified with Methodism in the metropolis. They regularly visited the sick and those in prison, and thus witnessed appalling scenes of disease and every species of misery; but the Lord greatly blessed their labours.

Amongst those whom they were the means of leading to the Saviour were some of the lowest and worst of criminals. One of these was a Romanist, under sentence of death, named Huggins, of most forbidding and repulsive appearance, who seemed at first quite callous and utterly insensible to his awful position. At length he was roused to a sense of his terrible state, became intensely anxious, and then God spoke peace to his soul. Even the external transformation was marvellous, his face shone with happiness, and his whole frame partook of the joy of his spirit. The change had a most salutary effect on his fellow culprits, also under sentence of death, one of whom prayed earnestly when proceeding to the place of execution: "O Lord, give me an item of it" — that is of the pardon which he knew his companion possessed. At the gallows Huggins broke out in prayer and praise, and exhortation. "Hold your tongue, I say," vociferated a priest. "Sir," said Huggins, "the Lord encourages me, and I cannot be silent," and in this happy frame he was soon translated to the Paradise of God.

The Society in Dublin became increasingly lively and zealous, and some of the people desired to enlarge the work. A prayer meeting was therefore begun at Dolphin's barn, where the preaching room secured by Charles Wesley had been given up, after the erection of the chapel in Whitefriar street. The people flocked to it, and soon the place became too strait for them. They then took an unoccupied weaver's shop, and had it suitably fitted up. Here Henry Moore preached his first sermon. When the preacher visited the place, he found twenty-six persons had been brought into the Society, all of whom were either under conviction of sin, or happy in the knowledge of God.[1]

Meanwhile, the Rev. E. Smyth having no further inducement to remain in Ballyculter, removed with his family to Downpatrick. Here he began at once to hold services in the open air; his extraordinary zeal, eventful history, superior talents, and gentlemanly appearance, all contributed to give success to his meetings. He did not, however, confine his labours to the town; but travelled through the country, preaching, holding love-feasts, and administering the Sacraments. Thus numerous Societies were formed. Mrs. Smyth writes concerning him — "The success that attends his words is really amazing; there is scarce any place that he has preached that he has not had seals to his ministry, and these not a few. Many witness at the love-feasts, that he is their father in Christ."

---

(1) *Life of the Rev. H. Moore*, pp. 16-42.

The death of the junior preacher on the Lisburn circuit, John Harrison, a young man of great piety and promise, added considerably to the labours of Mr. Smyth. Hence we find Mr. Wesley writing to Mr. Benson as follows — "If there is a preacher to spare, let him step over as soon as possible from Portpatrick, and supply the place of that good young man, John Harrison, in the Lisburn circuit. Mr. Smyth calls aloud for help. He is zealous and active, but is quite overborne."[2]

The British Conference met on August the 5th, when the total membership in Ireland reported was five thousand two hundred and eleven, being an increase of four hundred and thirteen on the previous year.

Messrs. R. Watkinson and J. Prickard[3] were appointed to the Londonderry circuit, a portion of which evidently having been cut off to form a new circuit, of which Ballyshannon was the head. Through the instrumentality of these excellent brethren the good work greatly prospered, especially at Coleraine, the rector of the parish, the Rev. Mr. Boyd, being favourable to the cause, and kind and attentive to the preachers.

Messrs. Jer. and John Brettel, and J. Hern, were stationed in Lisburn. Mr. Jer. Brettel says, they had thirty-three places to preach at, and many of them had been but recently visited by the preachers. In Lisburn they had a lively Society, some of whom were persons of deep piety. Through the circuit great numbers attended the services, and much labour and instruction were necessary, with God's blessing, to improve the minds of the people and direct them in the right way.

The Limerick circuit requiring an additional preacher, Mr. Myles was appointed to labour there. He bore his own expenses during the year, and the Lord blessed his labours and those of the Assistant, Mr. John Watson, so that upwards of one hundred members were added to the Society.[4]

It was in Dublin, however, that the events of most stirring interest took place. The contention that had long existed in the Society, and had been lulled into a calm, was now increasing and about to burst in a storm. On the day on which Mr. Hampson, senior, the Assistant of the circuit, landed at Dublin from the British Conference, a charge of preaching false doctrine was preferred against his colleague, Mr. Bradburn, by Mr. Solomon Walker, a gentleman of considerable influence and wealth in connection with the

---

(2) *Wesley's Works*, xii, pp. 426-27.

(3) Mistaken for Mr. Pritchard in the Minutes of the Irish Conference.

(4) *Arminian Magazine*, 1797, p. 212.

Society. The particulars of the charge are not now available; but their nature may be inferred from what follows. Mr. Hampson in a pamphlet entitled, "The Case Stated," after severely censuring the time at which this charge was made, and the manner in which it was supported by others than Mr. Walker; and after eloquently asserting his colleague's orthodoxy, good temper and usefulness, affirms that Mr. Bradburn's arguments against Calvinism had been so powerful, that some lukewarm people had been made uneasy under them, and could not sleep quite so soundly as they used to do, for they were convinced that if what he said was true, they had been prophesying smooth things, and crying peace, peace, when God had not spoken peace.

The matter was evidently reported to Mr. Wesley, who sent the following reply to Mr. Alexander Clark, dated September the 9th — "It is certain our preachers have a right to preach our doctrines, as my lady's have to preach theirs. None can blame them for this. But I blame all, even, that speak the truth otherwise than in love. Keenness of spirit and tartness of language are never to be commended. It is only in meekness that men are to instruct them that oppose themselves. But we are not allowed, on any account whatever, to return evil for evil, or railing for railing."[5]

Meanwhile the dispute had assumed another and more serious form, than that of simply accusing a Methodist preacher of being rather emphatic in his Arminianism. It became a question of moral character and conduct. Mr. Hampson called a meeting of the trustees of the Widows' Alms House, to elect a successor to Mr. Gaskell, deceased. The opportunity was seized by Messrs. Geoghegan and Hall, of accusing the treasurer, Mr. Martin, of cheating the charity, which, it was said, would be substantiated by a reference to the books. Mr. Martin was from home on account of his health at the time, and on his return the matter was at once investigated by Messrs. Walker, Deaves and Keene; and it was found that instead of defrauding the poor widows, for several years the treasurer had advanced money out of his own pocket towards the institution, which then owed him a considerable sum, and that the entries in the book on which the charges were based, had been surreptitiously made there by one of the accusers.

Here then was an undoubted case for discipline; but Mr. Hampson evidently considered that guilt was not confined to one person, and that the gross wrong done was only one indication out of many, of a bad spirit, which

---

(5) *The Western Pioneers*, pp. 45, 46.

others also had displayed: and therefore he acted with vigour, if not with sternness, by expelling four leaders for unchristian conduct. These were the Messrs. Clark, and probably Messrs. Geoghegan and Hall. Two of these, however, persisted in meeting their classes, and they were therefore read out publicly on a Sunday evening. Doubtless there was strong sympathy among the officers and members of the Society with those on whom discipline had been exercised, especially the Messrs. Clark, which was expressed in such a way that between expulsions and resignations, thirty-four members were lost to the Society, including Messrs. Walker and R. Hunt.

Numerous letters having been sent to Mr. Wesley, informing him of the state of affairs, and finding that all he could write was not sufficient to calm the troubled waters, he resolved to come himself and try what could be done. Accordingly he made a hurried visit to the city, arriving on Saturday, October the 4th, when Mr. M'Kenny met him, and brought him to his house.

The news of Wesley's arrival soon spread, the friends flocked from all quarters, and seemed equally surprised and pleased to see him. He found the congregations exceedingly large and the total membership unchanged, notwithstanding the losses sustained. When he met the excluded members and heard them at length, they pleaded their case with earnestness and calmness, but refused to be pacified. They were civil, even affectionate to him, but could never forgive the preachers who had expelled them, so that he could not desire them to return into the Society. They remained however friends at a distance, meeting in class by themselves, but regularly attending the preaching services in Whitefriar street chapel.

During this visit of Mr. Wesley to the metropolis, there was another visitor in the city, who subsequently took a very prominent position in connection with Irish Methodism. The Rev. Adam Averell, then a young man of twenty-one, who had been ordained deacon only two or three months, happened to call at the house of Mr. Persse, a barrister, found the family at dinner, and being asked to join them, consented. Immediately after he had taken his seat, Mr. Persse, addressing the gentleman who sat next him, said — "Well, Mr. Wesley, we interrupted you in the anecdote you were telling." The name of Wesley startled the young clergyman; he had often heard before of the founder of the Methodists, and now for the first time met him; and was not a little surprised to be informed by his host, that he considered Mr. Wesley "one of the greatest and best men of the age." In the evening Mr. Averell went with Mr. Persse to Whitefriar street chapel, sat in the pulpit, and heard

Wesley preach.[6]

On Sunday, October the 12th, the venerated evangelist took a solemn and affectionate leave of the members of Society, "more in number," and he was persuaded "more established in grace than they had been for twenty years."

But to return to Ulster. In Newtownbutler, although the Methodists were not exposed to brutal violence, yet for several years, after the first visits of the preachers, the Society made but little progress. A few very poor people were united in class and were favoured with an occasional sermon as the preachers passed through the town, but none of the Methodists were in circumstances to entertain the servants of God. At length, during this year, a brighter day dawned on the infant Society John Clarke, second son of James Clarke, of Cortrasna, having married his cousin Anne, a truly pious young woman, rented a house in Newtownbutler, and opened a shop. On the following Sunday morning, Mr. Horner, the Assistant of the Clones circuit, rode into the town, and preached in the house of a wheelwright named Trotten, when Mr. Clarke, seeing that the preacher was about to leave without partaking of any refreshments, invited him to his house, and desired that on his return he would come on the Saturday night, stop with him, and preach. From that time the itinerants regularly visited the town once a fortnight, and preached on Saturday evenings and Sunday mornings, which proved a source of strength and blessing not only to the Society in the town, but also to several small societies in the surrounding country, the members of which came to the Sabbath services. The meetings continued to be held in John Clarke's house for several years, and when the increase of his business rendered it necessary to enlarge his premises, he left the second floor in one room, so as to afford increased accommodation for public worship.[7]

In Downpatrick the Rev. E. Smyth having secured a suitable site for a preaching-house, collected the necessary funds, and set to work to have it built. In this erection he assisted in the manual labour; and had the satisfaction of conducting the opening service on the morning of Wednesday, November the 26th. In the evening Mr. Hern "preached with freedom from Revelation 3:20." In this work Mr. Smyth was greatly assisted by Mr. Thomas Tate, a gentleman of influence in the town, who was not a Methodist, but several members of his family were, including his son-in-law, Mr. George Moore, who was for many years the chief support of the cause in Downpatrick. When

---

(6) *Memoir of the Rev. A. Averell*, pp. 15, 16.

(7) *Irish Evangelist*, 1861, p. 14.

the preaching-house was completed, Mr Smyth and his family took up their abode in a small room adjoining, built for the accommodation of the preachers. Yet even in this obscure home, deprived of all the luxuries of life and many of its comforts, his delicately-reared young wife, although very weak in body, realized a deep and lasting happiness which raised her above every discomfort.

CHAPTER 8

1778

AT the beginning of 1778, Mr. Hugh Moore visited Drumbullion in the parish of Killashandra, where the Lord greatly blessed his labours; a prosperous society was formed, and a chapel soon erected. This building had a noteworthy history of its own. When the lease expired in 1798, the noble landlord took possession of the edifice and turned it into a school-house. The teacher was a Roman Catholic, and soon after his appointment, having declined to fulfil a matrimonial engagement with a young woman of his own communion, she in a spirit of retaliation set fire to the building, and it was burned to the ground. Little thus was gained by depriving the Methodists of their place of worship.[1]

On the Lisburn circuit the preachers persevered in their arduous and self-denying work. Frequently during the winter for want of room they had to preach out-of-doors, sometimes standing in the snow. Such excessive labours brought on an attack of fever, which nearly closed the career of Mr. Jeremiah Brettel. He had no pain, but slept perpetually. When roused from his sleep, and warned of his danger, he replied — "I shall live to go to England with Mr. Wesley," and immediately fell asleep again. Three days subsequently he was once more roused, and informed that the friends thought his recovery hopeless; he answered — "All things are possible to him that believeth," and slept again. He continued in this state for several weeks, and then slowly

---

(1) *Irish Evangelist*, 1861, p. 194.

began to recover. During his illness two deaths from the same complaint took place in the household of Mrs. Bennett, Broomhedge, by whom he was so kindly nursed — her eldest son and a servant maid — and both died happy in the Lord.[2]

On April 2nd Mr. Wesley arrived in Dublin, where he had the satisfaction to find that notwithstanding the recent separation, the members of the Society, while numerically undiminished, were more alive to God, and more united than they had been for some years.

Having spent five days in the metropolis, he set out for the country. At Tyrrell's Pass he preached to numerous congregations, and the power of the Lord was present to heal. At Mullingar the audience was much more serious than he had seen there before; at Longford the hearers were still more serious and not less numerous; and at Athlone he had a comfortable time, all being peace and harmony, and God spoke by His word both to wound and to heal. Some of the large congregation at Ballinasloe seemed much affected, as did many at Aughrim; and at Eyrecourt, the minister not only lent his church to the devoted evangelist, but also invited him to his house. At Birr the hearers were deeply attentive; many old friends assembled at Coolalough; and at Tullamore the commanding officer ordered all the soldiers to be present at the service, and attended himself with the rest of the officers.

At Portarlington Wesley had a very respectable yet attentive audience. At Mountmellick he preached in the church to a congregation much larger than when he was there before, and considerably more attentive. At Kilkenny, in consequence of the parliamentary election, and also the perpetual quarrels between the chief members of the Society, the congregation was small and dead. At Clonmel the preaching room being inadequate, and the weather unfavourable, the service was held in the largest room in the town. At Bandon, from the size and seriousness of the congregation he thought the work of God was much increased; but upon inquiry found the contrary; nearly one third of those were wanting, whom he had left in the Society three years previously, but those who remained seemed much in earnest. At Cork he found no increase in the membership, notwithstanding the glowing accounts he had received, yet many of the members were much alive to God. Here two companies of volunteers attended an evening service in the chapel, the gentlemen of the Aughrim Society dressed in scarlet filled the side galleries,

---

(2) *Wesleyan Methodist Magazine*, 1830, p. 656.

while the Independent Company, dressed in blue, occupied the front gallery and part of the body of the house, and all seemed to hear as for life.

At Kilfinnane, in the neighbourhood of which there was a considerable revival of the work of God, Wesley preached in a large vacant house secured for the purpose. At Limerick he found the congregations good and well sustained, and the Society appeared more alive to God and more loving than he had known them to be for many years. While in the city he wrote — "A Compassionate Address to the Inhabitants of Ireland," in which he refers to the general panic which prevailed concerning the desperate state of the nation. The fear of invasion from every side was making the people tremble. He laughs to scorn the report that General Washington had an army of 65,000 men; and says that "the French will as soon swallow up the sea" as swallow up old England; that the Spanish have not forgotten Havannah; that the Portuguese were "not such arrant fools" as to join in a confederacy with England's enemies; and that as to all *intestine vipers*, "there was no more need of being afraid of ten thousand White Boys than of ten thousand crows." "Blessed be God," he says, "there are still within the kingdom some thousands of regular troops, of horse as well as foot, who are ready to march wherever they shall be wanted; over and above the independent companies at Birr, at Mountmellick, at Bandon, and at Cork."[3]

Wesley preached to the poor people at Ballingarrane, who attended in large numbers, although the notice was short; and also to "the loving, earnest, simple-hearted" folk of Newmarket, who two months previously had been bereaved of good Philip Guier, their faithful and devoted spiritual father. At Ballinrobe there was a "numerous congregation, but most of them dead as stones;" at Hollymount there were more than the house could contain; and at Castlebar there was a lively, earnest people, upon whom the Lord graciously poured out His Spirit.

From this town Wesley drove to Sligo, accompanied by Messrs. Bradford and Delap, and two of the local brethren: when such was the state of the road, that twice he had to be carried on the shoulders of some of the peasantry over bogs, while the chaise was either being borne by others, or with no little difficulty and damage dragged through the mud. Having arrived at his destination he was thankful to find tokens of a gracious revival. It appears that after the recent division in the town the Methodists wisely abstained from

(3) *Wesley's Works*, XI., pp. 149-56.

entering into controversy with their former brethren, and gave themselves heartily to evangelistic work, labouring amongst both Protestants and Roman Catholics: in which efforts Charles Graham took a leading part. This brought on them the ire of the priests, who denounced them from the altars. Other means also were used by the opponents of the truth to accomplish their evil purpose. Thus as Graham went one Sabbath morning to meet a class, some distance from the town, a stalwart Romanist, instigated by altar denunciations, struck him on the side of the head: the servant of God, acting literally on the injunction of his Master, "turned to him the other also," and receiving a second blow, said — "It will be a mercy if you are able to lift that arm this day week." To the consternation of all who knew it the man was buried on that day week.[4] From that time forward preachers and leaders passed to their appointments unmolested. During this revival special prominence was given to the blessing of purity of heart. The whole circuit partook of the gracious influence, and numbers were led to seek and obtain the pearl of perfect love. Mr. Wesley found the congregations considerably increased, and the Society nearly doubled. For four years this good work continued to make steady progress, and the membership increased from four hundred and two this year to one thousand and ninety-eight in 1782, when a second division of the circuit took place.

At Swanlinbar Wesley preached in a large apartment designed for an assembly room, where rich and poor listened with great attention. At Belturbet he occupied the armoury, and the audience was large and serious. At Cavan, in the courthouse, the congregation was still larger; and at Cootehill, where the use of the Presbyterian meeting-house had been procured, he had an extraordinary audience consisting of all creeds and parties.

At Clones he preached in the fort to very large and increasing congregations: and observes — "There is something very peculiar in this people; they are more plain, open and earnest than most I have seen in the kingdom. Indeed, some of our Irish Societies — those in Athlone, Limerick, Castlebar, and Clones — have much of the spirit of our old Yorkshire Societies." Early morning meetings were regularly and numerously attended in this town; there was much life in the Society, and the zeal and consistency of the members had a good influence on the community at large. This was

(4) *The Apostle of Kerry*, p. 22.

particularly manifest in the case of horse-racing. There had been annual races in the neighbourhood, to which great crowds resorted, when a silver plate or cup purchased by public subscription was the chief object of competition. But such was the moral influence resulting from the conversion of so many respectable inhabitants, that sufficient subscriptions could not be raised, and the races ceased. Of the leading members, one was a cousin of the Rev. William Thompson, Mr. Andrew Thompson, a faithful and laborious leader, who went regularly six miles on the Sabbath morning to meet a class; another was Mr. Bernard Connolly, who when passing the chapel one evening was induced to enter, and the result was his conversion to God, so that he became very useful; and a third was Mr. John Armstrong, who had under his care a class for the religious instruction of youths, in which he was much acknowledged of God.[5]

But to return to Wesley. At Aghalun, Sidaire and Magheracolton there were large and attentive audiences. At Londonderry he found the Society a little smaller than it had been three years previously, and was surprised that more good had not been done, considering the size and seriousness of the congregations. At Kilrea he was the guest of Mr. Haughton, but the church being a mere heap of ruins, he preached in the new meeting-house to a very large auditory, some of whom seemed not a little affected, and all were seriously attentive.

At Coleraine the spacious preaching room could not contain a third of the congregation; but, standing at the door, he had them all before him in the barrack square. On the following day, having visited the Giant's Causeway in the morning, he witnessed a cheering and touching scene in the evening. A few days previously a young lady had joined the Society without the knowledge of her relatives: and having been informed that her sister was speaking to Mr. Wesley with the same object, she entered the room, ran and fell upon her neck, wept with holy joy, and then sank on her knees to praise God. Her sister could hardly bear it — she was in tears, and so were all present. These two young ladies were the Misses Young, and their becoming Methodists added much to the influence and success of the Society. One of them was afterwards united in marriage to Mr. Henry Moore, and the other to Mr. T. Rutherford. On Sunday Wesley having breakfasted with the Rev. Mr. Boyd, of whom he speaks in strong terms of commendation, read prayers

---

(5) *Irish Evangelist*, 1861, p. 193.

in the church, and administered the Lord's supper to an unprecedented number of communicants. The Right Hon. Richard Jackson, M.P., and his excellent lady, who were present, seemed to rejoice in showing him every mark of respect. In the evening the venerated evangelist preached to a wonderful congregation in the barrack square, many of whom were present at the five o'clock service next morning.

Having visited Ballymoney and Ballymena he arrived at Carrickfergus, where he met Messrs. J. Hern and William Black, who accompanied him round the circuit. Here, as the town-hall could not contain the audience, he occupied the market-house: and the people appeared more serious, and the Society more earnest than for many years. At Belfast he preached beside the new parish church of St. Anne's in Donegall street, to far the largest congregation he had seen in Ireland; but thought the spirit of the majority of his hearers was described in his text — "And Gallio cared for none of those things." This was the third time he applied this passage to the people of this town. While the venerable evangelist was thus proclaiming the message of mercy, a young soldier was engaged with a trooper in playing cards in adjoining public house, and saw the crowds passing to the service, but would not leave his game. Having lost all his money, in hope of getting back some he staked a new pair of shoes, which he lost, and then went home vexed and mortified. His name was Joseph Burgess, and he subsequently became a devoted and useful Methodist preacher.[6]

At Newtownards Wesley preached to five or six hundred people in the old church, and then proceeded to Kirkcubbin, where he was the guest of Joseph Napier, Esq., of St. Andrew's,[7] who fitted up a barn for the devoted evangelist to preach in, and also accompanied him in many of his ministrations.[8] He then went to Strangford and preached, standing on a rock which projected into a large cavity filled with people. He next visited Downpatrick, where he was the guest of Mr. Richardson, whose wife, mother and two daughters were all converted through Methodism. Close to the house of his host Wesley observed one of the most beautiful groves he had ever seen covering the side of a hill, and a circular space in the centre. He was most eager to preach in this delightful spot, and on the following day the

---

(6) *Memoirs of the Rev. J. Burgess*, pp. 13,14.

(7) Grandfather of the late Right Hon. Sir Joseph Napier, Bart., Lord Chancellor of Ireland.

(8) *Wesleyan Methodist Magazine*, 1864, p. 553.

desired opportunity was afforded. So taking his stand on a pedestal, from which had fallen a statue of St. Patrick, this modern apostle of Ireland proclaimed the Gospel to a vast multitude standing on the gradually rising ground before him, and listening with breathless attention to the message of salvation. The whole scene was one of intense interest and solemnity, and impressions for good were then made such as were never afterwards effaced.[9]

Downpatrick was at this time part of the Lisburn circuit, and it was not uncommon for some of the Society to walk to that town, a distance of twenty miles, to a love-feast. "The word of the Lord was precious in those days," and the love and unity of the people resembled that of the members of the early Church, when they "were of one heart and of one soul." Amongst these early Methodists were Mrs. Tate, her son-in-law, Mr. George Moore, for many years circuit steward, Miss Tate, Dr. Speers, Mr. Sloane, and Miss Kearns — names that should not be forgotten.

At Derryaghy Wesley preached to a lively congregation under the shade of a venerable yew tree, supposed to have flourished in the reign of King James, if not of Queen Elizabeth. At Lisburn, to which the brethren had flocked from all directions, he preached three times, presided at the quarterly meeting, and conducted the love-feast, when many of the people declared with all simplicity and yet with great propriety what God had done for their souls. At Ballinderry large numbers assembled to hear, though at very short notice; and there were four or five times as many at Lurgan in the evening, but "some of them wild as colts untamed." On the following morning he opened a small dwelling-house, which had been fitted up as a chapel, to the great joy of the little Society in the town. Mr. Miller, a local woollendraper, of whose ingenuity Wesley speaks at length, painted a representation of an angel pointing to Revelation 22:17, which was placed above the pulpit.[10]

At Derryanvil and Cockhill there were attentive congregations; and at Charlemont, where Wesley was the guest of the commanding-officer, Captain Tottenham, all the soldiers were present, in addition to large numbers from the surrounding country. At Armagh on Sunday morning the congregation was large and serious. It is probable that it is to this service William Black refers as one at which he was present, and of which he says — Mr. Wesley preached from Luke 20:36: and when he came to speak on the second clause, "For they are equal to angels, and are the children of God, being the children

(9) Unpublished MS.
(10) *Wesleyan Methodist Magazine*, 1827, p. 801.

of the resurrection," he repeated it several times, and his soul being so filled with rapture that he could not proceed, he burst into tears, saying, "Let us pray." An overwhelming influence fell upon the assembly. In the evening the audience was increased fourfold; but "there were many who behaved as if they had been in a bear garden." At Tanderagee, where he was the guest of Dr. Leslie, he preached in the courtyard, under the shade of a tall spreading tree, in the midst of a numerous congregation, who were still as night. Next evening there was a large audience at Newry; and then he returned to Dublin, where during the following week he visited as many as he could, and endeavoured to confirm their love to each other. He says that he had not known the Society for many years to be so united as it was then.

On July the 7th the Conference began, at which about twenty preachers were present. The increase in the membership during the year amounted to one hundred and twenty-five. Wm. Gill, Andrew Blair and Wm. Myles were received on trial. The question of leaving the Established Church was debated; but "after a full discussion of the point," says Wesley, "we all remained firm in our judgment, that it is our duty not to leave the Church wherein God has blessed us, and does bless us still." This discussion was brought about by the Rev. E. Smyth, who was most eager for a separation, and laboured with all his might to accomplish his purpose, but failed. "Is it our duty," it was asked, "to separate from the Church, considering the wickedness both of the clergy and the people?" "We conceive not," was the answer — 1. "Because both the priests and the people were full as wicked in the Jewish Church, and yet God never commanded the holy Israelites to separate from them. 2. Neither did our Lord command His disciples to separate from them: if He did not command just the contrary. 3. Hence it is clear *that* could not be the meaning of St. Paul's words, 'Come out from among them, and be ye separate.'" Wesley considered such questions then as only a diversion from the appropriate work of Methodism, and therefore reminded the Conference of its high calling by the additional question — "Have we a right view of our work?" It was answered: "Perhaps not. It is not to take care of this or that Society, or to preach so many times; but to save as many souls, and bring as many sinners to repentance as we can, and with all our power to build them up in that holiness, without which they cannot see the Lord."[11]

_____

(11) The following is the list of stations, taken from a copy of the Minutes in the hands of the Rev. Dr. Osborn: - Dublin - R. Watkinson, W. Eells; Waterford - T. Halliday, R. Armstrong; Cork - J. Hampson, sen., S. Bradburn; Limerick - A. Delap,

On the following Sunday Mr. Wesley conducted a covenant service. "It was a time never to be forgotten. God poured upon the assembly the Spirit of grace and of supplications, especially in singing that verse of the concluding hymn -

> 'To each the covenant blood apply,
> Which takes our sins away —
> And register our names on high,
> And keep us to that day.'"

On the three succeeding days Wesley visited many of those who had left the Society, but found them so deeply prejudiced that he could not advise them to return to it; and on July 19th he embarked for Liverpool, having spent more than fifteen weeks in Ireland.

On August the 4th that meeting of the British Conference began, which is memorable as the first at which the question of missions to the heathen was discussed. This debate arose in connection with a proposal to send missionaries to Africa, continued for several hours, and was marked by deep piety, sound sense, and powerful eloquence. The deepest impression, however, was made on the minds of all present, by the short speech of a young man far gone in consumption, who promptly offered himself as a missionary, and in unaffected language declared his readiness to go to Africa, or to any other part of the world to which it might please God and his brethren to send him.[12] That young man was an Irishman of great promise, James Gaffney,[13] who had travelled only two years, and was then received into full connexion; but his desire was not gratified, the way not being then open for such an undertaking; and in about eight months subsequently his pure and fervent spirit entered into everlasting light and glory.

Although the Rev. E. Smyth received no circuit appointment, he entered heartily into work for Christ in connection with Methodism. Having changed his residence from Downpatrick to Lurgan, he travelled through the kingdom,

---

J. Bredin; Castlebar - N. Price, W. Myles; Athlone - T. Payne, R. Boardman; Sligo - R. Lindsay, H. Moore; Clones - W. Boothby, J. Hern; Enniskillen - J. Price, G. Brown; Lisleen - J. Mayly, J. Howe, W. M'Cornock; Armagh - P. Mill, A. Blair, W. Gill; Londonderry - John Brettel, J. Gaffney; Belfast - T. Rutherford; Lisburn - J. Prickard, J. Hampson, jun. At the subsequent meeting of the Conference in England, however, Mr. Eells was appointed to Newcastle, and Mr. Rutherford to Dublin.

(12) *Methodist Magazine*, 1814, p. 508.
(13) *City Road Magazine*, 1875, p. 563.

preaching in the open air and in the chapels, holding love-feasts and administering the Sacraments, and his labours were much blessed.

On arriving in Dublin Mr. Rutherford says he found many persons who were deeply serious, and much alive to God, with whom he took sweet counsel, and his soul was both quickened and comforted. But during the winter his superintendent, Mr. Watkinson, was laid aside for seven weeks, and as there was no other preacher in the city to assist, he had to preach every night and three times each Sunday. This he found difficult and laborious; but it induced him to pray, to read, and to study hard, and the Lord helped him, so that he got through his work comfortably, and the people took knowledge that God was with him.[14]

Messrs. Hampson, sen., and Bradburn were appointed to Cork. The latter, who had just got married, says: "After a tedious and fatiguing journey, our reception in Cork was not very inviting; however, all is peace at present, and I am resolved to live to God, and do all the good in my power." He reached Bandon on July 30th, and after spending a month in that town, exchanged with Hampson, and went to Cork, where he wrote in his diary — "Though the accommodation in Bandon is very disagreeable, yet, as my lovely Betsy is content, with her I cannot but be happy. In Cork we have all we want, and are surrounded with friends, many of whom are old experienced Christians, and truly alive to God."

The Bandon accommodation referred to was the room already described as forming part of the first chapel. Other preachers also felt the discomfort of this room. But Bradburn found compensation in Cork, for of the time spent there he writes: "This month has been very pleasant, and I humbly trust some good has been done. I feel much pleasure in preaching; but by no means approve of addressing the same people every morning and evening without any change. Yet I find it useful, as it makes me read and study very closely. I feel an essential difference in this work, now that my mind is calm and happy, from when it was all confusion." This happiness did not continue, for he and Hampson quarrelled about the interchange: and Bradburn having referred the case to Wesley received the following reply — "I think you judge exactly right. You are called to obey *me* as a son in the Gospel. But who can prove that you are so-called to obey any other person? What I require (according to the twelfth rule of a helper) of John Hampson and you is, that

(14) *Methodist Magazine*, Dublin, 1808, p. 531.

each of you, in his turn, spend four weeks and no more — first at Cork and then at Bandon. When, therefore, you have been four weeks at Bandon, I desire you to return to Cork. And if John Hampson will not then go to Bandon, I will order one that will. Pray show this letter to Mr. Mackrill[15] whom I beg to assist you in this matter. Pass smoothly over the perverseness of those you have to do with, and go straight forward. It is abundantly sufficient that you have the testimony of a good conscience towards God."[16] This letter did not settle the quarrel. However, increase of experience brought a spirit of contentment.

Mr. Myles, who was stationed at Castlebar, says the people received him kindly, and he spent the year on the whole comfortably. The circuit was eighty miles in length, and embraced a part of each of the three provinces of Munster, Leinster and Connaught. The preachers regularly visited Castlebar, Ballinrobe, Tuam, Galway, Aughrim, Ballinasloe, Eyrecourt, Birr, Roscrea and Borrisnoe, besides many little villages and country places; but there were no societies in Tuam, Galway, or Ennis, and in many other places the members were few in number and the congregations small, the people being chiefly Roman Catholics.[17]

There is the following noteworthy entry in the diary of Mr. Hern, who was on the Clones circuit — "Kilmore, Friday, September 4th. This day, at the request of friends, hearing it was customary for the preachers to do so in this Society, I baptized a child, and God was remarkably present." It is certainly singular that such an act was performed by one of the itinerants at so early a period, and especially after the strong pronouncement of the preceding Conference against leaving the Church.

In Londonderry the Rev. J. Abraham, not feeling happy or comfortable in his work, after much thought and prayer, resigned his chaplaincy, and offered his services to Mr. Wesley as a Methodist preacher,[18] which were accepted, and he was regularly appointed to the City road chapel, London.

On the Coleraine circuit, at this period, a young man was brought under the sound of the Gospel, who in time proved one of the most illustrious of the sons of Irish Methodism — that youth was Adam Clarke, who then resided in the parish of Ballyaghran, or Agherton. One day a school-fellow said to

(15) One of the Cork leaders and stewards.
(16) *Life of S. Bradburn*, pp. 68-70.
(17) *Arminian Magazine*, 1797, p. 212.
(18) *Arminian Magazine*, 1788, pp. 609-10.

him: "Adam, let us go to Burnside, there is a Methodist preacher to be there this evening, and we shall have nice fun," and he consented, though without the slightest expectation of the promised diversion. He found many people assembled in a barn, and in a short time the preacher, Mr. John Brettel, entered, and with him, among others, Mr. Stephen Douthett of Coleraine. So deeply was the youth impressed, that he went again to the services, and thus entered upon his connection with Methodism, of which more again.

CHAPTER 9

1779

EARLY in 1779 Thomas Barber began his itinerancy as a missionary on the country parts of the Londonderry circuit, where he was owned as an instrument of grace to many. He mentions as scenes of his hallowed toil, Portrush, Bushmills, Ballyaghran, Beardiville, Portstewart and Mullaghacall, where he erected a small preaching-house, the first Methodist chapel in this district of country. At Ballycastle he was invited by a man in the neighbourhood to lodge at his house, where a door of usefulness seemed to be opened; but the next time the preacher came he received a message requesting him to come no more. The poor man could not bear the ridicule of his neighbours, so he walked in the counsel of the ungodly, and turned away the messenger of peace. It would have been well for that man and his family had he acted otherwise.[1]

Amongst those who went to hear the zealous and indefatigable evangelist was Mrs. Clarke, Adam's mother, who pronounced what she heard "the doctrine of the Reformation, true unadulterated Christianity," and urged her family to go and hear for themselves. Thus her husband was induced to attend the services, and being satisfied that what he heard was "the genuine doctrine of the Established Church," the preacher was invited to their house, which thenceforward became one of his regular stopping places. Through the preaching and godly counsels of Mr. Barber the mind of Adam became

(1) *Irish Evangelist*, 1862, p. 26.

gradually enlightened, his desires after God strengthened, and consequently his interest in Methodism increased. He rejoiced to see numbers attending the word preached, and a Society formed in the adjoining village of Mullaghacall, though at the time he had no intention of becoming a member. His mother, however, having gone to see how the meetings were conducted, was so favourably impressed that she desired her son to accompany her on the next day of meeting. This he did with some reluctance, listened with deep attention, and was not a little surprised to hear one of his neighbours, who had been a foolish trifler, testify — "I was once in darkness, but now I am light in the Lord: I was once a slave of sin, but now I am made free by the grace of Christ: I once felt the horrors of a guilty conscience, but now I know and feel that God has blotted out my sins." Adam began to feel very uneasy, and left the meeting dissatisfied with himself. Returning home, the leader, Mr. Andrew Hunter, of Coleraine, overtook him on the road, spoke faithfully to him, and earnestly urged him to give his heart to God, adding — "You may be a burning and shining light;" but little dreamed how remarkably his words would be realized. The young man earnestly and perseveringly sought the Saviour, and at length, as in anguish of soul, he pleaded for mercy, the Lord lifted on him the light of His countenance, so that he rejoiced in the God of his salvation.[2]

Adam Clarke had a school-fellow named Andrew Coleman, between whom and himself a warm friendship obtained. He was a young man of remarkable promise, had an amazingly comprehensive mind and retentive memory. He fathomed the depths of his studies, and could not be content with a superficial knowledge of any subject. At the age of fourteen he had not only the whole of the Book of Common Prayer by heart, but also had made himself such a master of the *Æneid* and of *Paradise Lost*, that on the mention of any line in either he could immediately tell the book in which it occurred and the number of the line. He also attended the ministry of Mr. Barber, his mind soon became enlightened as to the truth, and having earnestly sought redemption in the blood of Christ, he received it to the unspeakable joy of his heart. After some time he was employed as a leader, and at the earnest request of several began to hold meetings in different places through the country with great acceptance.[3]

Meanwhile on the Lisburn circuit an opening for preaching the word was

(2) *Life of A. Clarke, LL.D.*, pp. 84-99.
(3) Ibid., pp. 113-15.

obtained by Mr. Prickard at Kilkeel. At the time appointed for the service the house could not contain a quarter of those who desired to attend, so the faithful itinerant, irrespective of wind and weather, took his stand in the open air and preached for nearly an hour, while the hearers were as attentive as if they had been comfortably seated in church. This proved the beginning of a blessed work in the neighbourhood.

A severe trial, however, soon befell the Society on another part of the circuit. In February, 1779, the ship Lydia, richly laden with English and Irish manufactures, was wrecked near Sheepland, and all the crew except one perished. Many of the members of the Society went with the rest of the country people to plunder the wreck, and others either bought, or received presents of the stolen goods. When Mr. Prickard, the Assistant of the circuit, visited the neighbourhood, he found that every Society, except that at Strangford, had partaken more or less of the spoil. Feeling deeply the moral wrong of what was thus done, his duty seemed plain, to expel the guilty parties from the Society, and to urge the necessity of repentance and restitution. Accordingly on the following Sunday evening in the chapel at Downpatrick, he, with a bleeding heart, read out sixty-three who were implicated, adding that those who made restitution should be restored in due time, but those who declined to do so should have their names inserted in the general steward's book, with a record of their crime and obstinacy. This strict but faithful exercise of discipline proved beneficial; many of the offenders were deeply humbled before God, repented heartily of their sin, and made all the restitution they could, and even some who were not members, but attended the services, were convinced under the faithful preaching of the word, and desired also to unite in the act of indemnification. Mr. Prickard wrote to the owners of the vessel, stating the whole case, and desiring to know with whom he was to deposit what was restored. They replied, congratulating him on his connection with a people so open to conviction, and empowering him to allow salvage; but this he declined to do, considering the goods had been stolen. Thus the reproach that otherwise would have remained on the Methodists and prevented their usefulness was completely rolled away, and a most favourable impression created outside the Society.[4]

Valuable help was now rendered to the Society by the Rev. J. Creighton,

---

(4) *Lives of the Early Methodist Preachers, IV*, pp. 186-89.

who took an open and decided stand for Methodism, not confining his evangelistic labours to his own parish. Thus on the morning of March 31st, at Clones, in connection with the quarterly meeting, he preached in the open air: and then administered the Lord's supper in the chapel to upwards of three hundred persons, which proved to be a most remarkable time of God's power. In the afternoon Mr. Hern "preached in Mr. Armstrong's yard to a vast multitude." About a week later Mr. Creighton conducted a service on the hill of Knockninny, where a large concourse of people had assembled for a cock-fight. The poor Romanists who were present, however, were compelled by their priests to do penance for having listened to "a mad heretic." Other opportunities also were afforded the servant of God, in chapels, private houses and the open air, for proclaiming the glad tidings of salvation, which he faithfully and successfully availed himself of.

Owing to the death of Mr. Gaffney in Londonderry, at the request of Mr. Wesley, Henry Moore undertook to supply his place. Accordingly he set out for his circuit early in May, accompanied by the Rev. J. Abraham, who returned to his friends, not being considered by Mr. Wesley adapted to the work of the Methodist itinerancy. They spent the Sabbath *en route* at Clones, and were much cheered with what they saw there, the Society being "remarkable for the zeal, unanimity and love of its members." At Londonderry they found that Mr. John Brettel was about to start for England, leaving Mr. Barber to take his place. So Mr. Moore proceeded to Coleraine, the second place on the circuit, which even at this early period was the residence of one of the preachers, who had the charge of the adjoining country places, and interchanged with his colleague once in every three months. Mr. Moore says he never knew a Society more dead to the world, more alive to God, or more attached to Methodism, than in this town. The meetings were very lively, the congregations continued to increase, and there appeared to be a general pressing after holiness. He formed select bands, appointed a general meeting one evening in the week, preached himself every morning at five o'clock, and also frequently held meetings in the open air.[5]

Nor did this devoted young preacher confine his labours to his appointed round, but travelled to the regions beyond. Thus he visited Ballycastle, where he preached in the church green, and soon a little Society was formed of poor people, of whom a blacksmith and a shoemaker opened their houses to

---

(5) *Life of the Rev. H. Moore*, pp. 47-54.

receive the preachers. Liberty was then obtained to conduct the services in the court-house, and large congregations attended. In a place at some distance there were two men, nominal Protestants, who, feeling the Sunday heavy on their hands, went to the Roman Catholic chapel, where the priest warned his flock to beware of false prophets, and to show the dangers said they were come to Ballycastle. The curiosity of the two strangers being thus excited, they resolved to go and hear the Methodists for themselves. This resulted in the conversion of both. One became a useful local preacher, and t the other continued an attached member during a long life.[6]

In the course of this year, one of the itinerants preached in a field of Lieutenant Scott's, an officer of the yeomanry and a Methodist, who resided in the Derg country. Amongst those present were Mr. and Mrs. Robert Cather, of Carnony. As the servant of God spoke with deep feeling of the love of Christ, both of this worthy couple were convinced of sin, and soon after obtained peace in believing. They then opened their house to entertain the preachers. Mr. Cather gave up the use of tobacco in order to subscribe more liberally to the cause of God: and seeing a Christian professor return from the fair the worse of drink he resolved to give up the use of all intoxicating drinks. He died in peace in 1827, having been for forty-eight years a consistent and devoted member of the Society.[7]

Mr. Payne was at this time doing a noble work on the Athlone circuit. He writes to Mr. Wesley, that he had opened s seven new places in twenty-eight days, that he was invited to three more on his return to that neighbourhood, that in one parish alone he had preached in fourteen different places, and then went to Captain Armstrong's, Ballycumber, where he preached to about three hundred persons. "Upon the whole," he says, "there is a great prospect of much good, and a general desire that the preaching may be continued."[8]

The British Conference met on August the 3rd, when the reported increase of members in Ireland during the year amounted to six hundred and four. Although not named in the printed Minutes, the Rev. E. Smyth was appointed to the new chapel at Bath, being a part of the Bristol circuit, of which Mr. M'Nab was the Assistant.

William M'Cornock, who had been zealously labouring in the county of

(6) *Irish Evangelist*, 1862, p. 26.

(7) He was grandfather of the Rev. William and Dr. R. Cather.

(8) *Arminian Magazine*, 1789, pp. 385-86.

Donegal and had succeeded in forming several Societies, was called out into the itinerancy and appointed to the Enniskillen circuit. Although Methodism had been in the county of Fermanagh for sixteen or seventeen years, it was only now that it obtained a footing in the town of Enniskillen, where a few became members of the Society. They were much threatened by the inhabitants, yet no harm was done. At Drumbullion upwards of forty joined the Society, and at Florence Court the membership increased from about twelve to sixty.[9]

Of those who in this neighbourhood were brought under the influence of Methodism the most noteworthy was Daniel Bradshaw, Esq. He was a lineal descendant of the pious Bedell, Bishop of Kilmore, and in 1765, when about twenty years of age, purchased and made his residence at Violet Hill, where he was on friendly terms with the noble family of Cole. Here he got acquainted with the Methodists; and through the Divine blessing became anxious about his soul. Lord Enniskillen observing the change in his spirit, determined to draw him away from association with those who had caused this, as he thought, unnecessary seriousness; and with this object invited him to an entertainment at his house, to which Mr. Bradshaw went very reluctantly. But as soon as the frivolous amusements of the evening began, he slipped away, went to the usual preaching service, and before it concluded was enabled to believe with the heart unto righteousness. He immediately joined the Society, was soon appointed a leader, and opened his house for the preaching of the Gospel. In time that neighbourhood presented a changed appearance, new classes were formed, and the once Sabbath-breaking country became a land of prayer and praise. Lord Enniskillen and his family seeing the great moral transformation in the people, became favourable to Methodism, and his descendants have continued so to the present day. Mr. Bradshaw also during a long life gave clear and strong evidence of his deep love for God and sincere attachment to the Society.[10]

At this period the first regiment of dragoons was quartered in Lisburn, one of the non-commissioned officers of which was George Foster, a young man who had been led into folly and sin by ungodly companions, and enlisted in the army. He had a pious mother, who continued to plead earnestly for her wayward son, until the prayers of earth were lost in the praises of heaven.

(9) *Arminian Magazine*, 1785, p. 188.

(10) *Primitive Wesleyan Methodist Magazine*, 1852, pp. 317-19; and *Irish Evangelist*, 1861, p. 138.

On the very night her spirit entered endless felicity, Foster was roused to a sense of his state by a solemn and affecting dream. He thought that the day of judgment was come, and that the Judge looked at him with much displeasure, as he stood trembling with guilt and fear before the dread tribunal — a condemned sinner. He awoke, thankful that it was but a dream, and that there was still time for repentance. The vivid impressions then made were deepened by the sad intelligence of his mother's death; so he resolved to forsake sin, and seek the Lord with all his heart. He was thus led to become a member of the Methodist Society. Having found the Saviour, he spoke to his comrade, Joseph Burgess, who began to think seriously about the salvation of his soul, and to accompany Foster to the Methodist chapel. While listening to a sermon preached by Mr. Boothby, the Assistant on the circuit, Burgess also renounced his sinful practices, received the word with joy, and resolved to become a Methodist.[11]

Mr. Myles, who was then the junior preacher in Lisburn, says the people were of almost all religious persuasions, and each zealous for his own peculiar opinions. They frequently attended the Methodist services, and were eager to dispute with the preachers, especially with regard to Calvinism. But he very wisely, not having studied the subject thoroughly, abstained from controversy, and applied his mind to the careful examination of the works of Fletcher and Wesley.

Other preachers, however, did not escape so easily. Mr. Mill, a Scotchman, who entered the itinerancy in 1774, and spent four years in Ireland, was reluctantly drawn into a public discussion, apparently on the Armagh circuit. Four ministers who were opposed to Methodism openly and derisively challenged him, and Mr. R. Lindsay, an Irishman who had emigrated to America, where in 1774 he was received on trial, and after having laboured there a few years, returned to his native land. Accordingly, the challenge being accepted, a platform was erected in a field, and the discussion entered upon. During the debate, Mr. Mill especially displayed such thorough mastery of the subject in dispute, readiness of reply, and firmness of purpose, as completely to silence his opponents, and thus to strengthen and establish the Society in the neighbour hood, where it had been much distracted.

In some cases opposition assumed a more intolerant form, and the servants of God suffered open persecution. Once Mr. Mill was delivered from

(11) *Memoirs of the Rev. J. Burgess*, pp. 15-17.

his adversaries by fixing his eyes upon the most violent of them, until the miscreant crept away ashamed. At another time he wrenched a sword out of the hand of a villain, who rushed on him with savage fury while he was preaching.[12]

Mr. Wm. Myles refers to the encouraging opening for preaching at Kilkeel, on going to which on one occasion he was nearly involved in a serious row, through reproving a Roman Catholic for swearing. A mob gathered in the town and surrounded the house in the evening during the service, but did no other harm than to throw some stones.

He was also instrumental in introducing Methodism into Dromore. Having taken his stand in the street, he proceeded to call sinners to repentance, and as he was thus engaged an excise officer, under the influence of drink, came out of a public house, and having sworn that he would kill the preacher, drew a sword and made a thrust at him. But an inn-keeper perceiving his intention struck his arm, and thus frustrated the wicked purpose. Mr. Myles exhorted the congregation not to resent the assault, and finished his discourse in peace. A few weeks subsequently the excise man got into a quarrel and was killed. From that time the preachers met with no further molestation in the town, and a Society was formed.[13] Of this little band of devoted Christians the only information now available is, that the name of one of them was Maria M'Neill, who is remembered by some of the oldest inhabitants as a poor but respectable widow, who lived in Meeting street, and in whose house the services were conducted.

About this time there were four men — Tate, Shaw, Gallagher, and another — in Armagh under sentence of death for theft. Mr. Mill visited them, and was made a great blessing to Tate, who declared that God for Christ's sake had forgiven all his sins. The others at first seemed very hardened; but at length while Mr. Bates, who also evinced much interest in their spiritual welfare, showed them the evil of sin and its terrible consequences, Shaw became greatly agitated, and with tears inquired, "Do you think God will forgive me?" When the servant of the Lord returned, Tate exclaimed, "Glory to God, I still feel a sense of His pardoning love." "Are you ever tempted to doubt your acceptance?" inquired Mr. Bates. "Yes," said he, "but I look to Jesus, and the tempter flies." While they were speaking, Shaw came forward

(12) *Methodist Magazine*, Dublin, 1807, p. 292.
(13) *Arminian Magazine*, 1797, pp. 261-62.

and said that God had pardoned his sins, and other prisoners being present they exhorted them to repent and believe in the Lord Jesus. The day before their execution the Lord had mercy on Gallagher also, and gave him a sense of His favour. On the day on which they suffered the penalty of their crime, Messrs. Mill and Bates went to them early in the morning and continued with them until they were led forth to execution, when Tate bore a public testimony to his acceptance with God, through the merits of Christ Jesus. As thousands witnessed the happy end of these men, the news of it spread far and wide, and many who had been much prejudiced against Methodism resolved to go and hear for themselves, by which means much good resulted.[14]

In the South of Ireland also there were not wanting tokens of the Divine blessing. On October 27th, Mr. Bredin wrote to Mr. Wesley giving an account of the work on the Cork circuit. He says that when he arrived at Bandon he found the Society much scattered, as there had been no preaching there for a long time, no early morning service for several years, and no meetings of the children for more than twenty years. When he stated to the Society that he intended to resume these neglected services, he was told he need not attempt it; but he persevered, and the results were far beyond his expectations, the morning congregations being four times as large as those in Cork, and there were tokens of a great reformation amongst the children.

Mr. Bredin also visited Skibbereen, where no Methodist preacher had been before. As he knew no one in the town, committing his cause to God, he alighted at a house, and requested the occupant to go to the magistrate for the key of the courthouse. He did so, and the key was sent most courteously. A very large congregation assembled, including the collector of the town, who kept the people from making any disturbance. Having preached three times, Mr. Bredin returned to Bandon, and received a letter by the next post requesting him to return to the west as soon as he could do so conveniently, and promising that his expenses should be paid. As he could not do so immediately, Mr. Bradburn, the Assistant on the circuit, said he would go: and they subsequently arranged to visit the town once a fortnight[15] Such was the introduction of Methodism into Skibbereen, where the Society has had for many years a most interesting and flourishing cause.

---

(14) *Methodist Magazine*, Dublin, 1805, pp. 194-95.
(15) *Arminian Magazine*, 1789, pp. 611-13.

CHAPTER 10

1780

ABOUT the commencement of 1780 a great alarm was raised through the United Kingdom respecting a Bill which Parliament had passed in favour of the Roman Catholics, by which they were relieved from the rigour of certain penal statutes. A Protestant Association was formed to obtain a repeal of this Act, and pamphlets were published on both sides of the question. Amongst others, Wesley stated his sentiments on the subject in a letter, dated January the 21st, which he sent to the printer of the *Public Advertiser.* After premising that he wished no man to be persecuted for his religious principles, he laid down the general proposition, "That no Roman Catholic does or can give security to a Protestant Government for his allegiance and peaceable behaviour;" and rested his proof on the maxim, "No faith is to be kept with heretics," which was openly avowed by the Council of Constance, and never openly disclaimed; as well as on the acknowledgment by Roman Catholics of priestly absolution and the dispensing power of the Pope. "Although Wesley's views in relation to the Roman Catholic question were somewhat similar to those advocated by Milton and Locke, it would have been better had he not published them just then, and in connection with the Protestant Association. Out of the agitations of that body, with its monster petition to Parliament, arose the disgraceful Gordon riots, when bishops, peers and commoners were mobbed, Roman Catholic and Nonconformist chapels wrecked, and Wesley's own new chapel at City road, it is thought, had a narrow escape. Charles Wesley's illustrious schoolfellow, the great Lord Mansfield, saw his library and manuscripts in flames. This vandalism provoked the muse of Cowper, and the indignation of Charles Wesley expressed itself in satirical verse."

Several adversaries soon arose, the most conspicuous of whom was the Rev. Arthur O'Leary, a Roman Catholic priest, who published in the *Freeman's Journal,* "Remarks" on the letter of Mr. Wesley, as well as that of another signed "J. W.," in defence of the Protestant Association, to which Wesley replied. In this controversy O'Leary endeavoured in vain to explain away the obnoxious decree, and by shafts of wit and drollery to overcome his opponent. The decree of the Council could not be got over, and the reasoning of Mr. Wesley therefore remained unanswered, or as Mr. Skelton said, his proposition was a wall of adamant, and Mr. O'Leary's arguments were as boiled peas shot against it.[1] A few years subsequently, when Mr. Wesley was in Cork, he was invited to breakfast with Mr. O'Leary, and speaks thus candidly of his old antagonist: "I was not at all displeased at being disappointed. He was not the stiff, queer man that I expected, but of an easy, genteel carriage, and seems not to be wanting in either sense or learning."[2]

On February 26th Wesley wrote to Mr. Bradburn, congratulating him on having such "an honest and sensible fellow labourer" as Mr. Bredin, and expressing his hope to visit Ireland in spring.[3] His friends, however, advised him not to cross the channel, as they feared, on account of the recent controversy, the Irish would do him injury, so he gave up his intention for this year.

During the first six months of 1780 Mr. M'Cornock was on the Sligo circuit, and says he visited many places where the people never heard a Methodist preacher before, and was kindly received. He also went out of the circuit to Ballina and Killala, where the people were well pleased to hear the word of the Lord.[4]

In some instances the preachers had still to endure terrible persecution. Thus at Clara a magistrate, who could not prevail upon his wife and daughter to desist from attending the Methodist services, hired twenty-four Romanists, divided them into three companies, and stationed them on three roads leading to the place where the itinerant — probably Mr. Halliday — was about to preach, in order to waylay him. Thus the preacher, ignorant of any danger, suddenly found himself surrounded by eight ruffians, who knocked him down and beat him most cruelly with knotted sticks. They then produced a book, and insisted that he should swear upon it he never would preach in that place again, which he refused to do. They therefore drew their knives, swore they would cut the heart out of him, tore and cut all his clothes to pieces, and when they had stripped him naked, dragged him by the hair into a pond, beating him all the way, and then leaving him to perish. When he recovered his senses, naked and sorely bruised, he was just able to crawl to a friend's house at some distance.

---

(1) *Moore's Life of Wesley*, II., p. 277.

(2) *Wesley's Works*, IV., p. 374.

(3) Ibid. XIII., p. 124.

(4) *Arminian Magazine*, 1785, pp. 187-88.

On his next visit to this place, where there was a large congregation and a lively Society, the preacher was accompanied by Mr. Hall, who was then stationed on the adjoining circuit — Athlone — having gone there in the place of Mr. N. Price. On the first evening they met with no interruption; but on the following day, as they and some friends were on the road, three persons who ought to have been gentlemen, with their footmen, suddenly surrounded the Methodists, and one presenting a pistol at Mr. Hall, insisted that he should promise to leave that neighbourhood, and never return; but he firmly refused, so long as he regarded the salvation of his own soul and that of others. The miscreant then swore that he would lodge the contents of the pistol in his body; but the servant of God, nothing daunted, opened his breast, and said he would die rather than sin against his conscience. The rowdy, finding that threats failed, took a sword, and lifting it up to heaven, swore by the Eternal God he would cut the preacher in two; but the glittering of the sword frightened the horse, so that he suddenly sprang forward, which in all probability saved the life of the rider, who felt the weapon graze his back ere the saddle received the blow. The preacher then stood his ground, expostulated with his assailant, and expressed his willingness to answer to lawful authority if he had done anything contrary to law: so they arranged to go at once to a magistrate. But they had not gone far when the gentlemen espied a number of men in a field, whom they called to come with their spades and forks and beat the Methodists. The poor wretches readily responded, and sprang over the ditch, as fierce as tigers; but Mr. Hall told them that if they dared to assault him, they must expect to be punished according to law, which so confounded them that they were afraid to do anything, notwithstanding the terrible vociferations and execrations of those who incited them to lawlessness and cruelty. Meantime the wife of the magistrate having heard of the intentions of the young men, hastened to the place to prevent mischief, and as soon as they saw her one of them exclaimed, "Oh! we shall break her heart," and all spurred their horses and took to flight. The coolness and firmness of Mr. Hall so overcame his persecutors, that he was not hindered from preaching that evening. At the close of the service the members of Society, with many tears, entreated the preachers not to forsake them: and they promised; but the excitement, together with fatigue and exposure, brought on Mr. Hall an attack of fever, in which he lay for weeks deprived of reason.

Meanwhile the justice of the peace who, through vile calumnies, had been incensed against the Methodists, when he found that the violence of his son and nephews proved ineffectual in deterring the preachers from visiting that part of the country, and not being able to persuade his wife to desist from hearing them, compelled her to leave his house, so that for some time she resided with a relative at Mountrath. In that neighbourhood the magistrate had a connection who also held the commission of the peace, and this gentleman, together with a local clergyman, determined to attack the Methodists in the preaching-house; but having remained too long at their bottle, when they arrived the people had gone; so they broke open the door, and wreaked their vengeance on the benches and windows. The clergyman then thought they had done their duty and returned home; but the magistrate was not so easily satisfied. He found the house where the preacher, Mr. J. Hampson, jun., lodged, and entering it seized him by the throat. At that instant three young men ran to the rescue of the itinerant; but as the justice persisted in his hostile proceedings, they were obliged to settle the affair in his own way, in consequence of which he remained for some time subsequently under the doctor's care.

The lady above-mentioned was reduced to the disagreeable necessity of removing to Dublin, and obtaining a separate maintenance from her husband. He also sent his daughter to the metropolis, under the care of two of his sisters, with a strict charge not to suffer her to go near the Methodists. But the young lady eluded the vigilance of her aunts, and in her flight from them one morning providentially met with her mother going to the Methodist chapel. After they had been exercised for a season with many distresses, God mercifully interposed on their behalf. The daughter was married to a pious young gentleman of family and fortune, by whose wise and prudent conduct prejudice and misunderstandings were removed, and a happy reconciliation effected in each branch of the family.[5]

At the Conference Messrs. Pilmoor and Thomas were appointed to Dublin. Amongst those who heard the former preach his first sermon in entering on his new circuit was a young man named Walter Griffith, a native of Clogheen, in the county of Tipperary, who was then engaged in business in the city. Prompted by curiosity he went to Whitefriar street chapel, and was so impressed with the service that he resolved to become a Methodist, and soon after began to meet in Mr. John Dinnen's class. From this time his

---

(5) *Arminian Magazine*, 1793, p. 455-59.

soul was penetrated with a conviction of his guilt and depravity, and he sorrowed after a godly sort: but during several subsequent months severe temptations, arising from a naturally reserved disposition, and mistaken views of Divine truth, retarded him from finding that blessing which he ultimately obtained, and which laid the foundation of a most devoted and useful Christian career.[6]

At this period Mrs. Slacke, of Annadale, in the county Leitrim, was accustomed to visit Dublin, and enter with zest into the worldly amusements and festivities which obtained in the metropolis at certain seasons. On one of these occasions, about the year 1780, she lodged in the house of Alderman Exshaw, a printer and bookseller, with whom Bennett Dugdale, Matthias Joyce and Robert Napper lived as journeymen or apprentices. All three were truly devoted to God; and as they slept in the same room, it was their practice before retiring to rest to read and pray. Their room was immediately above the apartment occupied by Mrs. Slacke: so she frequently heard sounds which for some time she could not understand. At length, prompted by curiosity, she went quietly upstairs and listened at their door. Impressed first with the novelty, and then with the propriety, of such religious exercises, she was led to repeat her visits, until her conscience became awakened. Although a lady of most accomplished manners, and one who had mixed in fashionable society, she now discovered there was in religion something to make the soul happy, to which she was a stranger. Upon inquiry she found that the young men were members of the then much-despised Methodist Society, towards which she felt a strange attraction, that led her to venture to hear preaching in Whitefriar street chapel. The word was greatly blessed to her: she became earnestly desirous of salvation, and was enabled to accept Christ as her Saviour.

On her return home Mrs. Slacke resolved to exert her influence to introduce Methodism into the family and neighbourhood. But fully aware of her husband's prejudices, she felt it needful to proceed with great caution. She first prevailed on Mr. Slacke to invite to their house the Rev. J. Creighton, who not only came and preached, but also promised to return, and being very friendly with Mr. Blair, the preacher then stationed in Sligo, engaged him also to go to Annadale on his next visit. When the appointed time came Mr. Creighton preached in the morning, and after the service asked Mr.

(6) *Wesleyan Methodist Magazine*, 1827, p. 75.

Slacke if he had any objection to a Methodist preacher giving them a discourse in the evening. His heart had been touched by the sermon, and he consented, but inquired, "Where is he?" When Mr. Blair, whose appearance was very youthful, was pointed out to him, he expressed his astonishment, saying, "What, that boy a preacher!" Mr. Blair, who possessed more than ordinary ministerial talent, delivered a most impressive discourse, which was made a great blessing to Mr. Slacke and his family. Thenceforward the Methodist preachers regularly visited and were most kindly and hospitably entertained at Annadale.

From the time of Mrs. Slacke's conversion, her life was one of unostentatious but active devotion and benevolence. She became an intelligent, humble, and devoted witness of the doctrine of entire sanctification, as taught in the Word of God, and preached by the Wesleys. The Rev. A. Averell writes of her: "I never knew a more decided follower of the Saviour than was this truly lovely woman. With an elegant person, were united in her all that results from a liberal education, sound judgment, an enlarged knowledge of Divine truth, deep experience in the things of God, a cheerful and lively address, and a spirit sweetly tempered by love to God, and zeal for His glory."[7]

Thomas Payne and Thomas Barber were appointed to the Waterford circuit. During the year, as the result of the Divine blessing on the faithful labours of these excellent men, there was a very gracious and cheering revival in the city, especially amongst young people, many of whom, by their subsequent holy lives and peaceful deaths, testified to the reality of the blessed change they had experienced.[8] Among those who, at this time, were brought into connection with Methodism, was William Curry, then a young man. Mrs. Ball found him out, and persuaded him to meet in class. He was appointed by Mr. Wesley a leader in Dublin, and for about sixty years laboured for his Redeemer.[9]

This year the celebrated John Crickett was sent from England to labour on the Lisleen circuit. He was a plain, earnest, albeit somewhat eccentric and very old-fashioned Methodist preacher, chiefly remarkable for his great simplicity in worldly matters. Stories relating to him have long furnished a large contribution to the fund of Methodistical anecdote. Unsophisticated to

(7) *Memoir of Rev. A. Averell*, p. 166.
(8) *Minutes of the Irish Conference*, II., p. 175.
(9) *Primitive Wesleyan Methodist Magazine*, 1843, pp. 99, 100.

an astonishing degree, apparently unable to understand the ordinary conventionalities of society, he was, withal, a man of unaffected piety and of pulpit power. On his list of stopping places are the familiar names of Mr. Boyle, Mrs. Brown, Joseph Carson, Omagh; Joseph Gray, Lislap; and S. Steele, Magheracoltan.

Mr. Henry Moore was appointed Assistant of the Charlemont circuit, which he found was very extensive, without any provision for a married preacher in the shape of a residence; so as he and his wife could not get lodgings elsewhere, they settled in Tanderagee, where the people were very poor but very devoted, and their religion was exemplary and powerful. In, for the first time, going through his circuit, which required six weeks, he came to Glaslough on a Saturday, which was market day, and having no direction to any particular person, he let his horse walk slowly into the town, thinking that some member of the Society would probably recognize him. Accordingly he saw a lusty man leave one of the stalls, and placing himself right in his way, hold up his hand and vociferate, "I know what you are." "Do you?" said the preacher, "then perhaps you can tell where I am to go." "Follow me," cried the stranger, as he stalked forward and brought Mr. Moore to the house of Betty Brown, "an Israelite indeed," who entertained the preachers. On going to the stable to see after his horse, the servant of God was followed by his unknown guide, who immediately began to inform him of the distress of his soul, which was so great that he "roared by reason of the disquietness of his heart." Suitable counsel was then given to the poor penitent, who had grieved the Spirit of God.

The history of this man was most remarkable. His name was Bartley Campbell. He had been a Romanist, and had lived in the usual ungodly manner of the members of that Church then; but the Holy Spirit failed not "to convince him of sin, of righteousness, and of judgment;" and poor Bartley hardened not his heart. He went to the priest, made confession, was enjoined penance, and directed to repeat certain prayers, after which he received absolution; but he found this would not do: his distress increased, and, as he said, hell was open before his eyes. He applied to other priests, and faithfully performed what he was commanded, but only realized additional misery. He at length resolved he would go to Lough Derg, where it was supposed all sin could be expiated. He walked thither, a distance of about fifty miles: and having arrived, passed to the small island, half a mile from the shore, called St. Patrick's Purgatory, and applied to one of the priests in waiting, who prescribed the prayers and penances usually enjoined. These, though severe, he fulfilled with the greatest exactness, and then again received absolution. But, as in the former cases, it availed nothing. The cloud of the Divine displeasure remained, and guilt pressed still more heavily on his conscience. He returned to the priest, who inquired concerning the fulfilment of his instructions, all of which he was assured had been most faithfully attended to. "Did I not give you absolution?" said the priest. "You did, father." "And do you deny the authority of the Church?" "By no means," replied the poor man, "but my soul is in misery. What shall I do?" "Do," said the priest, "why, go to bed and sleep." "Sleep!" answered the awakened sinner, "no, father; perhaps I might awake in hell." The conversation abruptly ended with a threat of a good horsewhipping.

Poor Bartley, departing with his load of guilt, and seeking a retired place, cast himself on the ground, and gave vent to his anguish in loud cries and tears. After some time he found a desire to pray, and anguish gave utterance to his troubled spirit. He called upon Christ, pleaded His precious blood, and in a moment all his distress was gone, and an assurance given that the Lord had taken away his sins, so that the peace of God filled his soul. Having praised the riches of Divine grace, he returned in transport to the priest, crying out, "O, father, I am happy! I have found the cure!" His pastor replied with execrations, and a renewed threat of chastisement. Thus repelled, he thought of home; but recollecting having seen a number of persons performing their penances, he hastened to the place, told them of the cure, and of the jewel, as he called the knowledge of salvation, stating his own experience of the worthlessness of their penances, and of the willingness of Christ to save. But a cry arose that he was interrupting the penitents, and the priests, with a number of the votaries of superstition, hastening to the place, he was obliged to escape at the peril of his life. He reached home "a new creature," happy in God; and at once earnestly exhorted his wife to turn to the Lord, who, for Christ's sake, would give her the same happiness as he possessed. The poor woman answered only with tears, and really feared that he was gone mad. At length, being still in some degree under the influence of superstition, he thought of the place where God had spoken peace to his soul, and declared that his wife must go thither with him, and the Lord would make her happy there. Her lamentations availed not. Her pleading the two little ones only prompted the reply, "They shall go, too." He yoked his horse, carried out the bed, placed the mother and children on it, and set out on this extraordinary pilgrimage. Having arrived at the place, he brought the affrighted woman to the scene of his distress and deliverance, and earnestly exhorted her to call upon God, who, for Christ's sake, would forgive her sins, and make her happy in His love. But the godly sorrow that had brought him with strong cries and tears to the throne of grace, had no place in the heart of the almost distracted woman: so having spent some time there, poor Bartley saw that it was no use, and that he must return and betake himself to labour to gain "the meat that perisheth" for his family, and seek for himself "that meat which endureth unto everlasting life."

Shortly after he met with and related what the Lord had done for his soul to a priest who was much affected, and could only answer with tears. After a few visits he acknowledged that he experienced a similar work when a young man; but had lost the blessing, and long walked in darkness. Bartley exhorted him to look for the cure, be faithful with his flock, and tell them of the happiness that awaited them if they would turn to God. The priest became alarmed, and charged him not to speak a word to the people on that subject, for they could not bear it. "Father," cried the earnest man, "they will all go to hell, and you will go there too, if you hide the cure from them. I will tell all that I come near, and you will soon see what good will be done, only do not oppose me." The priest reiterated his admonitions, and Bartley departed, fully determined to speak and labour for the Lord.

Soon after the priest gave notice that he would celebrate mass in an old burial-ground in the neighbourhood. Bartley attended, and when the service concluded, he stepped up and said, "Father, you are to christen a bairn in the village; go, and leave the people to me. The dead souls you see are standing over the dead bodies, and I hope the Lord will awaken the uppermost." "Take care what you do," said the intimidated priest. "Make no disturbance, I charge you," and then left. Bartley began at once to lay before the staring multitude his own former miserable condition, and the efforts he had vainly made for deliverance. But when he came to speak from the fulness of his heart of the cure and the jewel, how Christ had blotted out his sins and given him to enjoy His love, so that, said he, "I am happy all the day long, and I no more fear to die than to go to sleep," the effect was astonishing. A general and piercing cry arose, almost the whole assembly fell on their knees, while some lay prostrate, groaning with deep anguish. The cry was heard at the village, the priest hurried to the spot, and demanded of the speaker how he dared thus to disturb his flock; but was only answered with earnest entreaties not to hinder the work of God. "You rascal," said the priest, "do you oppose the Church?" "No, father," he replied, "I have found the Church." "You villain," said the priest, "Begone!" and struck him on the head with his horsewhip. Poor Bartley felt "an old man's bone in him," and hardly knowing what he did, gave the priest a push that threw him over a grave, heels up and head down. A general commotion was the result, and the people, seeing that he had knocked the priest down, were all eager to lay hands on the culprit. Lamentations for sin gave place to execrations, and poor Bartley was obliged to fly for his life. Although he escaped the vengeance of the infuriated multitude, his conscience received a wound, and he went mourning all the day long, not knowing how to recover his happiness. Soon after he met with some of the Methodists, who understood his case, and encouraged him to come again to the "fountain opened for sin and uncleanness."

Such was his state of mind when he first met Mr. Moore; he continued with the Society, fully recovered his peace, and afterwards became very useful. He had a strong mind, great ardency of spirit, and was perfectly master of the Irish language. He could not be satisfied with any meeting where there were none convinced of sin, or enabled to rejoice in God their Saviour. He called it a sham fight.

On arriving at Newry Mr. Moore was requested by Mr. Kennedy to go and see a lady supposed to be dying, who had often expressed a wish to be thus visited, to which her husband, a Socinian, had objected, but now withdrew his objection. Mr. Moore accordingly went, and was introduced to a most interesting young lady, apparently approaching her end; but when he attempted to pray for her as a dying person, he felt so embarrassed that he could hardly utter a sentence without hesitation, and when he prayed for her recovery he had great liberty on leaving, her husband was hardly courteous, notwithstanding which the preacher repeated his visit, and again, in pleading with God, amazed all who were present by the importunity and confidence of his faith. On returning to the town at the end of six weeks he found that prayer had been answered in her restoration to health, that her husband had withdrawn all opposition, and she, having become a member of the Society, had obtained redemption through the blood of Christ.

Messrs. Carlill and Hall were stationed on the Lisburn circuit, where they had as favourable opportunities for being useful as could be expected, the congregations being large in general, and many new places received them gladly. However, Mr. Carlill, who had just come from England, though an excellent man, did not appreciate the Green Isle, which made his position neither pleasant to himself nor profitable to the people, so he only remained the year on this side of the channel; but Mr. Hall was happy and useful in his work. One of the most notable conversions of the year was that of a Deist, whom it pleased the Lord to awaken to a sense of his state and danger at one of the services, which some of his friends persuaded him to attend. The next time Mr. Hall preached, the earnest seeker obtained a knowledge of salvation by the remission of sins, and became a faithful witness of the truth, to the joy of his friends, and the astonishment of his Deistical acquaintances.[10]

CHAPTER 11

1781

THE Rev. J. Creighton, although still retaining his curacy, continued to make occasional preaching excursions through the surrounding country. Thus on January the 23rd, 1781, he preached at Ballyconnell to a large congregation, and while he met the Society two persons found peace, and one backslider was restored. Shortly after he preached again in the same place, there being then a great revival. On April the 25th he preached at Enniskillen, near the walls of the old castle, to a careless people. Some ladies strolled about, and diverted themselves in talking aloud during the service. In this town a chapel was built during the preceding year.

In June, at the Bishop's visitation, two doctors of divinity having entered into conversation with Mr. Creighton, passed some encomiums, which he did not expect on two sermons that he had published. They said his doctrines were Scriptural, and entirely in harmony with the teaching of the Church, but disapproved of his preaching outside his own parish. He took occasion subsequently to write to them on the subject, and received their replies. One of them was calm and friendly, reminding him that he had a family, and stating that the writer had spoken favourably of him to a nobleman who was related to a bishop, so he might expect promotion shortly. The other doctor,

---

(10) *Arminian Magazine*, 1793 p.621-22.

however, was very warm, and argued at length against irregular preaching. But neither the specious promises of the one, nor the plausible arguments of the other, made much impression on Mr. Creighton, who told them both that he never had any fruit to his labours until he became irregular, and that he was persuaded were he to confine himself to one congregation he would not only soon become useless, but also lose the life of God in his soul.

About this time Mr. Creighton began to preach at a place near Cavan, and continued to do so once a fortnight while he remained in this country. When a number of the hearers were awakened he explained to them the nature of the Society, and formed fourteen of them into a class on the first night. To these others were added, until after some time there were about four score, the greater part of whom had obtained remission of sins. Meantime the vicar of the parish sent for him, and threatened to complain of him to the Bishop, saying that if he and those fellows who were itinerating the country continued to go on thus the churches would soon be deserted. Mr. Creighton replied that their preaching tended rather to bring men into the churches; and that he must obey God rather than men, and therefore was determined to preach whenever and wherever it seemed to him to be right. Shortly after many who had been Presbyterians attended the church of his objector and received the Sacrament. Mr. Creighton also sent to him two Roman Catholics, to read their recantation as a proof that he was bringing the people into, and not driving them from the church. Opposition then arose from another quarter. Some Romanists waylaid the leader of the infant Society, Mr. Robert Creighton, to murder him, who, having received intimation of their intention, returned by another way, and thus escaped.

In August Mr. Creighton visited Bundoran, where he preached frequently in the cottages on the sea shore. On one occasion, as he conducted a service in the house of a Roman Catholic woman, several of her neighbours who were Romanists assembled in the kitchen and threatened to drive out all that were in the room, but they were restrained by Divine power.[1]

Mr. Creighton also seized the opportunity while in this neighbourhood of visiting the Society at Carricknahorna, where during the year the following valuable additions were made to the membership — three brothers, John, William and George M'Cornock and their four sisters; Thomas Elliott, and Anthony Lowry. John M'Cornock was appointed a leader, which office he

---

(1) *Arminian Magazine*, 1785, p. 398-400.

sustained with fidelity for upwards of half a century. William, a man of good strong sense, entered the itinerancy in 1787 and died in 1834 in great peace. Thomas Elliott was "a deeply pious and zealous man" with "good gifts," who in 1788 also entered the itinerancy, but the Lord was pleased to remove him in the prime of life. He died of consumption, brought on by excessive labours. Anthony Lowry was the Gaius of this country, and opened his house for the entertainment of the preachers.[2]

Meanwhile in the north death removed hence one of the most devoted and consistent of the members, Mrs. Johnstone, of Lisleen, truly "a mother in Israel," whose saintly life, faithful testimony, and self-denying charity ought never to be forgotten by Irish Methodists. Fourteen days after the removal of this excellent lady, and in the same district of country, Hugh Brown also was called to join the Church triumphant. Owing to the delicate state of his health he had been compelled to retire from the itinerancy three years previously. He suffered much from a nervous disorder, but his end was peace. But to pass from the north to the south of Ireland. At Bandon an important addition was made to the Society in Miss Alice Cambridge. Her father belonged to the Established Church, of which she ever considered herself a member: and her mother was a Presbyterian. Taken from school when very young, she had not the advantages of a liberal education; but subsequently endeavoured, as far as possible by reading, to supply this serious lack. She acquired a taste for light literature which could not tend to healthy mental culture, until in 1780 a severe trial, in the death of her mother, turned her attention to spiritual and eternal things.

Soon afterwards she began to attend the services in the Methodist preaching-house, and under a sermon preached by Mr. Myles was deeply convinced of sin. She then returned home to do what she had never done before — to pray: and continued for some time earnestly seeking the pardoning mercy of God, diligently using the means of grace, and greatly encouraged by the members of Society. At length, at a band meeting, as one of those present related her religious experience, the Lord lifted on Miss Cambridge the light of His countenance, so that she was enabled through grace to magnify the Lord, and rejoice in the God of her salvation. From that hour, as she could affirm many years after, not only did she never once doubt that God had then and there blotted out her sins and accepted her as His child,

---

(2) *Primitive Wesleyan Methodist Magazine*, 1840, p. 287-88.

but also she never thought or did anything which He gave her to know was wrong.

Feeling an earnest desire to bring others into the way of peace, the young convert went to her former companions, told them what the Lord had done for her soul, and urged them to seek the same priceless blessing. Some laughed at what seemed to them novel and foolish fancies; others listened with apparent attention, but continued to pursue their old course; and a few were led to believe in the Lord Jesus as their Saviour.

Miss Cambridge gave unmistakable evidence of the reality of the glorious change which the Lord had wrought, and of her determination to be fully devoted to Him, by an act which must have cost her a bitter pang. Having consented to marry a young man to whom she was much attached, but who had not given his heart to Jesus, she at once ended an engagement which was contrary to the Word of God, and could not be accompanied with the Divine blessing.

Entering upon her religious course in this spirit of complete submission to the will of God, Miss Cambridge could not fail to make rapid progress in holiness, becoming increasingly dead to the world and alive to God. As in prayer her soul was drawn out in earnest desire for more love and purity and power, she was often favoured with seasons of abundant spiritual blessing. As her love to God and desire for full conformity to His image increased, so did her zeal for the salvation of souls, but she knew not how to reach the unsaved. At first she thought, having been herself so blessed under the word, if she only could get them to the preaching-house to hear the gospel message, they would surely be made willing to receive salvation. So she invited her friends and neighbours. Many did respond, for the Lord gave her favour in the sight of the people, and often, with wistful eyes and praying heart, she would look round for tokens of spiritual anxiety, or religious concern, which she endeavoured to follow up with suitable words of counsel, of warning, or of encouragement. Thus some were led to the Saviour.

On April 12th Mr. Wesley with three of the preachers embarked for Dublin, intending to travel through the country as usual; but encountered a violent tempest for two days and two nights, when they were driven back into Holyhead harbour. Under these circumstances, the more he considered the subject the more he was convinced that it was not the will of God he should visit Ireland this year, so the project was for a second time abandoned.

Mr. Bredin was at this time stationed on the Athlone circuit, where many were drawn to hear him, and the word preached was accompanied with such power that several were convinced of sin and became members of the Society. Amongst others Miss Penington, then a girl of fourteen, afterwards Mrs. Burgess, was brought to see her sinful state, and consequent need of a saving interest in Christ. From Mr. Bredin she received a note of admission into the Society, and he seemed specially interested in her spiritual welfare and mental improvement. He had a choice collection of books, which were prized as his greatest earthly treasure, and it was no small proof of regard that he offered this young lady their unrestricted use.[3]

About this period one of the preachers was one day travelling from Armagh to Coleraine. Having crossed Ballinderry bridge he entered the county of Derry, and going up the hill to where the road is bounded by the church-yard wall, he disposed of his horse for the time, and commenced to sing. Soon a number of people from the village of Churchhill collected around him, and for the first time in this parish Christ was preached by a Methodist itinerant. Having concluded the service, the evangelist offered to preach there again in six weeks, if any person would provide a place for the purpose, which some one proposed to do. Mr. and Mrs. Averell, of Ballinderry, had been standing on the outskirts of the congregation, and as the people dispersed Mrs. Averell said to her husband: "There is no person attending to the stranger. You had better ask him to come in and take some refreshment." This was accordingly done, and the servant of God was further invited in coming again to stop at their house. From that time forward preaching was regularly established at Churchhill. Some time after a local preacher from Ballycastle visited the place, and his labours were greatly owned of God. He preached with power from Revelation 3:20, and then announced for a meeting at which he would read the rules of the Society. Having explained the nature and design of class-meeting, he invited those who desired "to flee from the wrath to come, and to be saved from their sins" to give him their names. Several were then enroled, and of these Mr. Averell's daughter Sarah, subsequently Mrs. Shillington, was the first. The class formed at this time is still in existence, and in the intervening period many have gone from it to various parts of the Lord's vineyard, irrespective of the numbers who have been removed to the Church triumphant.[4]

---

(3) *Irish Evangelist*, 1860, p. 98.

(4) *Memorials of T. A. Shillington*, pp. 44, 45.

During the spring of this year Adam Clarke was offered a situation by Mr. Bennett, a respectable linen merchant in Coleraine, which, with the consent of his parents, he accepted; and thus was placed in circumstances specially favourable to his growth in grace. He had the opportunity of sitting under a most instructive and powerful ministry several times in the week, and conversing with deeply religious and intelligent people. The preaching service at five o'clock in the morning he found particularly profitable. He met also with some valuable friends in that excellent Society, amongst whom was Mr R. Douthett, from whose conversation and almost parental tenderness he reaped the highest profit. Andrew and William Hunter cared much for his soul, and watched over him for good. He had also a useful companion in John M'Kenny, whose son became a devoted and successful missionary. Indeed the whole of the Society seemed to take a deep interest in his welfare, and endeavoured to promote it, believing that God had called him to do an important work in the Church. Miss Young, afterwards Mrs. Rutherford, by sending him suitable books, also rendered him much help. Adam Clarke and John M'Kenny were class mates: and on one occasion at least walked together to Ballymena, nearly thirty miles, to attend a quarterly meeting.[5] Young Clarke also was encouraged to engage in Christian work, and thus led to give exhortations at different places through the country, even then giving promise of his subsequent power and success as a public speaker.

At this time also, the Rev. E. Smyth, came to Dublin, where he remained for the following eighteen months, but does not appear to have been as extensively useful as formerly, there being but few traces now of his work.

At the following Conference the name of Mr. John Crook stands in the Minutes, with that of Mr. Pilmoor, for the metropolis; but he did not fill this appointment, being required elsewhere by Mr. Wesley.[6]

Mr. Zechariah Yewdall was appointed to Waterford with Mr. Lindsay. He was a pious Yorkshire man, who entered the itinerancy in 1779: and says he found on the circuit a lively people, the labours of his predecessors, Messrs. Payne and Barber having been much blessed. But in some parts the new preachers had much cause for discouragement, as many backsliders, by their disorderly conduct, brought reproach on the Society, and proved a stumbling-block to others. Several, however, were convinced of the evil of their course, and sought the Lord diligently until He restored unto them the joy of His

(5) *Irish Evangelist*, 1860, p. 92.
(6) *Methodist Magazine*, Dublin, 1808, p. 147.

salvation.[7] Evidently the preachers had trouble also about the chapel in Kilkenny, which some parties threatened to sell, on account of a debt that remained on it. Mr. Lindsay wrote on the subject to Mr. Wesley, who in reply said that if the property had not actually been made over to these parties, they could not sell it, that he was himself two hundred pounds in debt, but should anyone leave him a legacy it would be reserved for Kilkenny, and if he found a suitable preacher that could be spared he would send him to them.[8]

Mr. Myles was stationed in Belfast, where he says, although Mr. John Watson was appointed, he had no one to help him until Christmas; and that with daily travelling and constant work in regulating Societies, he had little time for reading. However, the Lord was with him, the Society prospered, and he spent the year with great satisfaction.

Messrs. Rutherford and Moore were appointed to the Lisburn circuit, where many persons were truly devoted, the people in general walked in the fear of the Lord, and the services were well attended. The spirit of Mr. Moore was stirred up within him at one of the annual Roman Catholic celebrations in Downpatrick, when he saw the infatuated multitude who loitered about the town when mass was over. He went out to the walks near the cathedral, and standing on an eminence gave out a hymn. Immediately the people flocked together from all directions, and he cried aloud — "He hath showed thee, O man, what is good; and what doth the Lord require of thee but to do justly, and to love mercy, and to walk humbly with thy God," contrasting the service to which they were subject with the requirements of God, and they heard with earnest attention to the close.[9] It is to be hoped that the seed sown that day in the Master's name brought forth fruit to the glory of Him who has said — "My word shall not return unto Me void."

(7) *Arminian Magazine*, 1795, p. 270.
(8) *Irish Evangelist*, 1874, p. 125.
(9) *Life of the Rev. H. Moore*, pp. 72, 73.

CHAPTER 12

1782

THE year 1782 opened well. On January 19th Wesley wrote to Miss Ritchie that he had very pleasing accounts from the brethren in various parts of England and Ireland, and of the abundant blessings which many received at the time of renewing their covenant with God. They thus realized foretastes of richer blessings yet to be obtained.[1]

At this period two young men named Nathaniel and Samuel Alcorn, who resided at Loughmuck, near Omagh, became members of the Society. Nathaniel having been convinced of sin as he listened to a member of the Society singing some hymn, subsequently while praying in a field realized peace and joy in believing. He then naturally identified himself with those who had been instrumental in leading him to decision for God. Many efforts were made to detach him from the people of his choice, but without success. He was soon appointed a leader, and after his marriage he invited to his house the messengers of salvation, who continued for nearly sixty years to preach the Gospel there, and scores of sinners were thus led to the Saviour. Samuel Alcorn entered the itinerancy in 1792. To mental gifts of a high order he added a popular address, fluency of speech, and an excellent voice for singing.

Evidently at about this time the incident occurred referred to in the following unique narrative: In 1837 a Christian lady visited Bushmills, where she one day met a stranger whose appearance greatly impressed her. He was above the middle height, overtopping most of his compeers, yet proportionately strong and muscular. His hair was grey, but the frosts of time had not untwined the curly bunches which in youth adorned what phrenologists would call a strongly marked forehead. After the usual first subjects on such occasions had been discussed, the lady ventured to allude to religious influence, and found he was no stranger to it. "My name," said he, "is John M'Conaghy. I hae twa dochters, an' had ance three as bonny boys as ever the sun shined on, but heaven tuck a fancy to them a'; ane by ane they drappit aff, till last Easter Sunday I buried the last o' them. A bright

---

(1) *Wesley's Works*, XIII, p. 62.

fellow he was; just five an' twenty years of age. An' he never married, but stuck by me an' the bit o' land I hae, and weel he kept me an' weel wad, had he been spared langer; but it's a' ower noo, an' we maun be content. I'm mair than fifty years amang the Methodists, the auldest ane o' them in these parts, an' I wish to tell ye hoo I cam' to be ane at a'. They had what we ca' tent meetings, an' had sic a meetin' in our kintra. I went to it, no' for loo o' my Maker, nor of the meetin', but for the loo o' as braw a lassie as ever lived, whose hoose was hard by where the preaching held. I looed her dearly, an' I maun tell ye she was aye in my head the time o' the sermon. When it was o'er up comes Adam Clarke, an' he says, 'Don't gang to the public-house noo to drink, but gang hame.' An' he tuck me by the hand an' he says, 'Promise me you won't gang there, but you will gang hame an' pray.' It was sair wark this; my bit o' a sweetheart wad expect me, and I tried to pull aff, but I cudna do it, an' I got sae frightened aboot death an' judgment an' sich like things, that I fairly set aff hame, cried to the Lord for mercy, got a wee pickle o' religious comfort, an' hae some o' it till the present."[2] "A word spoken in due season, how good it is!"

Mr. J. Bredin was then on the Londonderry circuit, to supply the place of one of the preachers, and he, believing that Adam Clarke was called of God to the work of the ministry, not only lent him books and directed his studies, but also invited him to Derry and persuaded him at New Buildings to enter upon his work as a preacher of the Gospel. Mr. Bredin then wrote concerning him to Mr. Wesley who offered to receive him into the Kingswood school, that he might be better fitted for his life work. Thus Providence opened up his path to the Wesleyan itinerancy, and Ireland gave to Methodism one of the most illustrious of commentators and powerful of preachers.

Towards the close of Mr. Pilmoor's second year in Dublin, Walter Griffith and a few of the most zealous young men in the Society agreed to meet together to pray for the revival of God's work every Sunday morning at five o'clock, and three days of the week at eight o'clock. The youthful band was soon joined by some of the leaders, and meetings were opened in the Infirmary, Channel row, and many other places in the city and its vicinity. Thus commenced prayer meetings in the metropolis, which subsequently were made with the Divine blessing means of everlasting good to thousands of immortal souls.[3]

---

(2) *Memorials of a Consecrated Life*, pp. 233-34.
(3) *Wesleyan Methodist Magazine*, 1827, p. 75.

Meantime the Rev. E. Smyth, who was stationed in Dublin, took lodgings at Killiney early in summer and began to hold meetings there, with tokens of the Lord's blessing. On June the 18th Mrs. Smyth writes — "I trust it was not in vain Mr. Smyth was sent into these parts, as there is already a noise and a shaking among the dry bones. We have a little congregation morning and evening on the Lord's day, and a prayer meeting every other day. Last Sunday an old woman cried aloud for mercy. A gauger's wife also and her daughter are seeking the Lord earnestly, and intend to join the Society on their return to Dublin."[4]

Mr. Wesley fully purposed up to May the 1st to visit Ireland this year,[5] but for some reason not given, changed his intention, and sent as his deputy the Rev. Dr. Coke, an honoured name, ever after dear to Ireland. This was the commencement of a new era in the history of Irish Methodism. Dr. Coke was directed to convene the Irish preachers, and to hold for the first time a regularly constituted Conference, similar to those held in England. During the visits of Mr. Wesley he had in almost if not every instance called together the preachers labouring in Ireland, and consulted with them as to the work in this country; but these occasional meetings did not control the affairs of the Society. No official record was published or apparently ever made of the proceedings, and at best nothing further was done than to receive reports and make suggestions to the British Conference. But now the preachers in Ireland had become so numerous, and the business had obtained an extent and gravity which rendered it expedient that the Irish ministers should receive a corporate status of their own, and hence the appointment of Dr. Coke.

These subsequent annual Conferences were for many years held in Whitefriar street chapel. The preachers generally rode to Dublin, and on arriving there was no small stir and much brotherly kindness, after a year's labours and dangers, and never were the messengers of the churches more heartily welcomed and entertained than by the Dublin Methodists. During the sessions of the Conference there was preaching each morning at five o'clock and at six, the President took the chair and opened the meeting with devotional exercises. Breakfast was at nine and dinner at four o'clock. The usual questions as to candidates, deaths, character, stations, membership and subscriptions were put and answered by those present. At the close the brethren hastened away to their respective appointments, travelling in little

---

(4) *The Religion of the Heart Delineated*, p. 256.
(5) *Wesley's Works*, XIII, p. 12.

companies by stages, at which they preached, and were hospitably entertained by the people.

This year the Conference met at the end of June, or early in July, but the Minutes have not been preserved. A brief record, however, was made by Mr. Myles, who was present, and having travelled five years was received into full connexion. He was the first thus accepted in Ireland, and received the usual mark of acknowledgment, the Large Minutes, with a suitable inscription, signed by the President. The number of circuits was only one more than at the previous Conference in 1778; but the membership had increased from five thousand three hundred and thirty-six to six thousand five hundred and twelve, or an addition of near twelve hundred. At the close of the Conference Dr. Coke read the minutes and enforced on the preachers the necessity of maintaining them, which they engaged to do; and it was agreed that thenceforward a yearly Conference should be held in Dublin.[6]

Dr. Coke soon became intimately acquainted with the details of Methodism on this side of the channel; and both preachers and people ever found in him not only a most uncompromising opponent to every moral or Methodistical irregularity, but also a faithful counsellor and a loving friend. They knew his worth, and to this day revere his memory.

Mr. W. M'Cornock was appointed to the Lisleen circuit. He says that in October he made a missionary tour of about one hundred and thirty miles; but the severity of the weather and the country being strange to him, he suffered much. Once he had to swim his horse over an arm of the sea. At another time, having to ride about twenty miles, he was benighted on a mountain, but providentially led by the barking of a dog to a house where he was kindly received. Here he embraced the opportunity of giving an exhortation, and uniting in prayer with the people, and had reason to believe it was not in vain.[7]

Mr. Burgess, who had been raised to the rank of quartermaster, was at this time in Belturbet, and found much enjoyment and profit in association with the Methodists of the town. They were few in number, he says, and mostly poor; but some of them rich in faith. Two are specially worthy of notice, John Ferguson, "an Israelite indeed," a pattern of meekness, simplicity and love, under whose roof those who "feared the Lord spoke often one to another," united in fervent supplications, and enjoyed rich tokens of the

(6) *Wesleyan Methodist Magazine*, 1831, p. 293.

(7) *Arminian Magazine*, 1785, pp. 188-89.

Divine favour. The principal support of Methodism in the town was Mrs. Alice Dawes, a widow of much industry and integrity of character, who gladly received the preachers, and fitted up a room on purpose for their accommodation. It was her delight to minister to the wants of the servants of God, and to them it was no small advantage to be favoured with the care, the counsels, and the prayers of such "a mother in Israel." Very soon after this a little chapel was built in this town.

Mr. Moore was appointed a second time to the Londonderry circuit, but did not remain the year there, as he had to remove to Dublin to settle some family affairs, so another preacher took his place, and he left the circuit under the care of his colleague, Mr. Crickett. Through his labours a young man was converted, named Blakely Dowling, who became a member of the Society, and in 1790 entered the itinerancy. He was distinguished by a steady and settled devotedness to God's service; while Christian simplicity and humility adorned his public life.

Not long after this Methodism was introduced into Walshestown. On one occasion Mr. Barber was announced to preach there, but having been delayed longer than usual at Killyleagh, from whence he came by water, the service was commenced by Mr. David Thompson. The place was crowded to excess, and after a short time Mr. Barber arrived. When he began to preach a solemn awe rested on the people, and as he proceeded the Spirit was poured out more abundantly, until many cried aloud for mercy. The meeting continued until midnight and amongst those converted that night were two young ladies who, before the congregation, embraced each other with mutual joy.[8]

At Manorhamilton a valuable addition to the Society was made in Mr. John Crawford, of Deerpark. At the time of his conversion he knew nothing of Methodism, but soon after heard of a people called Swaddlers, to whom all manner of evil was ascribed, and resolved to attend one of their meetings and judge for himself. The truths of the Gospel and his own experience were so clearly and accurately described in the sermon he heard that he concluded at once that the Methodists were the people of God; and being invited to class-meeting his opinion was so confirmed he made up his mind that thenceforth this people would be his people, and their God his God. In a short time he was appointed a leader, and after seventy years' acquaintance with the doctrines and discipline of the Society, said — "I bless God for such

(8) *Primitive Wesleyan Methodist Magazine*, 1829, p. 263.

a system, and will praise Him for it through all eternity."[9]

Messrs. Yewdall and Boardman were appointed to Cork. The former hastened to his circuit, and was much encouraged to find both a friendly people and large congregations. But Mr. Boardman remained at Limerick until the latter end of September, and then came to Cork, where he had laboured before, and was much beloved by the people. On the Sunday morning after his arrival he preached from "Though He slay me, yet will I trust in Him." It was a very solemn meeting, and a reverential awe filled the hearts of the people. His work was almost done. After service, on his way to a friend's house for dinner, he was suddenly struck blind. Soon after he seemed to recover. Then he had a fit which deprived him of both speech and understanding; but a physician who was called in apprehended no danger, although there were symptoms of apoplexy. Being somewhat better next day, Mr. Boardman preached on that and the following evenings. His mind was calm and serene. On Friday he attended the meeting for intercession at noon, and was observed to pray with uncommon freedom and power for the success of the Gospel, and for his brethren in the ministry. After the meeting he went to a friend's house in the city; but as soon as he got there lost the power of speech, and was taken in a carriage to his own house. From that time he sank until about nine o'clock, when he expired in the arms of two of the brethren, and in the presence of many of his friends, who commended him to God with sorrowful hearts.

On receiving the sad tidings of Mr. Boardman's death, Mr. Yewdall, who was at Bandon, at once hastened to Cork, and found the whole Society plunged in the deepest sorrow. On the Lord's day he preached the funeral sermon to a crowded congregation. The remains were placed in front of the pulpit, and next morning borne to the graveyard attached to the cathedral of St. Fin Barre, by friends, singing hymns as they passed through the streets, and accompanied by a great multitude.

Mr. Yewdall wrote to Mr. Wesley about a suitable epitaph, and received the following:-

"With zeal for God, with love of souls inspired,
Nor awed by dangers, nor by labours tired,
BOARDMAN in distant worlds proclaims the Word
To multitudes, and turns them to his Lord.

(9) *Primitive Wesleyan Methodist Magazine*, 1852, pp. 95-100.

> But soon the bloody waste of war he mourns,
> And, loyal, from rebellion's seat returns;
> Nor yet at home — on eagle pinions flies,
> And in a moment soars to Paradise!"[10]

For some unknown reason this was laid aside, and on the plain slab which covers the grave was placed the following inscription:—

"MR. RICHARD BOARDMAN,
Departed this life, October 4th, 1782.
Aetatis 44.

> Beneath this stone the dust of Boardman lies;
> His pious soul has soared above the skies,
> With eloquence divine he preached the Word
> To multitudes, and turned them to the Lord.
> His bright example strengthened what he taught,
> And devils trembled when for Christ he fought.
> With truth and Christian zeal he nations fired,
> And all who knew him mourned when he expired."[11]

Mr. Boardman's sudden death made a profound impression in the city, and many persons, who first went to the chapel to hear the funeral sermon were awakened to serious concern for their souls, and became regular hearers. Mrs. Ward, one of the leading members of the Society, in writing to Mr. Wesley, on October the 28th, says: "God has been glorified by the death of His servant, as well as by his life. Cork has not known such a revival for many years, as is now taking place in it. The congregations on Sunday evenings are so large that they cannot find room within, and many are obliged to stand in the yard, as far as the outer gate. The word is attended with power. Many old professors, who were luke-warm and settled on their lees, are stirred up. They hunger and thirst after righteousness, and are on stretch for purity of heart. Many who formerly partook of this blessing and lost their evidence are stirred up to seek it afresh, so that they cannot rest without it. Backsliders are restored, and new members added to our number."[12]

---

(10) *Wesley's Works*, XIII., p. 13.
(11) *The Western Pioneers*, p. 188.
(12) *Arminian Magazine*, 1790, p. 609.

Meantime Mr. Yewdall, being left alone on the circuit, overpowered with work, wrote for assistance to Mr. Wesley, who replied saying that he knew of none whom he could send, unless Mr. Rutherford, then in Dublin, could be persuaded to give up Mr. Blair, his colleague, and take "a poor invalid," John Mayly, then in the city in his stead; but this the leaders in the metropolis strongly objected to, and it was not until Christmas, when Wesley had exercised his authority by insisting on it, and when probably there was a prospect of getting Mr. Moore, that the proposal was carried out.

On December the 22nd, Mrs. Ward writes again: "The mercy of God, and His care of His vineyard, has been abundantly displayed among us. Could you see the unanimity and prosperity of our little Zion, your heart would rejoice. There is a universal revival in our bands and classes. God is in the midst of us, and all feel that uniting principle of life exciting us to provoke one another to love and good works. Our congregations are large on Sundays; and on week nights of late they are much increased and deeply serious. The select Society is again assembled. A general conviction rests on believers for holiness of heart; some who formerly experienced it, but had lost their evidence, are again restored; and others are brought into that rest which belongs to the people of God. Prayer meetings are in some places kept up, but not so generally as we could wish."[13]

Soon after Mr. Boardman was called hence to the home above, he was followed by another honoured servant of God, Mr. Swindells, whose end also was sudden. The health of this devoted evangelist had become exceedingly delicate, as he suffered for a long time from a very painful disorder, and thus was not able to do even the work then assigned to a supernumerary. Hence his name only occasionally appears on the list of stations. Yet he continued faithfully and zealously to work for God, as strength and opportunity were afforded him. His heart and fresh continued to decline for years, and his sufferings were excruciating. Still his patience was unwearied, and each interval of pain was employed in praise and heavenly conversation. About the middle of October, having returned to England, he was at Stockport. One evening he took tea at a Mr. Lavender's, in company with Miss Ritchie, Mr. Jeremiah Brettel, and others. He was cheerful and related some of the scenes through which he had passed. Among the rest, that once near Cork he was taken by a violent mob to the bank of a river, where they purposed to drown

(13) *Arminian Magazine*, 1790, p. 666.

him; but one of their number — the most resolute — said the preacher would swim out; but he would take him to a better place. Then going a short distance, he showed him a way across a field, and protested that not a man should touch him. Having spent a pleasant evening, Mr. Swindells accompanied Mr. Brettel to the chapel, and sat with him in the pulpit during the service. He continued apparently in the same state of health for a few days, until the 21st, when as he was walking to and fro in the parlour of a Mr. Whitaker, he sank down and died. Sudden death to him no doubt was sudden glory.

CHAPTER 13

1783

IN Cork the labours of Mr. Blair were accompanied with the Divine blessing in a remarkable manner, so that the good work continued to deepen and spread until within a few months nearly two hundred were added to the Society in the city.

Notwithstanding the revival in Cork, and although the chapel was crowded with hearers all through the winter, it was several months before there were any tokens of a deep work at Bandon. As some of the leaders seemed cold the preachers endeavoured to revive them by meeting them and their classes frequently, and also by preaching in the plainest and strongest manner, and their labours were not in vain. At length about sixty were added to the membership. Amongst these were fourteen young men belonging to a troop of horse then quartered in the town. A Society in London for distributing religious books amongst the military sent a number of Bibles for that purpose. On the day appointed for giving them Mr. Yewdall preached on the importance of searching the Scriptures, exhorted his hearers to carefully read and meditate on the word of God, and had every reason to believe that the word spoken and distributed was attended with the Divine blessing to many of the soldiers in Cork and Bandon.[1]

---

(1) *Arminian Magazine*, 1795, pp. 317-18.

The brethren on this circuit being much revived evinced their zeal by spreading the knowledge of the truth in other places. A subscription list was opened to defray any extra expenses that might be incurred. Inishannon, which appears to have been abandoned, got another trial, and Methodism was introduced to the villages of Newcestown, Castletown and Ballyneen, and a number of neighbouring farmsteads. As these places lay within a few miles of Bandon, the residents had occasional opportunities of hearing the Methodist preachers. Among the first to open their hearts to the truth and their homes to its messengers were Richard Dawson, of Mossgrove, and Benjamin Hosford, of Bengour. The latter was a Presbyterian; was trained to be a wool-comber in Bandon, where he heard Mr. Wesley preach; and while still a youth went to take charge of his father's small farm at Farranmareen, adjoining Bengour. About this time a local preacher from Bandon visited the place, and preached in the house of a weaver named Bennett, the people sitting on the looms during the service. This house is still standing. Thenceforth this was a regular appointment for the preachers, who, when they visited the place stayed alternately with Benjamin Hosford, his brother Joseph, and a man named Welply. Soon a small chapel was built at Bengour, which, in 1835 gave place to a better one erected at Rushfield, a short distance off. A daughter of Welply's had married a Mr. Anglin and these were the first to receive the preacher at Ballyneen. This is a small village in Ballymoney, one of the three parishes which were known as "the Paradise of Parsons." The fortunate incumbents, it seems, had large incomes and little to do, and so spent no small portion of their time in rounds of social festivities. Other workers however found something to do. After occasional meetings in Anglin's house, the preachers secured a large room in which to hold their services, and then came to the village once a fortnight. Many of the names of Hosford, Dawson, Welply, Roberts and Fuller joined the Society, and welcomed the evangelists to their homes. A member of the last named, Mrs. Elizabeth Fuller, died at Castletown, near Ballyneen, in 1867, having reached the venerable age of one hundred and two. She heard Wesley preach several times, and was the last connecting link in these parts of the Methodists of the eighteenth and nineteenth centuries. By the death of "Old Aunt Betty," as she was popularly called, many a good story has been lost, for no one has preserved her reminiscences of early Methodism.[2]

---

(2) *Irish Christian Advocate*, 1883, p. 430.

In March Mr. Blair preached at Youghal, where the chief magistrate granted the use of the courthouse, and the inhabitants in general gave attention to the word: so that in a short time a Society was formed of about sixty persons, many of whom, there was good reason to believe, experienced the life and power of true religion.

At Skibbereen, where the preachers obtained the use of the town-hall, a small Society was also formed. Mr. Yewdall, a few miles from the town, met with a clergyman who was most desirous for the spiritual welfare of those under his care, invited the preachers to his parish, and procured a suitable room for the services. Many attended and good was done.[3]

A young lady also who five years previously had been converted at Bandon, was this year married to Captain Evans, of Ardraly, in the parish of Aghadown, and invited the preachers to her house, which became a centre of religious light in the neighbourhood. Twenty years subsequently a chapel was built here, eighteen years before one was erected in Skibbereen.[4]

Mr. Yewdall visited Dunmanway, a town where they had never heard a Methodist preacher before, and he was received with open arms. The people were so eager to gratify their curiosity that "they had hardly patience to wait until he lighted from his horse," and they compelled him to remain with them four days, during which they not only received him with generous hospitality, but also received the truth in love. From this time the preachers continued to visit the town regularly once a fortnight, and soon formed a Society of thirty persons, who gave satisfactory evidence of their desire to flee from the wrath to come and abandon all sin. Of those who then became Methodists, one was Mrs. Ellen Wolfe, who during the remaining sixty-three years of her protracted life adorned the doctrine of the Lord her Saviour.[5] Another was Mrs. Elizabeth Atkins, who through the first sermon of Mr Blair in the town was deeply impressed, and determined to cast in her lot with the Society. This resolution she carried out when the next preacher came to the neighbourhood. During the first few visits of the itinerants they were entertained by a poor man named Patterson, who a short time previously had removed from Ballyneen, where he had heard and embraced the Gospel. But Mrs. Atkins, being in better circumstances, opened her house for the reception of the messengers of truth, and to the close of her long and exemplary life it

(3) *Arminian Magazine*, 1795, pp. 317-18.
(4) *Wesleyan Methodist Magazine*, 1847, p. 410.
(5) Ibid., p. 620.

was the home of the preachers.[6]

The success which attended the labours of the itinerants on this circuit in opening new places, encouraged them to attempt preaching at Bantry, where a few Protestant families resided, but the greater part of the inhabitants were Roman Catholics. Accordingly a few friends accompanied Mr. Yewdall thither, and went through the town, informing the people that there would be a service in the evening. The preacher took his stand in an open place, near the market cross, and a large congregation assembled; but as the ground happened to be the property of a gentleman who was not at home, his officious steward, under pretence that his master would be displeased, compelled them to remove to the market-place. Here the service had not proceeded far, when another interruption took place, through a sea captain engaging a man to blow a French horn; but he was prevailed upon to desist, so that the preacher concluded without further interference. Not having succeeded in obtaining lodgings in the inn, the Methodists took up their residence in a private house belonging to a Roman Catholic, who treated them with the greatest civility. At six o'clock next morning Mr. Yewdall preached again before the door of his host to a quiet congregation, many of whom were Romanists, and behaved far better than those called Protestants. At the end of a fortnight the zealous itinerant returned to the town, and found that during his absence the priest had been very energetic in his attempts to excite the people to commence a riot, if the Methodists should venture to preach there again, threatened any that dare to attend with excommunication, and procured a poor half-witted fellow to harangue the people in the street, as a counter attraction. Seeing that it would be dangerous to preach out of doors, Mr. Yewdall obtained the use of a large dining room in the inn, which was filled with an attentive audience. The priest came in, intending to make disturbance, but the gentlemen present would not suffer him. Next morning the congregation was increasingly attentive, and Mr. Yewdall was enabled to speak with much liberty.[7]

While thus the work was gloriously prospering in the south, in the extreme north it seemed to languish. Hence, on February the 10th Mr. Moore having removed to Dublin, Mr. Wesley wrote to Mr. Crickett, who had charge of the Londonderry circuit, as follows:— "Many years ago, the Society at Barnard Castle, as large as that at Derry, was remarkably dead. When Samuel

---

(6) Ibid, 1840, p. 255.

(7) *Arminian Magazine*, 1795, pp. 318-19.

Meggot, now with God, came to them, he advised them to keep a day of fasting and prayer. A flame broke out, and spread through all the circuit; nor is it extinguished to this day. I advise you to do the same at Derry. On Sunday evening reprove strongly their unfaithfulness and unfruitfulness: and desire all that fear God to humble themselves with fasting on the Friday following. I am much inclined to hope a flame will break out in Londonderry likewise. But you must immediately resume the form at least of a Methodist Society. I positively forbid you or any preacher to be a leader; rather put the most insignificant person in each class to be the leader of it, and try if you cannot persuade three men, if no more, and three women, to meet in band. Hope to the end. You shall see better days. The plainer you speak the more good you will do. Derry will bear plain dealing."[8] How far Mr. Crickett attended to these instructions, or with what results, does not appear.

Soon after writing the above Mr. Wesley left London for Ireland, intending to make his usual tour; but was attacked in Bristol with the disease which brought him so near death in 1775. This so weakened him that he could only visit Dublin, where he arrived on April the 13th, and was the guest of Mr. H. Brooke.

On April the 29th the Conference began, and continued until May the 2nd. "All was peace and love." "We had an exceedingly happy Conference," writes Wesley. "I wish all our English preachers were of the same spirit with the Irish, among whom there is no jarring string. I never saw such simplicity and teachableness run through a body of preachers before."[9]

On the following Sunday evening the Society met to renew their covenant with God, and to receive the Lord's supper; the Saviour was graciously present, and manifested Himself in power to many.[10] Mr. Moore says that he had the great privilege of hearing Mr. Wesley preach almost every day, and learned more concerning the apostolic direction about "rightly dividing the word of truth" than in all his previous studies.[11]

While in the city Wesley seized the opportunity of waiting on Lady Arabella Denny at her beautiful residence, now known as Lisaniskea, Blackrock. The philanthropic character of this noble lady is well known. In 1765 she was presented with the freedom of the city of Dublin as a mark of

(8) *Wesley's Works*, XIV., p. 361.
(9) *Wesley's Works*, XII, p. 151.
(10) *Wesleyan Methodist Magazine*, 1851, p. 527.
(11) *Life of the Rev. H. Moore*, p. 76.

esteem "for her ladyship, for her many great charities and constant care of the poor foundling children in the city workhouse." She also founded the Magdalene Asylum in Leeson street, which was opened in 1766, and was the first institution of the kind in Ireland. Her ladyship died in 1792, aged eighty-five years.

Wesley being unable to make his usual tour, embarked for Holyhead on May the 8th, having remained about three weeks in Ireland, and delegated to Dr. Coke the work of visiting the Societies.

No details have been published of the doctor's excursion. Doubtless it was then, as he journeyed through the country, he first met our friend Bartley Campbell, who became at once a great favourite with the worthy doctor, heralding him from place to place, and with amazing success collecting the people to hear him preach.

For some time the leading Methodists in Dublin were most wishful that the Rev. J. W. and Mrs. Fletcher should visit the city, and in April, 1782, sent a request earnestly urging them to do so. But on account of the delicate state of Mr. Fletcher's health, his long absence from his parish, and his curate being at Kingswood, he was compelled to decline going just then. The friends in Dublin, however, availed themselves of the presence of Dr. Coke to send with him this year a renewal of the invitation, and Mr. and Mrs. Fletcher judged it improper any longer to withhold consent, lest, in disregarding the solicitations of a willing people, they should disobey the summons of God. So they accepted the invitation, and in August, 1783, arrived in Dublin, where they continued for about six weeks.

Application was made to the rector of St. Andrew's to allow Mr. Fletcher to preach in his church, which was immediately granted. The house was crowded to excess, and the earnestness and power of the preacher astonished the congregation, some of whom seemed to doubt if he were not more than human. But, alas! when it became known that he preached on the evening of the same day in the Methodist chapel, the pulpits of the churches, with the exception of that of the French church, were immediately closed against him. Notwithstanding, however, the intolerant spirit thus manifested, Mr. Fletcher's labours were wonderfully owned of God.

The expectations in regard to this period, though high, were more than realized: for a more blessed and fruitful visit has scarcely ever been made by a Christian minister to a Christian Church since the days of the apostles. Mr. Fletcher's public and private ministrations were attended with marvellous power, numbers of careless persons were awakened, and desire for the blessing of holiness was excited and intensified in professing Christians.

Amongst the many who during this visit were either converted or awakened to a concern for their souls that resulted in their conversion, were Michael Murphy, who entered the itinerancy in 1788, James Stuart, who began to travel in 1792, and Miss Sarah Moore, afterwards wife of Mr. Myles.

Mr. Fletcher frequently preached in the French church to the descendants of the Huguenots, who had sought in this country an asylum from the sword of persecution. Amongst his auditors on these occasions were sometimes many persons who did not understand a sentence of what he spoke, as he preached in French, and on being asked their reason for attending the services, replied, "We went to look at him, for heaven seemed to beam from his countenance."

While in Dublin, Mr. and Mrs. Fletcher were entertained by Mr. and Mrs. Smyth, and under their hospitable roof had the opportunity of meeting with many truly pious persons of different religious denominations. These social gatherings — or "drawing-room meetings," as they are now designated — proved means of rich spiritual blessing, and initiated a series of reunions probably unsurpassed in their power for good in the history of Methodism.

It should also be recorded that Mr. Fletcher established the prayer and class meetings on Tuesdays and Thursdays at eleven o'clock, held on the lobby of Whitefriar street chapel, for the convenience of delicate and aged females, not able to go out in the evenings: and it was often remarked what special blessing attended these meetings.[12]

During the latter part of the visit of Mr. and Mrs. Fletcher the devoted Lady Mary Fitzgerald was also the guest of Mrs. Smyth, with whom she cultivated the closest intimacy and friendship, until severed by death. Her ladyship's stay in Ireland was not of long continuance, and she returned to England with Mr. and Mrs. Fletcher and Mrs. Smyth. She was a woman of deep piety and singular devotedness to God. Her unhappy marriage with George Fitzgerald, Esq., of Turlough park, County Mayo, proved the fruitful source of many of those afflictions which she was called to endure in the early part of her life.

When Mr. Fletcher was about to leave, knowing the scanty pittance he received from his parish, it was thought but an act of common honesty to

---

(12) *Smith's History of Methodism in Ireland,* p. 195.

refund him the expense he had been at in coming to Ireland, and to bear his charges back again to Madeley. Accordingly on the last evening of his visit the stewards and trustees united to press his acceptance of a small purse, not as a present, but as a debt justly due. But he firmly and absolutely refused it. At length, they being very urgent with him, he took the purse in his hand and said - "Must I accept it? and may I do what I please with it?" "Yes, yes," all replied. "God be praised, then!" said he, raising his eyes towards heaven. "What a mercy is here! I heard some of you complaining that your Poor's Fund was never so low before; take this purse, God has sent it to you, and bestowed it upon your poor. You cannot deny me; it is sacred to them. God be praised! I heartily thank you, my dear, kind brethren."

Mrs. Fletcher expressed her deep conviction — "a faith riveted in her heart" — that before long there would be a great revival of the work of God in Dublin. These expectations were fully realized, and a large addition to the Society took place, as it gradually and steadily increased from about five hundred members to upwards of one thousand.

While Mr. and Mrs. Fletcher were in the metropolis, the Rev. J. Creighton, with his family, arrived there *en route* to London. Having been invited by Mr. Wesley to join him, he had resigned his curacy, and was appointed to officiate in City road chapel, as one of the resident clergymen.[13]

At the Irish Conference Messrs. Moore, Blair and Yewdall were stationed in Cork; but the British Conference appointed Mr. Lawrence Kane to take the place of Mr. Yewdall, who returned to England. Mr. Moore says that his reception on the circuit was very encouraging, and a door of usefulness was opened. The Lord greatly blessed the preaching of the word, and a considerable number of the members were led to seek the full salvation of God.

At Dunmanway there was a good prospect. A large room, which had been used as a workshop, was secured, and was well filled; a considerable number, also, had been received into the Society, who seemed desirous to experience all the blessings of the Gospel. Here the following remarkable incident occurred: The town was on the property of Sir Richard E. Cox, Bart., a young man of most profligate habits. He was much displeased at the moral change which had taken place in the inhabitants, and with the preachers, who in his opinion had caused it: and had frequently threatened to stop their proceedings.

---

(13) *Arminian Magazine*, 1785, p. 402.

A good man observed — "He may certainly do so, if the Lord permit, for no man can resist him; he is greater in Dunmanway than King George himself." This wild youth at length resolved that he would throw the preacher who next came to the town into the lake in front of his own residence. But when the time of Mr. Moore's going there arrived, the Lord had most awfully thwarted the execution of this wicked purpose. Living by himself, and being at a loss for a pastime on the Lord's day, Sir Richard determined to have an excursion on the lake. One of the oars of his boat, however, had been broken, and to supply its place timber was procured, and a piece sawn from it in the church-yard during divine service. He embarked with a young gentleman, one of his companions, and having sailed for a little while, said he would see in how short a time the rowers could make the circuit of the lake. They then struck off, and he remained, with watch in hand, for some time observing them; but the slowness of the motion annoyed him, and after many oaths and imprecations, he pulled one of the men from the bench and took his place, saying he would show them how to row. He dipped too deeply in the water, and making a violent pull, the new made oar snapped like a twig, and he was precipitated backward into the lake. Though upwards of three hundred people soon collected on the shore, and every effort was made to save him, it was in vain. The body was recovered next day, much swollen and disfigured, a short time before Mr. Moore entered the town.[14] The Methodists saw in the untimely fate of the young Baronet a signal mark of the displeasure of Providence. "If Sir Richard had not taken out his boat," they said, "and made arrangements to drown one of the preachers, he would not have been drowned himself." "It was because he laid his horsewhip across the shoulders of a priest," said the Roman Catholics. "No," replied the Episcopalians, "it was because the oar which he used was made on Sunday, and from a branch cut off one of the venerable elms in the church-yard."[15] The appalling accident, however, was overruled for good, as all opposition to the truth ended, and the word of the Lord had free course and was glorified.

The remainder of the year, says Mr. Moore, was one of the happiest he ever experienced, believers were built up in their most holy faith, while his labours and those of his colleagues were much owned of the Lord in the salvation of souls. The itinerants made excursions into the surrounding country, and preached in new places wherever opportunity opened. Thus on

(14) *Life of the Rev. H. Moore*, pp. 78, 79.
(15) *Irish Christian Advocate*, 1883, p. 359.

one occasion Mr. Moore visited Cappoquin. Having heard that there was a detachment of dragoons there, in which was a Methodist class, he wrote to the quartermaster, who was a member of the Society, and informed him of his intention. Accordingly he was met about a quarter of a mile from his destination by a friend sent to conduct him. "I am afraid," said the stranger, "you will not be able to do any good in the town, the people are mostly Catholics and very wicked, and the Protestants are little better." "Are they worse than dead in sin?" inquired Mr. Moore, and then added, "If they are no worse we know One that can undertake for that." His companion brightened up, and having seen the preacher safe in his quarters, cheerfully left to publish through the town the service in the evening, when a large congregation assembled, most of whom were Romanists. The commanding officer also and all the soldiers, not on duty, attended. Mr. Moore preached again on the following morning, and announced that he would return to the town on a certain day.

When the time came he was met by his former guide, who with a rather discontented air accosted him thus — "O, Mr. Moore, I have bad news for you. The priest has been here, and when he heard of you he preached for the first time these twelve months, and warned all his people not to hear you." Mr. Moore, being curious to know something more about the sermon, his friend said — "He took for his text Revelation 20:7, 'And when the thousand years are expired, Satan shall be loosed out of his prison, and shall go out to deceive the nations;' and addressed his audience thus: 'O you brute beasts, you ought to be the greatest people in the world, as you are the only Church: and yet you are nothing but beasts. You think the Church knows nothing of these men who are going about preaching, because you do not know them. But you see, here they are. The Church knows all about them. I will read the passage again to you.' So he did, and then continued, 'Now you beasts, who are running after these servants of the devil, when I come here again I shall know how to deal with you. I will put out the candle upon every one of you.'" After this luminous exhortation it might be expected that there would have been but few with courage sufficient to resist the *brutum fulmen*, yet notwithstanding the threats, the congregation was good, and much spiritual power was realized.[16]

Some time during this year a young man named Meade Leahy joined

(16) *Life of the Rev. H. Moore*, pp. 78-80.

the Society at Kinsale, of which he continued a consistent and useful member for nearly fifty years. His natural disposition was warm, and his manner considered by some eccentric; but sanctified by Divine grace, these helped to make him an efficient and active leader. His house was ever open for the messengers of mercy, and there they found a comfortable home. It was his custom to go to the preaching-house an hour previous to the beginning of the service, and spend the intervening time in communion with God.[17]

Another event which occurred at this period is worthy of notice. Mr. Thomas Gilpin, who had resided in England, and been converted through the ministry of Mr. Wesley, came with his family to Tullyroan. He was a pious and zealous local preacher, and as his residence was but a mile from Derryscollop, he found in this village ample opportunity for usefulness. He established regular Sunday preaching there, and also travelled much through the surrounding country, where his labours were greatly blessed. In this work he was assisted by his sons, Thomas and William.[18] Mr. Gilpin caught the disease, which terminated his life, by preaching a funeral sermon in the open air with his uncovered head exposed to the cold and rain. While on his deathbed, knowing that his end was approaching, he said to his son William — "I bequeath to you the care of the people among whom I have been labouring. Be faithful, and strive to promote their salvation." Again, addressing all his children, he said — "I have endeavoured to instruct you in religion by precept and example, and am now going to my Father's kingdom; if you all be faithful to death, I shall meet you with joy at the right hand of God; but if not, I shall see you on the left, and seeing you there shall give me no pain, for where I am going pain can never enter." His last words were — "My Father, my Father, the chariot of Israel and the horsemen thereof."[19]

The Methodists of Ireland have been identified with the foreign missionary operations of the Society from their commencement, contributing liberally their worldly substance, and giving their sons and daughters to carry on the sacred work. By a remarkable Providence this country had the privilege of co-operating in the first mission formed by the Society, that in the West Indies, long before any Wesleyan missionary had arrived there. At this time a venerable man lived in Waterford, a member of the Society, who was too far advanced in life to engage in business, and was with his wife supported

---

(17) *Primitive Wesleyan Methodist Magazine*, 1883, p. 411.
(18) His son William entered the itinerancy in England in 1779.
(19) *Primitive Wesleyan Methodist Magazine*, 1849, pp. 31, 32.

by two sons, whom, with the rest of his children, he had brought up in the fear of the Lord. Some persons persuaded these young men, that if they went to America they would certainly make their fortune. From this they became restless, and this year induced their parents to accompany them to the New World. As their means were very limited, the two young men entered into an engagement with the captain of a schooner bound for Virginia, by which they empowered him to sell their services for such a period as would be sufficient to indemnify him for their passage, and that of their parents. When they were about to embark, another of the old man's sons came to take a last farewell, but was so affected at the thought of seeing them no more, that he also bound himself as his brothers had done: so they all bade adieu to their native land together.

The captain was a most inhuman and wicked man. No sooner were the poor people at sea than they were treated like slaves, and obliged to submit to hardships unknown to the lowest sailors. Their voyage was long and stormy; and this, in addition to the indignities to which the emigrants were obliged to submit, rendered their situation deplorable in the extreme. When they drew near the destined port, a violent storm arose, which carried away one of the masts, and eventually drove them to the West Indies. Having sprung a leak, they drifted, a floating wreck, into a harbour in Antigua, after having been at sea thirteen weeks. The vessel remained for repair; the poor passengers went on shore, and the old man having learned that there were Methodists in the island, enquired for the preaching-house; and there he found real and active friends, who, as soon as they knew the circumstances of the case, immediately ransomed the whole family. The three brothers were provided with good situations, and the father, having gifts as well as grace, was employed in instructing the negroes and holding meetings.[20] Under the superintendence of Mr. Baxter, with the assistance of Mrs. Gilbert, and the subordinate instrumentality of the old Irish emigrant, the cause prospered; so that there were under their care at this time upwards of one thousand members. Three years later, in 1786, when Dr. Coke first visited the island, he found as the result of the Divine blessing on their united labours nearly two thousand members in Society.

As a young Englishman named Robert Blake, who had entered the itinerancy in 1778, and was appointed to Limerick at the Conference of 1782,

---

(20) *Arminian Magazine*, 1791, pp. 499-501.

left his circuit three times without the consent of the Assistant, and "stupidly and saucily affronted almost all the leaders,"[21] Matthias Joyce was sent by Mr. Wesley to supply his place. Mr. Joyce says that during the short time he travelled the circuit he had severe trials, but the Lord comforted him in the midst of all.

At the Conference this year he was stationed at Ballyconnell with Messrs. R. Armstrong and J. Kerr; but the numerous privations and discouragements in connection with the work so affected him that he resolved to return home. So he saddled his horse and rode away from one of his appointments, but with such a sense of guilt, that he feared each moment he would fall and break his neck, and when met and reasoned with by several members of the Society, was prevailed upon to resume his labours. His wife also, as a true helpmate, wrote to encourage him to persevere in the Lord's work. She said — "Are you afraid of the devil, who is himself held in chains by your Master?" Is not God on your side? Then fear not. This temptation is for the trial of your faith. The Lord will make your cup to overflow after it, and bless you in His own way.[22] Thus an eminently devoted and useful servant of God was saved to the Connexion. On this circuit towards the close of the year a blessed revival commenced in the neighbourhood of Aghalun. One Sunday morning in November as one of the leaders, James Shearman, narrated his experience in class, a man present, Thomas Berney, was deeply impressed, and from that time several sought for redemption in the blood of Christ. At the love-feast on the 28th Berney expressed his determination to serve God before all, and fervently desired an interest in their prayers; and on the following Sunday was filled with peace and joy unspeakable. A profound impression was then made on the minds of many, which proved the beginning of a glorious and long continued revival movement, during which large numbers were led to decide for God.[23] Thus "the wilderness became a fruitful field, and the fruitful field was counted for a forest."

(21) *Wesley's Works*, XIII, p. 14.

(22) *Lives of Early Methodist Preachers*, IV, pp. 264-68.

(23) *Arminian Magazine*, 1786, pp. 54, 55.

CHAPTER 14

1784

THE good work in Fermanagh referred to at the close of the last chapter continued to deepen and spread during the whole of the year 1784. Numerous openings were obtained for preaching the glorious Gospel, the services were largely attended, and at nearly every meeting there were persons convinced of sin or converted to God. On some occasions such was the distress of the people that the preacher was unable to proceed with his sermon, and had recourse to prayer. Amongst those converted were some of the Irvines, Beattys, Dunbars, Mitchells, Halls, Johnstons, Grahams, Littles and Armstrongs, families long identified with Methodism in this district of country, and in America.[1]

A few local preachers, led by Messrs. William Armstrong and George Henderson, of Drumbulcan, formed a plan to carry on the work on the northern part of the Enniskillen circuit, by which means access was obtained to numerous places and families where Methodism had not been known before. It was no uncommon thing for these zealous brethren to travel twenty or thirty miles to preach, and in many instances openings were thus made for those who had entered the itinerancy. In connection with this special effort Robert Crozier, of Trory, was led to religious decision, and soon began to work for Christ, giving indications of those talents which when cultivated proved him to be one of the remarkable men of his day.[2] With an unattractive countenance he had a mind of great excellence, keen, analytic and transparent.

In January the Methodist Missionary Society was formed in London, and from the first report issued this year it appears that the income amounted to £66 3s, including £14 14s subscribed in Dublin.[3] Mrs. Kirchhoffer (misspelled Kirkover), £2 2s; Mr. Henry Brooke, £2 2s; Master and Miss Blatchford, £4 4s; Mr. D'Olier, £2 2s; Mrs. Smyth, £2 2s; and Mrs. King, £2 2s.

In Cork the good work continued to prosper greatly. Thus on April the

---

(1) *Arminian Magazine*, 1786, pp. 55, 56.
(2) Unpublished *Gleanings of Methodism in Fermanagh*.
(3) Tyerman's *Wesley*, III., pp. 480-81.

17th Mrs. Ward writes — "I have not in the twenty-one years that I have been in Society seen such times; our people have the power and life of religion increasing daily among them; their only contention is to provoke each other to love and good works. The fire not only spreads from heart to heart, but Cork and the county of Cork are growing almost too small for it; five new places have been visited. The people here receive the word gladly, and there is a prospect of much good being done among them. They are growing in grace and in the knowledge of God in the country Societies, as well as in number. Much of this great good is owing to those servants of God who labour among us. No time, no weather makes any interruption in their plan: their labours are abundant, and the blessing on them as great. They love and prefer each the other to himself, while their ministry, instead of growing stale, increases daily in power and usefulness. Do not think I exaggerate. I speak rather short of the truth; I am not partial to any man; but God continues to bless their united labours, and the work spreads and deepens in their hands."[4]

At Waterford a young man named John Langley was convinced of sin through a sermon preached by Mr. J. Price, became a member of the Society, and gave himself unreservedly to the Lord. Soon afterwards he removed to London, became connected with City road chapel, and there as a leader and also a visitor of the Strangers' Friend Society, did a good work for Christ. He died in great peace in 1814, and his remains were interred in the graveyard at City road.[5]

During the spring Dr. Coke paid his third visit to Ireland;[6] but as usual few details are available. He was in Dublin at the end of April, and wrote that he had met the classes, and had no doubt but there was a considerable revival in the Society. One of Mrs. King's classes, especially, afforded evidence of it, more than any class he had ever met.[7]

He also visited and had a large congregation in Prosperous, a small town in the county of Kildare, founded in 1775 by a younger brother of Mr. Henry Brooke, of Dublin. Here Captain Brooke established a cotton factory, in which about two thousand operatives were employed; amongst whom he invited the Methodist preachers to labour, and afforded them every facility for regularly preaching. As the majority of the workers were Romanists, he

(4) *Arminian Magazine*, 1791, pp. 553-54.
(5) *Methodist Magazine*, London, 1814, pp. 335-36.
(6) Tyerman's *Life of Fletcher*, p. 540.
(7) Etheridge's *Life of Dr. Coke*, p. 79.

also provided a room for the priest to celebrate mass in, on condition that he should neither say or do anything to prevent his people from attending the Methodist services, which was readily promised. In carrying on this vast undertaking Captain Brooke soon exceeded the limits of his own means, and, on application to Parliament for assistance, received a loan of £25,000 for twelve years, without interest; but in 1786, having again occasion to apply for help, either in the shape of a fresh loan or an extension of time, his petition was rejected, and the works consequently were discontinued, thus throwing more than fourteen hundred looms idle. On the failure of his fortune in Ireland, Captain Brooke was in 1788 appointed Governor of St. Helena, and shortly after raised to the rank of colonel. In recognition of his important services here he received the thanks of the King and Government through Mr. Dundas, and was presented by Marquess Wellesley, Governor of India, in full assembly, with a diamond-hilted sword.

But to return to Dr. Coke. He was evidently much concerned about the appointment of the Assistant in Dublin for the ensuing year, and hence wrote to Mr. Wesley for his advice, as follows: "I really do not know one preacher in Ireland, of those who are to remain, who appears to me to be every way qualified to be Assistant of the Dublin circuit. I sincerely wish you would send one from England; but he should be a thorough Methodist. What do you think of James Rogers? If you would make him a promise that he shall return to England, after two years in Dublin, I think he will come; and Andrew Blair can fill his place for a month or three weeks, while he steps over the channel and marries Miss Roe. Henry Moore would do, but London is of still more importance; and our Cork friends would be angry if he was removed to any other place in Ireland."[8]

The Conference met on July the 6th, with Dr. Coke for its president. Five preachers were received on trial, including Walter Griffith, James M'Donald, and William Hammett; and the increase of membership reported was three hundred and seventy-four.

A few months previous to the Conference Mr. Wesley had executed and enroled in Chancery a Deed of Declaration, which has ever since been regarded as the Magna Charta of Methodism. The nature of this document must now be considered.

In the Large Minutes of 1763 it was enjoined that every chapel should

(8) Ibid., p. 80.

be settled according to a certain form given, to the effect that the trustees for the time being should permit Wesley himself, and such other persons as he might appoint, to have the free use of the premises, to preach there God's Holy Word. In case of his death the same right was secured to his brother Charles, and on his decease to the Rev. W. Grimshaw. After the death of these three clergymen, the chapels were to be held in trust for the sole use of such persons as might be appointed to them at the yearly Conference of the people called Methodists, provided that they preached no other doctrines than those contained in Wesley's Notes on the New Testament and his four volumes of Sermons.

As yet, however, there was no legal definition of what was meant by the terms "Conference of the people called Methodists," and to supply this defect, by declaring what persons were members of the Conference, and how the succession and identity of it were to be continued, Wesley in February, 1784, executed his famous Deed of Declaration, which a few days afterwards was enroled in the High Court of Chancery.

This document states that the Conference had always consisted of Methodist preachers, whom Wesley had annually invited to meet him for the following purposes: to advise with him for the promotion of the Gospel of Christ; to appoint preachers and exhorters in connexion with him to the use of chapels; to expel unworthy preachers: and to admit others on probation.

The deed then gives the names and addresses of one hundred preachers, who were declared to be the members of the Conference, and proceeds to state:— They were to assemble yearly at London, Bristol, or any other place which they might think proper: and their first business was to fill up all vacancies occasioned by death or other circumstances. No act was to be valid unless forty members were present. The Conference should not continue less than five days, or more than three weeks. They were to elect a president and a secretary from their own number. Any member absenting himself from two successive annual assemblies without leave, and not appearing on the first day of the third, forfeited his position. The Conference had power to admit preachers on trial, to receive them into full connexion, and for sufficient cause to expel them. The members should not appoint any person to preach in their chapels who was not either one of their number, admitted into connexion with them, or received on trial; nor appoint any preacher, except ordained ministers of the Church of England for more than three years successively to one place. They might send one or more members of their body as delegates to Ireland, or anywhere else out of Great Britain, to act on their behalf, and with all the powers they possessed. Whenever the Conference should be reduced below the number of forty members, and continue so for three years, or whenever the members should decline or neglect to meet for three successive years, the Conference should be extinguished, and all its powers, privileges and advantages should cease.

The hundred preachers appointed by Mr. Wesley included the following eleven then stationed in Ireland — Messrs. Rutherford, Jackson, Henry Moore, Blair, Watkinson, N. Price, Lindsay, G. Brown, Barber, Foster and Crook; and three Irishmen who had appointments in England — Messrs. Creighton, Myles and Thompson, not to mention Mr. Wright, who, though a Scotchman, was one of the fruits of Irish Methodism. Many of the preachers in England, who were not included in the hundred selected, were greatly offended, and some in consequence withdrew from the Connexion; but in Ireland and among the Irish preachers no such feeling appears to have existed. That the Deed Poll was cordially accepted is evident from the following important resolution which passed the Conference this year — "Whereas, a deed poll has been lately enroled in his Majesty's High Court of Chancery in London by the Rev. John Wesley, for the specification and establishment of the Conference of the people called Methodists; and whereas, an anonymous appeal has been circulated among the Societies with the design of depreciating and destroying the force of the said deed; we, the preachers in Conference assembled, do testify that we do approve of the said deed, do prefer it to the former plan of government set forth in the Large Minutes of Conference, and are willing to submit to its regulations and to support it, and that we also do condemn the said anonymous appeal as false and inflammatory."[9]

The proposal of Dr. Coke with regard to the metropolis evidently met with the approval of Wesley, as it was carried out by the appointment of Messrs. Rogers and Blair, an arrangement which was signally owned of the Lord. On August the 19th Mr. Rogers was married to the saintly Hester Anne Roe, and soon after, with his bride, hastened to Dublin. Here they were cordially welcomed by the people, and were not many days in the city before they were fully satisfied that their coming was of the Lord. They found a people fully prepared to receive the Gospel of peace. Within six weeks several

---

(9) *Minutes of the Irish Conference*, I. p. 27.

found mercy, and publicly returned thanks to Almighty God for a sense of His pardoning love, and many more were awakened.[10]

In the meantime Mrs. King was married to Mr. J. Johnson, of Lisburn, and thus Mrs. Rogers arrived just in time to take her place and follow up her work. The hopes of all were encouraged to expect a glorious revival, for which a general Spirit of supplication was given, and God answered in a wonderful manner. As it was manifestly a time of refreshing from the presence of the Lord, it was thought expedient at the love-feast on October the 13th to give notes of admittance to many who were not members, so that nearly seven hundred were present: and a feast of love it was, such as many will praise God for to all eternity. After several had spoken with great freedom and simplicity, a poor penitent with tears besought the people to pray for her. The kindlings of love which had been felt before then became a flame: the power of God descended of a truth, and in every part of the house were heard cries for mercy or songs of praise. Not one remained unaffected, at least seven were justified, and several who had come with only a faint desire after God were deeply convinced of sin. Next night others were pardoned, amongst whom was "dear sister Rudd," a poor nervous woman, who had been a seeker for twenty-one years, but now obtained "the knowledge of salvation by the remission of sins." A young man also who had indulged himself in all kinds of sins with greediness, and, according to his own expression, "believed no God more supreme than himself," strayed into the chapel just as Mr. Rogers announced his text — "Believe on the Lord Jesus Christ and thou shall be saved" — was pricked in his heart, and led to cry for mercy. On another occasion a man and his wife came to the service who had been anxious inquirers seven years, and were both set at liberty in the same instant, and rejoiced together with exceeding great joy. Another person who had been a backslider ten years, and fell first into Antinomian principles, and then into gross sin, got into despair, and many times attempted to put an end to his life, but was prevented by an overruling Providence. On November the 12th, having pointed a loaded pistol at his own breast, intending to discharge it, the inquiry came with power to his heart, "Why will ye die?" He instantly dropped the weapon, fell on his knees, and afterwards came to the preachers, who encouraged him to look to Jesus. On the Tuesday following, at the prayer-meeting he obtained some hope, and

(10) *Lives of Early Methodist Preachers*, IV. pp. 315-16.

that night under Mr. Blair's preaching was set at liberty, which he told with unspeakable gratitude.

On November the 18th there was in Gravel walk chapel another love-feast, which proved a more wonderful season than even the previous one. Nine at least were justified, and many lukewarm professors greatly revived. This glorious work continued to deepen and spread. Amongst others converted was a Jew, who from being according to his sect a Pharisee, became zealous in his love for Jesus, though at the risk of life, for his own mother and other relatives attempted to murder him.[11] In answer to earnest prayer, through the instrumentality of this devoted son of Abraham, his sister was led to believe in the despised Nazarene, and became a living and dying witness of His power to save. On her death-bed, her mother having sent a message to the effect that if she renounced Christ, she would receive her and be as kind to her as ever, the young Jewess, true to her Christian profession, replied: "No, I will never renounce Christ, I would not for a thousand worlds. I never knew happiness until I knew Him. He is my Lord, my God, and my Saviour, and I am going to be happy with Him for ever," and in holy triumph her ransomed spirit entered into the new Jerusalem.[12]

On Christmas morning the chapel in Whitefriar street was well-filled at four o'clock. The people continued during preaching, exhortation, and prayer until eight. "It was a memorable season, and the power of God was manifest to the whole congregation."[13]

Amongst the many who at this period were converted in the metropolis, and subsequently occupied influential positions in the Society, were Messrs. Roger Lamb,[14] George Gallagher,[15] William Curry,[16] and John Parkington.[17] To these should be added the name of another, Thomas Holy, Esq., of Sheffield. During a visit to Dublin this year, one of the devoted women of the Society, Mrs. Ayckbown, was so owned in leading him to the exercise of saving faith, that he subsequently gratefully subscribed himself as her son in the Gospel.[18]

(11) *Experience of Mrs. H. A. Rogers*, pp. 133-36.

(12) *Arminian Magazine*, 1788, pp. 461-65.

(13) *Lives of early Methodist Preachers*, IV., p. 318.

(14) *Wesleyan Methodist Magazine*, 1831, p. 729.

(15) *Primitive Wesleyan Methodist Magazine*, 1844, p. 76.

(16) Ibid., 1843, p. 99.

(17) *Wesleyan Methodist Magazine*, 1824, p. 214.

(18) *Wesleyan Methodist Magazine*, 1832, p. 4.

A free school for forty boys was also opened, and for seven years was conducted on the lobby of Whitefriar street chapel. The first master was Mr. Richard Condy, who had entered the itinerancy in 1776, and was held in high esteem by Mr. Wesley; but subsequently was compelled to retire for a time on account of his health.

But to pass from the metropolis and take a brief glance at the work in the provinces. The appointment of the Assistant on the Cork circuit this year was left by the Irish Conference in the hands of their English brethren, who sent Christopher Peacock, a native of Yorkshire, who had been converted through the preaching of Mr. Rogers, and in 1781 was received on trial. He is described as "a precious devoted labourer, highly favoured of God and man." He and his colleague, Mr. Thomas Davis, followed strictly in the lines of their excellent predecessors, and by continuing the same plan both of doctrine and discipline greatly furthered the work. Nearly one hundred were added to the Society, and many truly converted.[19]

The charge of the Limerick circuit was given to Mr. John Leech, a native of Lancashire, who began to travel in 1773, and now for the first time visited Ireland. Here he found an intelligent loving people, who received him with affection, and showed him much kindness. He gave himself up to God and His work, determined to do all the good he could, and had the satisfaction of seeing that his labours were not in vain in the Lord.[20] One of those converted through his ministry was Mr.Thomas Gloster, who became a member of the Society, and after a long mental struggle was filled with peace and joy in believing. For nearly sixty years he walked with God, and his whole spirit and deportment evinced the character of a genuine disciple. For forty-two years he sustained the office of a leader, fulfilling its duties with zeal and fidelity.[21] Some men of influence in the city joined the Society, while a good work was carried on in the country, where the Societies and congregations had been small.

Up to this period no permanent Society had been formed in the town of Wexford; but in September Mr. Deaves came to reside there, and at once requested Mr. Tattershall, the Assistant on the Waterford circuit, to visit the neighbourhood, which he did, and formed a class of ten members. The second name enroled was that of Mr. William Gurley, who was asked the following

---

(19) *Arminian Magazine*, 1786, p. 600.
(20) *Methodist Magazine*, Dublin, 1812, p. 386.
(21) *Wesleyan Methodist Magazine*, 1843, p. 611.

questions: "What are your motives for uniting with the Methodist Society? Do you believe in the forgiveness of sins, and the witness of the Holy Spirit? Do you believe in a further state of grace to be attained in this life? Do you believe it possible to continue in that state of holiness? Do you believe it possible to fall from that state?"[22] Little probably did the preacher think that the new member he then received into the Society would in the course of time be amongst the first to plant the Cross in the wilds of a western state, and that he would live to proclaim to thousands in the new world the blessed truths he had heard from the Irish itinerants. Yet so it proved.

The appointments to Charlemont were J. Crook, J. Mayly, and W. Griffith, who had a most prosperous year. The circuit then embraced the whole of the county Armagh, and a large part of Tyrone, requiring the preachers six weeks to go the round, though seldom remaining more than one night in any place.[23] Of Mr. Crook it is said, "the hand of the Lord was with him, and many believed and turned to the Lord."

The reception of Mr. Griffith was not very encouraging. On arriving at his first appointment his host accosted him with, "Who sent you here?" but added, "Since you are come, we will not turn you out." At this and at several other places which the young preacher visited that week, he found small congregations, dull societies, and very poor accommodation. On the following Sunday he went to Armagh, and on speaking of his intention to preach in the open air, the steward of the Society warmly opposed it. Mr. Griffith produced the Large Minutes, and read the regulation respecting preaching out of doors; but the official argued that on that day especially it would be improper, as several corps of volunteers were in town, that Lord Charlemont was expected every moment, and that the whole place was in great confusion. All these reasons, however, had no weight with Mr. Griffith, and so as soon as the cathedral service was over, he took his stand on the steps of the market-house and preached to a great multitude. All the men of the Society were of the same mind as the steward, and therefore did not attend; but the women with more courage and zeal, stood nobly by their preacher, and the Lord so helped him that he felt encouraged to continue such efforts for doing good.

At this time the Society and congregation in Newry were very small, and the services were held in a wretched and obscure garret. On Mr. Griffith's

---

(22) *Memoir of the Rev. W. Gurley*, pp. 31, 32.

(23) *Irish Evangelist*, 1860, p. 73.

second visit to the town he proposed to preach here also in the open air; but was strongly opposed by the wife of the Society steward, who told him that he ought to be thankful that he had the garret to preach in; that better preachers than he had occupied it; and added with due emphasis, "If Mr. Wesley had sent us preachers fit to preach in the street, we should have had no objection!" This, however, did not prevent the devoted evangelist from going to the market-house, where he addressed a considerable congregation. So long as the weather permitted services were conducted out of doors, and the fruit was apparent in a large increase to the congregation and Society.[24] During this year no less than two hundred and fifty-nine members were added to the Society on this circuit.

There were tokens of prosperity also in many other parts of Ireland. Some years previously a young man named Joseph Prosser was converted in Limerick, became a Methodist, and for more than forty years adorned his Christian profession. Early in life he settled in Tipperary, soon after which he and another Christian friend applied to Mr. Wesley for a preacher to visit the town, and thus a Society was formed there. Mr. Prosser during this year was enabled to carry out a resolution he had long formed, of erecting a house for the worship of God. This he did on his own property, and entirely at his own expense, and thus proved a means of much blessing in the neighbourhood.[25]

It was at this period that Methodism was introduced into Westport, where a young lady, who subsequently became Mrs. Laurence, and her father's family, were among the first that received the glad tidings of salvation, and became members of the Society. Mrs. Laurence continued a steady and consistent follower of the Lord Jesus until the end of life, being a period of fifty-six years.[26]

A Society was also formed at Letterkenny, where a Miss Mary Brown resided, who in 1779 was married to Mr. James Elliott. At this time she was visited with a severe affliction, which proved the means of bringing her to an experimental knowledge of the truth; and thus she was one of the first in the town whose names were enroled as members. On the evening on which the preacher formed the class, he was much surprised and cheered to hear her give a clear account of her conversion; and her subsequent consistent

---

(24) *Wesleyan Methodist Magazine*, 1827, pp., 78, 79.
(25) *Primitive Wesleyan Methodist Magazine*, 1823, pp. 367-69.
(26) *Wesleyan Methodist Magazine*, 1840, p. 502.

life attested the truth and reality of the profession she made.[27]

In addition to these encouraging openings for preaching the truth and new Societies that were formed, there were one or two interesting and remarkable conversions that should be noticed. Thus, one Sunday afternoon during the year a respectable young man in passing through the main street of Downpatrick observed a crowd of people standing round a preacher. Some were laughing, some talking, and others listening attentively. The preacher was Mr. George Brown, and the youth was James M'Kee Byron. The latter joined the congregation, listened with respectful attention, was deeply convinced of the error of his way, and determined to yield himself up to God. On the following Sabbath he heard Mr. W. Hammett deliver a powerful discourse on the Prodigal Son, in which he drew so correct a picture of young Byron's former life, that he concluded the preacher must have had some previous knowledge respecting him. After the public service the members of the Society and any seriously disposed persons being invited to remain, the anxious inquirer thankfully embraced the opportunity, and found this meeting even more profitable than that which had preceded it. He was led to realize the love of God in Christ Jesus to sinners; and from that time resolved, "this people shall be my people, and their God shall be my God." He accompanied the preachers to their country appointments, and on one occasion, at a love-feast at Strangford, the Lord manifested Himself to him so powerfully that he was constrained to break out in fervent praise. Soon after he spoke of Christ to his father, and urged on him the duty of family prayer, which had previously been neglected. The parent consented if the son would conduct it, which he gladly did; the Lord heard prayer, and both father and mother were soon converted, joined the Society, and continued until death to adorn their religious profession. Mr. Byron began to exhort at prayer meetings, and at length to preach.[28] He was summoned by Mr. Wesley to enter the itinerancy, and travelled in England for thirty-eight years with general acceptance and considerable success.

In Wexford a young man named Ramsey was under sentence of execution. He was the son of respectable parents, and heir to considerable property; but being over-indulged in childhood, contracted an ungovernable temper, which, as he grew older, broke out into various excesses, such as drinking, swearing, gambling and the like, until at last he became a highway robber,

---

(27) *Primitive Wesleyan Methodist Magazine*, 1827, pp. 355-58.
(28) *Wesleyan Methodist Magazine*, 1829, pp. 577-78.

was seized by the authorities and condemned to death. He was then visited by Mr. Tattershall, the Assistant on the Waterford circuit, to whom at first he appeared very hardened; but on his second visit the wretched culprit wept bitterly. Subsequently the Romanists perplexed him greatly, striving to induce him to receive a priest, and thus obtain a full absolution. Special prayer was offered for him by all the Societies on the circuit, and not in vain. When Mr. Tattershall visited him in order to sit up with him during his last night on earth, it appeared that two days previously while some of the local brethren were singing the hymn beginning — "O Thou that hearest when sinners cry," he obtained peace with God, and said he was satisfied to die and go to his Saviour. From this time he gave clear and satisfactory evidence of the reality of his conversion, rejoiced in the Lord his Saviour, and his last testimony produced a most profound and, it is to be hoped, lasting impression.[29]

CHAPTER 15

1785

ON the first Sunday in 1785 the Society in Dublin, with several other friends, met to renew their covenant with God, and it proved a most solemn season. Mr. Rogers says that he seldom remembered to have felt more of the Divine presence than at this time. Five were reconciled to God by faith in the blood of Christ, and on the Thursday and Friday evenings following, while the nature of the covenant was further explained, others stepped into the glorious liberty of the children of God. Thus the good work continued to extend and prosper.[1]

Nor was there any abatement in the blessed revival in Fermanagh. For months very few days elapsed without one or more finding peace with God. On February the 6th, although the snow on the ground was deep, a large congregation assembled, and one young woman who had forded a river, stood, wet as she was, all the time of the service, weeping bitterly, until the Lord refreshed her soul with His heavenly benediction. On Thursday the 24th

---

(29) *Arminian Magazine*, 1786, pp. 485-90.

(1) *Lives of Early Methodist Preachers*, IV., p. 318.

three souls were set at liberty. The case of one of these was peculiar. A few weeks before she had so violently opposed her husband joining the Society as even to strike him. He did not retaliate, but immediately advertised all he had for sale. She was then much frightened, asked his pardon, and promised never more to oppose his going where he thought right; but he said "Nay, you must go with me and hear for yourself," which she did, and soon after gave her heart to God. On April the 17th Messrs. Hetherington and Mitchell, after they had preached at Kilmore, held a love-feast, at which it pleased God to display His saving power in a wonderful manner. On the 24th as Mr. Mitchell conducted a service the people were so deeply affected that they could not sing, but bitterly wept. Many were convinced of sin, and some obtained the pardoning mercy of God. On June the 13th there was a love-feast, from the beginning of which many testified freely to what the Lord had done for their souls, amongst whom was a boy eight years old, as well as several other children. At length recourse was made to prayer, and the Lord poured out His Holy Spirit abundantly. Those who had not decided for God began to weep and some to cry aloud for mercy. The preachers were obliged to separate and go from one place to another to exhort and comfort the mourners, and thus there was prayer in four or five different parts of the house at the same time. About twenty-five or thirty obtained a sense of sins forgiven, and very many were convinced of the remains of sin, and led to seek earnestly entire sanctification. On Saturday the 18th a field meeting was held near Belleek by Messrs. Barber, Joseph Armstrong, and Mitchell, when the Spirit of the Lord descended in a gracious manner. There was a shaking among the dry bones, so that many were convinced of their guilt, and others of their need of purity of heart.[2]

On April the 11th Mr. Wesley, accompanied by Mr. Whitfield, arrived in Dublin, where he found "such a resting-place at our own house" as he had never found in Ireland before, and two such preachers with two such wives as he knew not where to find again. But what specially gladdened his heart was the evidence of spiritual prosperity. The morning congregations were at least one-third larger than when he was formerly in the city, and those on the week evenings as numerous as those that had been wont to assemble on the Sundays. On examining the Society he says he never found it in such a state before. The number of members was seven hundred, about two hundred

(2) *Arminian Magazine*, 1786, pp. 260-63.

of whom had been added during the previous few months. Many of these he believed loved God with all their hearts, and their number increased daily. At the various services "the overwhelming power of saving grace" was realized. The number of children converted was remarkable. Thirteen or fourteen girls in one class rejoiced in God their Saviour, and were "as serious and staid in their whole behaviour as if they were thirty or forty years old." At St. Patrick's there was such a number of communicants as had scarcely ever been seen there before.

Having spent a week in Dublin Wesley set out for the provinces. At Prosperous, where he preached in a very large room, there was not nearly sufficient accommodation for the congregation. Here a Society of about fifty members had been formed. At Edenderry the audience was uncommonly large and attentive. At Tyrrell's Pass he found a small society, all that remained of a once numerous and devoted people. At Coolalough, or more correctly Brackagh Castle, the new residence to which the Handys had removed, alas! the cause had undergone a similar reverse, while Mr. S. Handy had passed to the home above six years previously. But at Athlone the scene was entirely changed; for many years there had not been so much life in the Society, many of the old dead members were revived, many were added to their number, and harmony and love prevailed. At Ballinasloe he preached in the open air to a numerous congregation of Catholics and Protestants, who were equally attentive. As he entered Aughrim, the rector, who was waiting at his gate to welcome the venerable evangelist, desired him to use his house both then and whenever he pleased, so he preached there in the evening, and it was thoroughly filled; but the Society was "well nigh shrunk into nothing," which he traced to "the baneful influence of riches." At Eyrecourt also the minister gave him the use of his church, but the people seemed to understand little of religion.

As Wesley had not the privilege of using the church at Birr, where he was the guest of Mr. Marshall, he stood in the square, and the audience was exceedingly large, but many of them were "wild as untamed colts." He was in hope that the work would revive in this town, more especially as the Lord had here restored one of the most eminent backsliders in the kingdom. While in Birr he administered the Lord's supper to the members of the Society.[3] At Tullamore, where he was the guest of Mr. and Mrs. Burgess,[4] he preached

---

(3) *Primitive Wesleyan Methodist Magazine*, 1844, p. 256.
(4) *Memoirs of the Rev. T. Burgess*, p. 26.

in the church, the soldiers with their officers attended, and the Lord was graciously present. At Portarlington, as the house could not contain a third of the hearers, Wesley removed to the market-house, where the word proved quick and powerful, and very few appeared unaffected. At Mountmellick he preached in the church to such a congregation as probably was never there before; but the majority of them seemed to care for none of those things. At Kilkenny in the evening the audience was similar to that at Mountmellick; but those who attended in the morning were of a nobler spirit, and he found uncommon liberty among them.

Wesley's visit to Waterford this year was one of the most encouraging and successful he had paid to the city. He was the guest of Mr. Deaves, and preached three times to numerous congregations in the court-house, which he speaks of as "one of the largest in the kingdom." On Sunday he went to the cathedral, "one of the most elegant churches in Ireland," where "the whole service was performed with the utmost solemnity," and at its close the senior prebendary, Dr. Fall, invited him to dinner, and requested him to stay at his house on his next visit to the city. In the afternoon the venerable evangelist preached on 1st Corinthians 13 "at the head of the Mall to a Moorfield's congregation, all quiet and attentive." A love-feast was also held in an upper room of a private house, during which a woman burst into tears, and requested Mr. Wesley to pray for her. She and Mr. Gurley, from Wexford, then knelt down. The venerable servant of God prayed earnestly for them, and both were made happy in the love of Christ.[5] At the concluding service, early on the following morning, all the congregation "appeared to have a real concern for their salvation."

At Youghal the court-house was filled from end to end, and such was the attention of all that Wesley had hopes many would bring forth fruit to perfection. Next day he set out for Cork, and was met at Middleton by thirty equestrians,[6] members of the Society, led by George Howe. Accompanied by this devoted escort, the venerable evangelist rode through a well cultivated country to the city. Here he found the Society had greatly prospered, the congregations were exceedingly large, and the membership numbered four hundred. There was no disturbance now: God having made even their adversaries to be at peace with them. While in the city he appointed Andrew

(5) *Memoir of the Rev. William Gurley*, p. 34.
(6) One of these, William Seymour, having been spared to the patriarchal age of ninety-seven, was gathered home so recently as 1863.

Laffan, George Howe and Jas. Johnson stewards.[7] "How," enquires Wesley, "shall we keep up the flame that is now kindled, not only in Cork but in many parts of the nation? Not by sitting still, but by stirring up the gift of God that is in them; by uninterrupted watchfulness; by warning everyone, and exhorting everyone; and by besieging the throne with the power of prayer."

On May the 9th, at noon, Wesley preached at Kinsale in the old bowling green. All conducted themselves with propriety but a few officers who walked up and down, and talked during the whole service. On the evening of that day he reached Bandon, and preached in the Main street to a very numerous congregation, "but some of them were better clothed than taught, for they laughed and talked a great part of the time." At Kilfinnane, it being too stormy to preach out of doors, he occupied the assembly room.

On arriving at Limerick Wesley found that many of his old friends had been removed to the Church triumphant. On Sunday he was present at the service in the cathedral, which continued four hours, although it concluded a little sooner on account of his assistance at the Lord's supper. In the evening he took his stand near the custom-house, where a great multitude assembled, many of whom were "Wild as the untaught Indian's brood," so that he deemed it advisable to remove to the chapel. Next day he re-established the select Society, which had been quite neglected. At Kilchreest he was the guest of Colonel Pearse, but found the society uncongenial. Next day hearing that a little girl had sat up all night, and then walked two miles to see him, he took her into his chaise, and was surprised to find that she had been two years in possession of purity of heart, and was continually rejoicing in God. Her name was Mary Brooke, and from the time of her conversion for sixty years she adorned the Gospel of Christ.[8]

At Ballinrobe Wesley visited the charter school; but found no master or mistress; the children were ragged and dirty, three beds had to serve for fifteen boys, and five for nineteen girls, and only five farthings a day was allowed the master for the sustenance of each of the hunger-bitten pupils. Wesley was so disgusted with the thing that he reported the case to the Commissioners in Dublin. At Castlebar, where a second chapel was built this year, he received a cordial welcome. On Sunday evening he preached to a numerous congregation, and afterwards administered the Lord's supper to the Society,

(7) *Irish Christian Advocate*, 1883, p. 301.
(8) *Wesleyan Methodist Magazine*, 1845, p. 401.

two clergymen being present, one of whom enjoyed the peace of God, and the other was earnestly seeking it. At Sligo he found a sad reaction had taken place after the gracious revival with which this circuit had been visited, his congregations being by "far the worst" he had seen since he came into the country, and their behaviour exceedingly improper.

At Manorhamilton, where he was the guest of Mr. Bradham, one of the earliest and most influential Methodists in this neighbourhood,[9] he preached in the court-house. At Florence Court the audience was so large that he was obliged to take his stand out of doors. At Swanlinbar the service was held in the assembly room, and at its close a Mr. Pollock[10] invited the venerable evangelist to his house, where he was the means of sowing the seed of eternal life in the family, and its fruits appear to the present day.[11] At Ballyconnell, where a chapel had been built two years previously, called by Wesley "our melancholy house," he preached in the church, which was very full. At Killashandra a large number of people attended, and at Kilmore, where he was the guest of Mr. R. Creighton, as no house there could contain half the congregation, he was obliged to preach in the open air, and "the Lord sent therewith a gracious rain on the souls of them that feared Him." At Cavan the service was held in the ball-room; and at Ballyhaise in the yard of the inn, where a large audience assembled.

At Clones, where he says the new preaching-house was exceedingly neat, but far too small to contain the congregation, the Society was such as he had hardly seen in Ireland, making it a point to conform to all the rules, great and small. When he preached there were about two thousand present, amongst whom was a lad named Charles Mayne, who had not previously been present at a service outside a church.[12] His father, a gentleman of respectability and influence, resided near Cootehill, and his eldest brother subsequently rose to be one of the judges on the Irish bench. The youth who was greatly charmed with the heavenly appearance of the preacher, which he could never afterwards forget, was induced to return to the Methodist services, and thus was led to give his heart to God. His friends alarmed at the prospect of having Methodism introduced into the family, removed him from the town, and by various tempting offers sought to dissuade him from

(9) Ibid., 1833, p. 822.

(10) His nephew, William Pollock, entered the itinerancy in 1813.

(11) *Irish Evangelist*, 1876, p. 90.

(12) *A Mite to the Treasury*, p. 4.

his choice; but in vain, for his heart was fixed.[13]

But to return to Wesley. He next visited Caledon, where a convenient preaching-house had recently been erected, which after the seats had been removed, just contained the congregation. The power of the Lord was unusually present, many were cut to the heart, and refused to be comforted till God spoke peace to their souls, and many more rejoiced with joy unspeakable. At Armagh no building could contain the vast audiences which assembled in Mr. M'Geough's avenue, where they crowded together regardless of wind and weather. At this period there was in the neighbourhood a great increase of the work of God, many new societies were formed, and old members quickened into spiritual life. John Noble especially entered with great zeal into the work, holding services in every place where he could get access. He was a native of the county of Donegal, had been converted about seven years, and was a man of strong intellect, uncompromising honesty and firmness, mighty in the Scriptures, and well-known for his attachment to Methodism.[14]

At Blackwatertown Wesley preached in Mr. Roe's yard to "a large and elegant congregation," and in the evening to one still larger at Charlemont. He then proceeded to the residence of the Rev. Charles Caulfield, the rector of Killyman, in which a numerous and deeply-affected audience assembled. Mr. Caulfield was a true Christian, and a faithful friend to Methodism. He invited the preachers to his house, and gave them all the support and encouragement in his power.[15]

In writing to his brother from Killyman, Wesley says — "The patriots here are nobody. They are quite scattered, and have no design, bad or good. All is still in Ireland; only the work of God flourishes, spreading and deepening on every side."[16]

At Londonderry the Society appeared better established than it had been for many years. At Coleraine there was a larger congregation than even at Clones, and the people seemed to him more intelligent than most he had met with. On the following day he preached in one of the Presbyterian meeting-houses at noon and in the evening. At Ballymoney he discoursed in the court-house to a very civil and dull auditory, and from thence went to Ballymena,

(13) *Irish Evangelist*, 1861, p. 193.
(14) Unpublished sketch of John Noble, by James M'Keown.
(15) *Primitive Wesleyan Methodist Magazine*, 1839, p. 209.
(16) *Wesley's Works*, XII., p. 153.

where a chapel had been built four years previously. At Antrim, in the court-house, there was a large staring audience; and at Belfast, in the Linen-hall, the hearers were not only numerous but admirably behaved, which was rather a novelty to him in this town. At Downpatrick the preaching-house being too small, he repaired to the grove, where the congregation was as large as in Belfast, but much more awakened. At Ballynahinch, in the linen-hall, there was a numerous audience. At Lisburn he considered the Society the most lively he had seen for some time, owing chiefly to the good providence of God in bringing Mrs. Johnson hither. He preached in the Presbyterian meeting-house, and also in the open air to about seven or eight thousand persons. At Lurgan the service was held in the church-yard; and at Tanderagee, where he was the guest of Dr. Leslie, in a grove, several clergymen being amongst the auditory.

At Derryanvil, where a chapel had been built in the previous year, Wesley occupied a shady orchard, and the audience was exceedingly large, but still larger at Grange. At Richhill, where there were many backsliders, he preached from "How shall I give thee up, Ephraim!" At Newry, where he "never before had any tolerable place to preach in," the Presbyterians offered the use of their large and handsome meeting-house, which was well filled. This very year, however, a chapel was built in William street, on ground given by a Mr. Boyd, who had joined the Society, and whose consistent conduct greatly strengthened it. A few others here also were distinguished by their upright and steady walk, including Mr. Thomas Kennedy, the steward of the Society; Miss Brown, subsequently wife of Mr. J. M'Donald, and Mr. John Smith, who afterwards removed to Dublin.[17]

At Drogheda Wesley preached in the linen-hall to a large audience, and the Mayor and some of the aldermen saw that none made any disturbance. He then gave a short account of the rise of Methodism, which so satisfied the people that he believed there would be no more persecution of the Society in the town. On June the 18th he returned to Dublin, where he found the good cause continued to flourish. On the day following he wrote to his brother, saying: "The work of God, almost in every part of this kingdom, is in a prosperous state. Here is a set of excellent young preachers. Nine in ten of them are much devoted to God. I think, number for number, they exceed their fellow-labourers in England. Those in Dublin particularly are burning

---

(17) *Irish Evangelist*, 1868, p. 25.

and shining lights."[18] And again, four days later, "Ireland is full as quiet as England; and our Societies were never so much alive as they are now."[19]

The Conference met on July the 1st, when most of the preachers in Ireland were present. Four candidates were received on trial, including John Dinnen and Andrew Coleman. The membership showed an increase of one thousand three hundred and ninety. To the inquiry with regard to the Yearly Collection, how was this expended? there was given the satisfactory reply: "In supplying the deficiencies and wants of the preachers, as far as it would go." As there had been great loss through mismanagement in the sale of books, various resolutions were adopted to prevent a recurrence of this. The allowance of each preacher was fixed at £12 per annum, with eighteen-pence a week for each child. Each circuit was required to bear the expenses of its preachers to and from the Conference. Permission was also given to erect new chapels at Waterford, Londonderry, and Prosperous.[20] The sittings concluded on July the 6th; and Wesley says he remembered few such Conferences, either in England or Ireland, so perfectly unanimous were all the preachers, and so determined to give themselves up to God. On the 10th he set sail from Dublin, having spent three months in Ireland.

Reference has been made to the work in Newfoundland, begun by Mr. Coughlan, who, when his health failed, returned to England. For twelve years the people in that distant region were deprived of the presence and labours of a settled ministry. At length they wrote for a preacher to Mr. Wesley, and he at the British Conference, this year, appointed an Irishman, John M'Geary, as a missionary to Newfoundland. Thus Irish Methodism gave to Eastern British America, as it had done to the States, its first lay preacher and its first itinerant.

Mr. Griffith was this year appointed to Waterford by the Conference, but by Mr. Wesley's directions sent to Athlone. When he arrived in this town, he found a party in the Society violently opposed to the Assistant, Mr. Joyce: and having made himself familiar with the merits of the dispute, he conscientiously espoused the cause of his injured brother, and prudently exerted himself to support him, and to convince his opposers of the impropriety and culpability of their proceedings. In some instances he was successful, and in others his fidelity caused those who had been his friends

---

(18) *Wesley's Works*, XII., p. 153.

(19) Ibid, p. 154.

(20) *Minutes of the Irish Conference*, I., pp. 27-30.

to become his enemies; but he had the satisfaction to know that his endeavours had contributed to smooth the path of a worthy fellow-labourer, and to prevent mischief in the Society.[21]

The preachers on this circuit were favoured with a blessed revival and extension of the work of God, particularly at Longford, Cleggill, Loughan, and Killashee, in which places the Societies were awakened to deeper spiritual life, and doubled in number. At Newtownforbes, where the services were held on the Sunday afternoon, a society was formed, consisting of more than fifty members, most of whom were led into the enjoyment of the pardoning love of God. The clergyman of the parish opposed the Society, privately exerting himself to prevent the people attending the services: and when that did not succeed, declared open war from the pulpit. Mr. Griffith happened to be present when this ecclesiastic preached a sermon with the intention of exposing the alleged errors of the Methodists. In the course of this learned theological disquisition, he said that repentance was an habitual course of holiness, and that a person who continued in that course for a number of years might have some hope in the end; but for any man to profess to be awakened in a moment, and after having been for a while in distress to pretend to know his sins forgiven, was enthusiasm bordering on blasphemy! When the service concluded, Mr. Griffith was followed by nearly the whole of the congregation to the place where he preached, and took the opportunity of stating and applying the true gospel plan of salvation, temperately refuting the erroneous teaching of the sermon to which they had just listened. The minister's wife and brother were present, and doubtless informed him of what was said: for, when Mr. Griffith returned to the town, the clergyman apologized from the pulpit for his former discourse, and admitted that all he had said on that occasion might not be correct, nor would he attempt to vindicate it. From that time his opposition to Methodism ceased.[22]

Mr. Leech was appointed to Castlebar with Mr. John Watson. On his arrival his colleague took sick, and was unable to leave the town the whole year, therefore the labour of the circuit devolved on Mr. Leech, who exerted himself greatly, and his labours were crowned with the Divine blessing. He succeeded in obtaining several new preaching places, in forming a number of Societies, and also in making such financial arrangements, that at the end of the year instead of there being a deficiency on the circuit accounts, to be

(21) *Wesleyan Methodist Magazine*, 1827, p. 79.
(22) Ibid., pp. 145-46.

paid out of the Yearly Collection, there was a surplus to give to the help of those in need.[23]

Mr. J. M'Donald was appointed to assist Mr. Crook on the Charlemont circuit. Here the work continued to prosper, and new Societies were formed in different places. The principal of these was Dungannon, where, although there had been preaching there for nearly twenty years, no class had been formed, and there was no place for the services except in the open air. However the itinerants continued to visit the town regularly once a fortnight, and preached in the market square. This year the Lord awakened several who were formed into a class met by Hercules Hall, of Castlecaulfield, in the house of Michael Cross, in Irish street.[24] Mr. Hall was an honest, simple-minded, devoted man, who not only met the class on the Sabbath mornings, but also held a weekly prayer meeting. Having to enter the town by Irish street, the wicked and ungodly shoemakers who resided in that locality, with many others who knew well the hour of his coming, prepared for his reception not only with bad words, but also with every kind of missile that came in their way. All this did not deter him from doing his duty. The members met only a short time in the house of Cross, when they removed to another, which proved equally unsuitable. It was therefore found necessary to take a place at a rent for the services, and accordingly a room was secured in the house of Dr. Temple, Market square. They had not met here, however, more than a month when the Lord was pleased to increase their number to thirty, and in the course of four months the Society was further increased to about eighty. Some of the most abandoned characters in the town were converted to God: and the enemy of souls seeing his kingdom suffer, raised a storm of persecution against the Society. The preachers were held up by the ministers of the town as false prophets, the work was grossly misrepresented, and many of the members suffered in their families. Still the work of the Lord prospered. Mr. Hall got assistance. Mr. Jonathan Turner, then of Castlecaulfield, and Mr. James Heather, then of Killyman, were also appointed to meet classes and hold public meetings in the town. Mr. Turner was a zealous local preacher, as well as a devoted and faithful leader, of great tenderness, love and sympathy. Mr. Heather belonged originally to the Society

---

(23) *Methodist Magazine*, Dublin, 1812, p. 386.

(24) This first class consisted of the following members:— Richard Simmons, Geo. Appleby, Charles Chichester, Michael Cross, Prudence Cross, Hugh Brown and George Morrow.

of Friends, but when the love of God was shed abroad in his heart, he laid aside to a great extent the peculiarities of that communion. He is described by Dr. Coke as "nine parts a Methodist, and one a Quaker." He was truly devoted to God, and sustained the offices of leader and local preacher with much acceptance and success.[25]

In another part of this circuit, called Newtownhamilton, the preachers had the use of the Presbyterian meeting-house, with the hearty concurrence of the minister, the Rev. Mr. M'Comb, and the principal members of his congregation. "I have," said that venerable minister, "been striving in vain for many years to do my congregation good, and if the Methodists can be of any use to them, they are welcome to the use of my house." The Rev. Mr. Martin also, the Episcopalian minister, was very friendly, and frequently entertained the preachers. Notwithstanding this generous help, scarcely any good was done here for many years. However, the Lord so prospered the work in other parts of the circuit that at Christmas it was found necessary to get an additional preacher. Then the places on the round were so numerous that they could not be visited by each preacher more frequently than once in eight weeks; but through the judicious superintendence of Mr. Crook, each Society was properly regulated and disciplined.[26]

About this year the preachers first visited Banbridge. Two young women, named Walsh, who had resided in Newry and removed to this town, prevailed on John Bradford, the man in whose house they lodged, to allow his stable to be used for a Methodist service, and then invited one of the preachers in Lisburn to hold a meeting. Mr. J. Kerr, the Assistant on the circuit, was the first to respond to this invitation. Amongst his hearers was a lad named John Kinnear, who accompanied his aunt. She soon after became a member of the Society, and brought her nephew to the class. The mind of the boy was thus impressed with Divine truth, so as to lead to the consecration of his life to the service of God. He became, for more than fifty years, the pillar of Methodism in this town.[27]

At this period the Society at Inishannon was greatly revived and increased. Amongst those added to the membership was Sylvanus Robinson, then only fourteen years of age, who used to walk to Bandon nearly every Sunday evening. In a few years he removed to this town where he entered into

(25) *Primitive Wesleyan Methodist Magazine*, 1839, pp. 201-13.
(26) *Methodist Magazine*, Dublin, 1808, pp. 148-49.
(27) *Irish Evangelist*, 1868, p. 143.

business, and also married Miss Lovell, a Methodist. He was then appointed a leader, several times acted as steward, and when the present chapel was built was elected a trustee. He remained a steadfast and devoted Methodist to the end of life, and was greatly beloved by all who knew him for his consistent, upright and kindly character. His children were trained up in the fear of God, and still live to revere his memory. His power in prayer at the public service was very remarkable. One of the walls of his bedroom at the spot where he used to pray, was stained with breath, so long and frequent were his private devotions. His death accorded with his life. At the age of sixty-seven he passed away, saying "Glory! Glory! Glory!"[28]

In November Mr. Wesley wrote to Samuel Bates, expressing his willingness to receive him into the itinerancy, and he, accepting this as an indication of the will of Providence, set out at once for the Limerick circuit, where he was cheered with manifest tokens of the Lord's blessing, more especially at Kilfinnane, Adare, and the city of Limerick. In each of these places the work of the Lord was revived, and numbers were converted, who were thus led to unite themselves with the people of God.[29]

CHAPTER 16

1786

IN 1784 Robert Raikes published an account of his plan for Sunday schools. This sketch arrested the attention of Mr. Wesley, who inserted the entire article in the January number of the *Arminian Magazine* for 1785, and also exhorted his people to adopt the new institution. This did much to excite an interest in regard to the work in Ireland as well as in England.

At this period a number of persons of respectability and wealth in Dublin were brought more or less under the influence of Methodism, and quickened into spiritual life. Amongst these was a young gentleman of eighteen, Arthur Guinness (father of the late Sir Benjamin Lee Guinness), to whom in part at least is to be ascribed the honour of founding the first Sunday school in our

(28) *Irish Christian Advocate*, 1883, p. 301.
(29) *Methodist Magazine*, Dublin, 1805, p. 206.

metropolis. A meeting was held in the vestry of St. Catherine's church, on 11th January, 1786, at which two clergymen and Mr. Guinness were present, when it was resolved that a school be formed and certain rules drawn out. This school was opened on the 22nd of the month, when the attendance was only six males and four females, but the numbers rapidly increased. Similar schools were soon opened in the North Strand and other portions of the city.[1]

Mr. Peacock had been appointed at the last Conference to labour in Dublin, and his ministry was attended with great success; but it pleased the Lord to call him hence in the midst of his usefulness, and in the full vigour of life. He finished his course with joy on February the 15th, in the thirty-fourth year of his age.

Application was at once made to Mr. Wesley to fill up the vacancy, but he was unable to do so, as all the preachers were engaged. Mr. Rogers and the Society therefore, fearing lest the good work, which still continued, should suffer, made it a subject of special prayer, and the Lord answered them. The congregations continued very large, the prayer meetings and classes exceedingly lively, and scarcely a week passed in which some were not awakened and led to join the Society.[2]

In the midst of this glorious revival the Society was cheered with the presence, and blessed with the labours of the devoted Miss Ritchie, who had been strongly urged by Mr. Wesley to visit the metropolis. She says so plainly did the cloud move towards Dublin, that she never undertook a journey with stronger assurance of being in the very way wherein the Lord would have her to go. While in the city she was actively employed in Christian work, from which others as well as herself appear to have derived much benefit. Her engagements multiplied so fast that it was almost too much for her strength; but the Lord sustained her. After a visit of three months she left, expressing great thankfulness to God, and also to her friends for their kindness.[3] The number of persons who were brought to a saving knowledge of God during this year in Dublin was at least one hundred and seventy-eight, and the net increase in the membership two hundred.[4]

In the provinces, also, Methodism continued to extend and prosper. The 1st dragoons were at this time quartered in Nenagh. Mr. Burgess therefore

---

(1) *Biographic Sketches of La Touche*, pp. 390-95.

(2) *Lives of Early Methodist Preachers*, IV, p. 320.

(3) *Memoirs of Mrs. Mortimer*, p. 1045.

(4) *Lives of Early Methodist Preachers*, IV. p. 321.

invited Mr. Leech, who was in Castlebar, to come to the town, which thenceforward was regularly visited by the preachers. One of the first-fruits of the labours of the Society was the conversion of Mrs. Hardy, a cousin of George Foster, through whose influence she was led to attend the services, from which time she was a steady and consistent member of the Society. Her family also participated in the happy effects of her decision for God; her son Joseph having been converted, became a leader, and rendered valuable aid to the cause.[5]

In Armagh the Society, which for nearly twenty years had been bearing reproach, and struggling against most adverse circumstances, began at length to feel itself straitened for room, and able to take a step so bold and so significant as the erection of a place of worship. A suitable site was secured on the north side of Abbey street, close to the scene of Wesley's first service in the city, and a neat little preaching-house built. It was forty feet in length and twenty in breadth, and as regards comfort and accommodation was a great improvement on the little room in Thomas street, previously in use.[6]

Reference has already been made, in the list of preachers who came out from the Derg country, to a young man named Matthew Stewart, who was born at Drumclamph, grew up a wild and thoughtless youth, and enlisted in a regiment of dragoons. Having been led to attend some of the Methodist services, the Gospel became the power of God unto his salvation, and he began to direct others to the Saviour. In 1785 he was quartered in Athlone, where he was introduced to Mr. Wesley, and encouraged by him to persevere in his efforts to save souls. Soon after Stewart obtained his discharge, and returned to his native place.

In the meantime, however, Mr. Wesley, whose attention had long been directed to part of the county of Donegal as a sadly neglected and isolated district of country, sent this young man five guineas, and wrote to him to the following effect:— "Go to that country and see what you can do. When you have spent the enclosed, and stand in need of more, apply to your affectionate friend, J. Wesley." Receiving this as the direction of Providence, Stewart went and preached at Ardara, the Glenties, and several other places in that neighbourhood, where many of the inhabitants attended his ministry, several were converted, and Societies were formed, which continue to this day.[7]

(5) *Memoirs of the Rev. Jas. Burgess*, p. 27.

(6) *Irish Evangelist*, 1861, p. 121.   (7) Ibid., 1862, p. 234.

When Mr. Stewart arrived at Ardara, for want of more suitable accommodation he was obliged to put up at a public house, where the parish priest and the rector happened to be at the time enjoying themselves together over their glasses. When they heard of the arrival of the stranger they at once interviewed him, and inquired if he was a commercial traveller. He said No. They asked if he was an excise officer, to which also he answered in the negative. They said — "What are you? and what did you come here for?" He replied that he was a Methodist, and that he came to preach the Gospel. Then answered the priest — "You are not wanted here. My friend, the rector, looks after his people, I look after mine, and we get on quietly and nicely together! No one else is wanted." But Mr. Stewart expressed his determination to preach in the fair next day, which he did; and Mr. James Pearson, who resided in the town, hearing of it, invited the servant of God to his house, where from that day to the present the Methodist preachers have always had a most hearty welcome and a comfortable home.[8]

After Mr. Stewart had been some time in this part of the country he preached one evening at the house of a farmer, a few miles from Ardara, where a very powerful man, a Roman Catholic, frequently interrupted him, and with most awful imprecations, swore he would have the preacher's heart's blood before he crossed Bainbane mountain, knowing that Mr. Stewart had an appointment next day which rendered it necessary that he should travel in that direction. The brave evangelist rose early on the following morning, and prepared to set out on his journey. His hostess urged him to wait for breakfast, but he declined, saying: "I will eat nothing until I know what the Lord will do with me." Although there was a good road over the mountain, yet for some miles there was then no dwelling-houses. Lifting his heart to God in prayer, Mr. Stewart proceeded on his lonely way, not meeting with or seeing any person until he had passed the highest part of the mountain road, and descended on its southern side. Having travelled about a mile from the summit of the hill, he saw at some distance from him two men standing on the road, and a third lying on the ground — dead. The two men informed the preacher, that about fifteen minutes before he made his appearance they had been working at the turf, a short distance off, when the deceased came to the place. They saw him stagger and fall, and ran to his assistance, but when they reached him he was dead. "Last night," said Mr. Stewart, "that

---

(8) Unpublished Notes.

man swore with an awful imprecation he would have my heart's blood before I crossed this mountain." That evening the servant of God preached about two miles further on, and the body of the dead man was brought into the next house to that in which the service was conducted. This awful occurrence made such a profound impression on the inhabitants of the neighbourhood that the preacher met with no more persecution there. Mr. Stewart was appointed to a circuit in 1788.[9]

While this earnest evangelist laboured with success in the county of Donegal, Mr. Barber did a good work a little further south in the same county and in Leitrim. A considerable awakening took place, during the progress of which many were turned from darkness to light, and from the power of Satan unto God. Thus Mr. Barber was the means of introducing Methodism into Ballintra, Boyney, and Dartry.[10] Amongst the members of the first class at Ballintra were the following devoted and exemplary women: Mrs. Sarah Cockburn, Mrs. Luscinda Mowbry, Mrs. Vair, and Mrs. Thompson.[11]

At Boyney, about two miles from Ballyshannon, John Bell was the first to receive the itinerants, and soon after David Thompson and his wife were made partakers of the grace of God, became members of the Society, and invited the preachers to their house. This worthy couple adorned their Christian profession, testified that the blood of Jesus Christ cleanseth from all sin, and at the close of life left behind them a seed to serve the Lord.

From Boyney Methodism extended to Dartry, where the preachers were received by Mr. George Curry, a son-in-law of Mr. and Mrs. Thompson. It was not without peril that he opened his house to the messengers of peace, as his ungodly neighbours resolved that the preachers should not visit that part of the country if they could prevent it. So one evening, soon after Mr. Barber arrived, tidings came that there were six or seven men coming to kill him. Mrs. Curry, in a state of great alarm, hastened to inform the preacher, who replied with great composure — "Don't fear, my sister, they will not hurt one hair of my head." As soon as the men entered the house Mr. Barber requested them to be seated, which they refused to do; but, being overcome by his quiet and gentle spirit, were about to leave when he said — "Let us pray." During this solemn exercise some of them knelt down, while the rest stood, and all then went peaceably away. But that night Mr. Barber's horse

---

(9) *Irish Evangelist*, 1862, p. 234.
(10) *Primitive Wesleyan Methodist Magazine*, 1840, p. 288.
(11) Her son, Mr. Wm. Thompson, entered the itinerancy in 1804.

was dreadfully mangled, being deprived of his ears, mane and tail, and the sign of the cross cut in several parts of the body.[12]

Passing further south to the Athlone circuit. While Mr. Griffith preached one Sabbath morning at Cleggill, he observed in the congregation a young man weeping most bitterly, and at the close of the service sent for him. In conversation he found that he had been deeply convinced of sin through the ministry of Mr. Joyce, at Mountmellick, and for some time had been almost driven to despair; but on that morning the cloud broke and a ray of hope appeared. A few days later he obtained a clear sense of the pardon of his sins. That young man was Zechariah Worrell, who entered the itinerancy in 1796.

Mr. Griffith was also the means of leading the Rev. Adam Averell, then resident in Athlone, to see the way of God more perfectly, which proved the first step towards his entering the Methodist Connexion, in which he was for many years an esteemed and useful minister. The curate of the parish alarmed at the growing prosperity of Methodism in the town, and wishing to preserve Mr. Averell from the imputation then beginning to be cast upon him of being a Methodist, requested him to preach against this dangerous heresy; but he, very wisely, was unwilling to comply with the request without further acquaintance with the doctrines of Methodism. Just at this juncture, in the good providence of God, he made the acquaintance of Mr. Griffith, and resolved to qualify himself for the task by obtaining from him the necessary information. He therefore proposed a number of questions relating to the peculiar teaching of the Methodists, in answer to all of which Mr. Griffith took great pains to give the fullest satisfaction; and on returning to his lodgings sent Mr. Averell a copy of Wesley's *"Appeal to Men of Reason and Religion,"* which he read with much interest, astonishment and profit. "Are not these," thought he, "the very doctrines that our enlightened ancestors rescued from Popish error and superstition? Are they not the truths contained in the articles and liturgy of the Church? Are they not the very views that God so often gave me while upon my knees before Him?" The contemplated sermon was never preached, and Mr. Griffith was looked upon ever after as his father in the Gospel.[13]

During the spring Mr. Griffith visited his parents at Clogheen, and seized the opportunity of preaching there. The congregation consisted chiefly of

(12) *Primitive Wesleyan Methodist Magazine*, 1840, pp. 206-7.
(13) *Memoir of the Rev. A. Averell*, pp. 21-24.

Roman Catholics, who listened with the greatest attention; and some of them proposed that he should preach in the Catholic chapel, but this of course could not be. The priest declared war against the Methodists, but his threats did not deter the people from coming again in large numbers to hear.[14]

On the Charlemont circuit the blessed work continued to prosper greatly. The faithful itinerants stationed on this round preached in their turn at Portadown every second Sunday on their way from Kilmoriarty to Lurgan; and after some time were invited to the house of James Lemon, a chandler, where in spring a small class was formed, consisting of persons in very humble circumstances, whose first payment of quarterage was only five shillings and eight pence, and this sum was not exceeded for several years. The first leader was John Hamilton, who came from Newmills, near Gilford. About this time Messrs. J. Noble and J. Heather began to visit Portadown, and preached in the house of Mr. Richard Atkinson, a baker, who was friendly to Methodism, although not a member of the Society. It is also stated that meetings were held in a place which was resorted to for public amusement, known by the name of "the cockpit."[15] Such was the origin of Methodism in the town which now contains so large and influential a Society.

Amongst those brought under the influence of the truth on the circuit was a young man named William Read, of Moy, who for sixty-five years sustained with great efficiency the offices of leader and local preacher, and was made the honoured instrument of much good for miles round the town in which he lived.[16] Another, in the neighbourhood of Dungannon, was a youth named David Stuart, who soon after went out to the island of St. Vincent, where he amassed a considerable amount of wealth. Dr. Coke makes honourable mention of Mr. Stuart's kindness towards himself and the missionaries who accompanied him to that island, and the servants of God always found a most affectionate welcome in the house of Mr. Stuart. He returned to Europe in 1797, settled in London, and identified himself with the City road Society. Having no children, he at his death in 1807 left upwards of £10,000 to Methodism — £3,200 being invested to pay the annual rent on the City road premises, and £7,000 to assist the Superannuated Preachers' Fund. Such is one of several instances of valuable financial assistance the Connexion in England derived through Irish Methodism.

---

(14) *Wesleyan Methodist Magazine*, 1827, pp. 146-48.

(15) *Memorial of T. A. Shillington*, pp. 15-16.

(16) *Wesleyan Methodist Magazine*, 1853, p. 669.

At this period the following two interesting conversions took place: Brian M'Maken acted as herd for a number of families near Newtownstewart. The itinerants were accustomed to visit this neighbourhood, and through a sermon preached by Mr. Joseph Armstrong, this poor ignorant Romanist was so deeply convinced of his sinful state that when he returned home he was unable to conceal his distress: on seeing which his wife said to him — "Brian, what ails ye? You are good for nothin'." "Molly, wisha,"[17] said he, "I'm afeer'd I'll lose my sowl." "Lose yer sowl, man! an' how's that? What have ye been doin'? Have ye been robbin' or murtherin' inybody? Are ye not the bist man in the counthry, and don't ye attind to all yer dues an' duties?" "Och, in throth, I think God Almighty is lookin' at me ivery minnit, an' is angry wid me." "Why, Brian, what makes ye think that?" "Bekays I'm all dirty widin." "Thin go to the priesht an' tell him all about it." The hint was promptly taken, and his reverence, perceiving at once how matters stood, exclaimed — "Oh, you dog, you have been to hear the Methodists; nothing better could come of it!" "'Tis thim," said Brian, "that did it on me intirely. I'll niver go near thim agin." The priest scolded him well for listening to the preaching of a heretic, and then enjoined certain severe penances. These having failed to quiet the conscience of the awakened sinner, he was ordered to go to Lough Derg, where he went through the appointed stations, walking so many times on his bare knees round a series of circles of sharp stones, and repeating certain prayers. On returning home his wife said — "Well, Brian, ye won't lose yer sowl now." "Och, dear," he replied, "I'm dirtier, an' God is angrier than iver." "Thin," said she, "go and see father Tom again." The priest told M'Maken he must try and get his spirits up: and as there was to be a dance that night he should go, and, added his reverence, "don't forget to take a drop, it will do you good." The poor man supposing that any advice from the clergy was right, went, and did take the drop — but it was a drop too much. He returned home late, and his wife was awakened by him rolling on the floor, and roaring — "I'll lose my sowl." She became alarmed and began to cry, and together they wept and prayed, as well as they knew how until morning. That day, during the time of service, Brian being led by his employment to the house where the Methodist meetings were held, notwithstanding his resolution to the contrary, approached the door to hear the singing, then waited for the prayer, and lastly ventured in. The text was

(17) My dear.

— "What must I do to be saved?" and the preacher considered the state of an awakened sinner, and the advices given to relieve his distress. "Amongst the rest," remarked the servant of God, "he is told by the priest to go to Lough Derg and he will be saved." "Och, I declare," said Brian, audibly, "it's meself shure. Haven't I been there?" "Sometimes he is asked to go and drink to drive away his sorrow." "Oh! an' wasn't it only yistherday the priesht towld me to do that same, an' the devil's advice it was, too;" and there and then, before the congregation, the poor man stated the whole of what had passed between him and his clergy. The preacher told him that he could never be happy until he was converted and obtained the forgiveness of his sins, adding, "kneel down, and we will pray for you." The whole congregation then joined in calling upon God to have mercy upon the penitent, who, after some time, leaped up, clapped his hands, and said — "I have got it — I have got it! I know He is not angry wid me now! Oh, sir, will ye come and convart Molly?" The preacher replied, that he would go and talk with her next morning; but Brian could with difficulty wait so long. As soon as he got home, he exclaimed — "Oh, Molly, I'm all clane widin, shure I'm converted; God is not angry wid me now." "Brian, wisha," said his wife, "who converted ye?" "Oh," said he, "it was the Lord Jesus." "Would He convart me?" said she, "for I'm as bad as ye." "He would convart all the world," replied Brian. The preacher visited Molly, and explained to her the plan of salvation by Christ Jesus, and she also was soon brought to enjoy the power and comfort of religion. Brian could not rest now without telling the priest. He was advised not to go; but go he would, and in his own way told of the happiness of his soul. The priest ridiculed him, and threatened him with excommunication; to which Brian replied — "Ye may save yerself the trouble; ye could do nothin' for me in my distris, and I'll niver come near ye more." Brian and Molly suffered much from their bigoted neighbours; but held on their way, brought up their children in the fear of the Lord, and at length passed in triumph to the Paradise of God.[18]

Andrew Coleman, who had been appointed to the Sligo circuit, found the work arduous; but laboured to the utmost of his power. At length, however, he fell into decline, brought on, it is said, by sleeping in a damp bed. On his return home he received every attention that his friends and the Coleraine Society could render; but sank rapidly. He had the happiness of

(18) *Wesleyan Methodist Magazine*, 1823, pp. 809-10; and *Irish Evangelist*, 1871, pp. 26, 27.

seeing his mother and grandmother brought to an acquaintance with the truth before his departure: and his last words to them, as his redeemed spirit prepared to take its flight, were — "Follow me." The evening before he died he desired to be carried out on a chair to see the setting sun, which he beheld with pleasure until it sank beneath the horizon: when he exclaimed, "This sun has been partially obscured to me, but it shall be no more so for ever;" and about the time it re-illuminated the horizon, his happy soul soared away to regions of eternal light and glory. Mr. West preached the funeral sermon out of doors to an audience that no house could contain; and the high estimation in which the deceased was held was evinced by the many thousands who followed his remains to the grave.[19] His death brings to remembrance that of the youthful Spencer, thus sung by Montgomery:-

> "The loveliest star of evening's train
> Sets early in the western main,
> And leaves the world in night;
> The brightest star of morning's host,
> Scarce-risen, in brighter beams is lost;
> Thus sunk his form on ocean's coast,
> Thus sprang his soul to light."

Mr. Wesley having arranged that either he or Dr. Coke should visit Ireland every year, the latter made an excursion through the country; but the only record of this visit to the provinces we have found, is an unimportant entry in the steward's book of the Cork circuit, dated May the 24th.[20] But having gone through the Societies, he returned to Dublin in time to act for the third time as President of the Conference.

The preachers met on July the 7th. No less than ten young men were admitted on trial.[21] There were two deaths; and two ceased to be recognised as Methodist preachers. One of these was the fearless and once faithful Thomas Halliday, who had fallen a victim to strong drink. His case was a sad and painful one. A complaint brought on by fatigue, exposure, and the terrible abuse he had received, drove him to stimulants for relief: and at length

---

(19) *Life of Adam Clarke*, I., pp. 115-16.

(20) *Irish Christian Advocate*, 1883, p. 317.

(21) The name of an eleventh, D. Graham, is inserted in the Minutes of the Irish Conference, by mistake.

he became a slave to the intoxicating cup. His end should not be forgotten, and shews the depth and sincerity of his repentance. As his last moments approached, bitterly lamenting his sin, and earnestly imploring pardon, he said, "I will die on my bended knees, calling for mercy;" and thus, in the act and attitude of an humble supplicant at the throne of grace, his spirit passed into the more immediate presence of a merciful God.

The membership reported at the Conference showed the gratifying increase of two thousand five hundred and twenty-eight, which was spread over every circuit in the country except one. The subscriptions to the Foreign Missions — now for the first time reported to the Conference — amounted to £20 5s 6d. Mr. Wesley was earnestly requested, either himself or by his delegate, to appoint the circuit and Society stewards in the course of the annual visitation. The preachers were forbidden to become security for any chapel debts. A resolution also was passed strongly condemning various letters, some anonymous, and others signed Michael Moorhouse, which had been circulated with great diligence, to the disturbance of the Societies.[22]

Michael Moorhouse entered the itinerancy in 1773, and bore his share of the persecutions of his day; but became discontented, and in 1785 published a broadsheet of sixteen columns, in small type, entitled, "*An Appeal to Honest Men,*" and full of petty grievances, particularly with regard to the influence of Messrs. Wesley and Crook, and respecting his own appointments to inferior circuits. This year he left the work, and then embodied the wailings of his Appeal in an octavo volume of 128 pages, with the title, "*Defence of Mr. Michael Moorhouse, written by himself.*" He bitterly complains of Wesley for suffering some of the wives of preachers to dine on potatoes and buttermilk, while others were pampered with good cheer; and for allowing their husbands to wear great coats, and to use umbrellas on a rainy day. The *Monthly Review,* in noticing poor Moorhouse's notable production, quietly remarks:— "The labourer is certainly worthy of his hire, but in adjusting the hire of the labourer, a good deal must depend on the workman's skill: and if we are to judge of Master Michael Moorhouse's preaching abilities from his illiterate and silly performance, we do not see how his master could have afforded him higher wages: perhaps he might fare better if he were to return to his lawful occupation."[23]

Owing to the Divine blessing on the influence of Mr. and Mrs. Wm.

---

(22) *Minutes of the Irish Conference,* I., pp. 30-34.
(23) Tyerman's *Life and Times of Wesley,* III., p. 468.

Smyth, as well as on the labours of Mr. Fletcher and others, many influential persons in the metropolis were the subject of serious impressions, for whom it was considered desirable that some church should be erected in which the Gospel would be preached. Accordingly in July, 1784, the foundation stone of the Bethesda chapel was laid. It was built at the sole expense of Mr. Smyth, who on the day previous to its dedication, accompanied by a few friends, entered and, kneeling in the centre, besought God to bless the preaching of His Word in that place. The voice of prayer was heard and answered: and in the last great day very many, no doubt, will be found who were born there. The chapel was opened according to the forms of the Episcopal Church on June 25th, 1786; the Rev. Edward Smyth and the Rev. William Mann being the first chaplains. Mr. Smyth added to the premises a Female Orphan School and also a Penitentiary.[24]

At the Irish Conference Messrs. Rutherford and Joshua Keighley were appointed to Dublin; but at the subsequent meeting of that in London, Mr. Moore at his own desire was sent instead of Mr. Keighley.

At the British Conference three missionaries were appointed to accompany Dr. Coke to Nova Scotia, which ultimately led to the establishment of a mission in the West Indies. One of these was an Irishman, Mr. Hammett, who was stationed in St. Christopher's.

Messrs. Jonathan Brown, Joyce and Dinnen, were appointed to Cork. Mr. Brown had been eight years in the itinerancy and was a great favourite with Wesley, who had a high estimate of his suitability for the work. While on this circuit he was at one time pursued by two Popish miscreants, who had vowed to take summary vengeance on him if possible. There was no safety but in flight: and therefore, putting spurs to his horse, he urged the animal to his utmost speed. His pursuers were mounted on mules, one of which was equal in power to Mr. Brown's horse; but descending into a valley, where it is probable he would otherwise have been seized, the best mule fell, while the horse held on, and thus the rider escaped. He was ever afterwards fully persuaded that their intention was to murder him: and was often heard to relate the circumstance with gratitude to the Lord, his Preserver.[25]

Mr. Dinnen says that when he came to this circuit, Laurence Kane then lived at Youghal, his native place, and had been apprenticed as a ship-carpenter. He was a rigid Romanist, fond of cock-fighting and similar sports.

(24) *Life and Times of the Countess of Huntingdon*, II., pp. 201-2.
(25) *Wesleyan Methodist Magazine*, 1826, pp. 506-7.

One Sunday as Mr. Dinnen went into the court-house to preach, Kane, with some others, pelted him with snow-balls; but afterwards went to the service, and was deeply convinced of sin. He then sold his cocks, and walked to Cork barefooted to buy a Bible. Soon after he became a member of the Society, was converted, and maintained his steadfastness, though he endured violent persecution, especially from his relatives.[26] In 1795 he entered the itinerancy, and travelled for eight years, when he retired, in order by keeping an academy in Cork, he might be able to support his aged parents.[27]

Messrs. Leech and Griffith were stationed in Londonderry. In this city the former preached in the streets, lanes, and wherever he could get people to hear him. He had much opposition, principally from ministers among the Covenanters, who not only assailed the doctrinal teaching of Methodism, but also cast aspersions on the preachers, and especially on Mr. Wesley; but by so doing they defeated their own design, and lost credit with their own people. Mr. Leech's labours were greatly acknowledged in the conversion of a man condemned to death, who had murdered his wife. At first the wretched criminal appeared very hardened, then became truly penitent, and at length, having abandoned all the mummeries of Popery, was enabled to rejoice in the Lord his Saviour. The servant of Goa who had been with him the greater part of the previous day and night, proceeded with the condemned man to the place of execution, singing a hymn. When they arrived at the awful spot Mr. Leech addressed the multitude at the request of the sheriff, sang another hymn and prayed; and as the poor criminal ascended the ladder, he held out his hand to him, saying, "I am going to die a just death for a crime I committed, but am a monument of the pardoning love of God. My soul will soon be with Jesus, and though I have dishonoured Him on earth, I shall be glorified with Him in heaven."[28]

Meanwhile Mr. Griffith left the Athlone circuit. On his way, as he passed through Fintona, he observed a young man who looked at him very earnestly, and at length expressed a wish to speak. Mr. Griffith took him by the hand and inquired — "Do you love Jesus Christ?" The young man burst into tears and answered — "No, sir; and I fear I never shall," adding that he was the son of a pious man, in whose house for several years there had been

(26) Crook's *Centenary of American Methodism*, p. 66.

(27) He should not be confounded with another preacher of the same name, who began to travel in 1784.

(28) *Methodist Magazine*, Dublin, 1812, pp. 386-89.

preaching by the Methodists, and that a little before death he had called his son to his bed side and given him the following injunctions, which he promised to observe:— 1. To seek the Lord with all his heart. 2. To continue the preaching and class in his house. 3. Never to marry any but a religious woman. But he had broken his word in each of these particulars. Mr. Griffith advised him on returning home to invite the servants of God again to his house, to tell his wife with affection and firmness that he was determined at all hazards to keep his promise, to join the Society, and to begin in earnest to seek the kingdom of God; and then having commended him to God they parted. Nine months subsequently Mr. Griffith spent a night in Fintona, and rejoiced to find that the young man had strictly followed his advice, and was happy in God.

Mr. Griffith remained on the Londonderry circuit only a few weeks, and was then, by order of Mr. Wesley, removed to Coleraine, which had been formed into a separate circuit with three preachers on it. In this town he had the satisfaction to witness a considerable addition to the congregations. The Rev. Mr. Hazlett, the rector of a parish in the neighbourhood, was one of his regular hearers on week nights. This clergyman declared afterwards that during the first five weeks in which he attended the ministry of Mr. Griffith he had received more evangelical instruction than in all the studies of his previous life.

The country parts of the circuit, however, were in a deplorable condition, but soon improved through the faithful labours of Mr. Griffith. The first time he visited them five or six persons found peace with God. The case of one of these especially is worthy of record. As the itinerant ascended the hill contiguous to Ballinderry he saw two respectably dressed men approaching him, and heard one of them say with much earnestness to his companion — "That is the man. Did I not describe to you his person, dress, etc., as I saw him in my dream?" He then came forward and said to the preacher — "Welcome, thou servant of the Lord. I saw thee last night in a dream, and thou art come to show me the way of salvation." The next morning when Mr. Griffith preached in his house the Lord spoke peace to his soul.[29]

Mr. Thomas Roberts, a native of Cornwall, who was this year received on trial, and whose name was put down to Coleraine, was sent to Londonderry instead. At St. Ives he was joined by his friend, Mr. Benjamin

(29) *Wesleyan Methodist Magazine*, 1827, pp. 148-50.

Pearce, who was appointed to Lisburn. On August the 27th, they landed at Dunleary, and proceeded to Dublin, where they were received by the preachers and people with Christian cordiality. Mr. Roberts, having obtained a horse and the necessary equipments, commenced his journey northward. At Armagh he was met by Mr. Gustavus Armstrong, who greatly cheered the youthful and timid preacher. Mrs. Richardson, of Charlemont, received him as an angel of God, and showed him great hospitality. Journeying on he came to Dungannon and Cookstown, where he preached, and was favoured with the gracious presence of the Lord. At length he arrived at his destination, where he was heartily welcomed by Mr Leech, and also by Mrs. Knox, who received him as her own son. His acquaintance with Mr. Alexander Knox proved no small advantage, as that gentleman had been favoured with a liberal education, and in addition to extensive reading, possessed a fine taste and brilliant fancy, sanctified by Divine grace. The preaching of the ministers appointed to this circuit had for some time previously been confined chiefly to the city and its vicinity; but an additional preacher was sent to enter on new work, chiefly in the north of the county of Donegal. Therefore the two devoted men on this circuit travelled through a large extent of country, from Derry across Lough Swilly to Rathmelton, Rathmullan, Letterkenny, Raphoe, Strabane, Drumquin and many intermediate places, preaching generally in private houses, but often in the open air.[30] Thus sinners were converted, new Societies were formed, and of many districts of the country it might be truly said, "The wilderness and the solitary place were glad, and the desert rejoiced and blossomed as the rose."

(30) *Life and Remains of the Rev. T. Roberts*, pp. 24-57.

CHAPTER 17

1787

WM. M'ALLUM was born near Tanderagee in 1766. His parents were members of the Presbyterian Church, in the principles of which their children were educated. However, it pleased the Lord to bring them into connection with Methodism before the family were grown up, which proved a signal blessing. During the first six months in 1787 Mr. John Kerr was stationed on the circuit, and through his preaching William was convinced of sin, and for a season continued in a most distressing state of mind, without a sense of sins forgiven. At length, one Sunday morning in a love-feast at Derryanvil, when many were led to seek the Lord, Mr. Kerr and several others prayed earnestly for him, the Lord graciously heard and answered their united supplications, and the earnest seeker became a joyful possessor of the blessings of salvation. Soon after this he found the word of the Lord "like a fire in his bones," and began to hold meetings amongst his neighbours, which proved a blessing to many. Some time subsequently he removed to Manchester, became a local preacher, and in 1797 entered upon a brief but successful course of usefulness in connection with the British Conference.[1]

On Good Friday, April the 6th, Mr. Wesley arrived in Dublin, when he was the guest of Mr. Arthur Keene, about half a mile out of the city — "a pleasant, healthy spot, where were peace and love, and plenty of all things." On Easter Sunday he preached in the Bethesda. "Mr. Smyth read prayers, and gave out the hymns, which were sung by fifteen or twenty fine singers, the rest of the congregation listening with as much attention and devotion as they would have done to an opera." There were between seven and eight hundred communicants, and the power of God was in the midst of them. Whitefriar street chapel was well filled in the evening, and the Divine blessing was signally manifested.

Mr. Wesley found that the Society, which consisted of more than one thousand members, continued to increase in grace as well as in numbers. Even at Gravel walk, where the congregations used to be small enough, the house was crowded, although the soldiers, seventy of whom were members

---

(1) *Methodist Magazine*, Dublin, 1811, pp. 49-53.

of the Society, could not attend.

Having spent ten days in Dublin, Wesley set out for the provinces, accompanied by Mr. John Broadbent. At Prosperous the congregation was numerous; at Philipstown, which had been forsaken for nearly forty years, there was again a prospect of good; and at Tyrrell's Pass the chapel could not contain a fourth of the people, Protestants and Romanists, who flocked to hear.

At Keenagh he was the guest of Mr. Alexander Kingston,[2] a son-in-law of Mrs. Johnstone, of Lisleen. For many years the preachers here had seemed to be beating the air, but now the Lord so blessed the labours of "poor John Bredin, just tottering over the grave," that there was a lively, vigorous Society, rapidly increasing both in grace and in numbers. At Longford a large number of people assembled in the town-hall, and Wesley says he had much liberty of speech in addressing them, and seldom saw an audience more affected. At Athlone he "found a congregation of deeper experience" than any he had seen since leaving Dublin, the work of God having much increased in the town. At Ballinasloe, as the usual preaching place proved insufficient, many occupied the passage and staircase, and all within hearing distance seemed to receive the word gladly. At Aughrim the church was well filled, the Lord enabled His servant to reach the hearts of his hearers, both Roman Catholics and Protestants, and a deep and wide-spread impression seemed made in the town. Here a chapel had been built in the previous year on the property and at the sole cost of Mr. John Handy. In the church at Eyrecourt the audience was neither large or serious. At Birr, where a gracious revival had taken place, and several additions made to the Society, the congregations were increased, and they listened with much attention. At Tullamore Wesley preached in the assembly room, and on the following morning in the parlour of his host, good old Matthew Moore, whom he thought would soon join the Church above. The chapel at Portarlington and the church were both filled with serious audiences. From thence he went to Kilkenny, where the cause had been so very low that scarcely any Society was left. Providentially, the town having been visited by some cavalry, in which were several men full of faith and love, the work of God revived and prospered, and now the preaching-house was quite filled.

Having left Mr. Kane at Kilkenny for two or three days to follow up the good work there, Wesley proceeded to Carlow, where he was the guest of Mr. and Mrs. Burgess, then quartered in the town,[3] and preached in the assembly room to large congregations. Soon afterwards the Society having obtained the lease of a site, erected a chapel, which with slight enlargement still stands; showing, by the placing of all its windows in the rear, that it was built in troublous times.[4]

At Newtownbarry Wesley rejoiced to meet three devoted Christian ladies, Mrs. Cookman, Mrs. Henry Moore, and Miss Acton, who had come all the way from Dublin to see him. Miss Acton, the youngest daughter of William Acton, Esq., of West Aston, County Wicklow, and niece of Sir Lawrence Parsons, of Birr Castle, was a lady of highly cultivated mind, who to the regret of her aristocratic relatives had become a Methodist. Her love and zeal for God and His cause were almost boundless, and led to such exertions of body and mind as her feeble frame was unable to bear. She had a valuable property, which, after providing herself with the mere necessaries of life, was devoted to religious and charitable purposes. Her last illness was accompanied with much pain, but her happy spirit sustained by Divine grace, rose superior to physical suffering, and in 1794 she gloriously triumphed over death.[5]

But to return to Wesley. At Enniscorthy the use of the assembly room was granted, but a clergyman succeeded in getting the arrangement cancelled, so the venerable evangelist took his stand in a large yard, and preached there to three or four times as many as the room could have contained. At Wexford, "high and low, rich and poor, flocked" to the assembly room, and it seemed as if many of them were ripe for the Gospel. At the close of the service, as Mr. Gurley conducted him to his lodgings, a drunken Romanist came up to them with a thorny shrub in his hand, which he thrust in front of Mr. Wesley, saying, "O Sir, see what a fine smell this bush has." Mr. Gurley saw at once the malicious design, and said, "Begone! you scoundrel, or I will knock you down." The would-be assailant was alarmed, and fled. Wesley then enquired why the man had attempted to hurt him, and his companion replied, "You know the devil hates you, and so do his children."[6]

At Old Ross Wesley preached in the church to a large congregation of plain, country people. At Waterford he had an immense number of hearers

(3) *Memoirs of the Rev. J. Burgess*, p. 28.
(4) *Irish Evangelist*, 1869, p. 15.
(5) *Memoir of the Rev. A. Averell*, pp. 33, 34.
(6) *Memoir of the Rev. William Gurley*, p. 37.

in the court-house, while a file of musketeers, ordered by the Mayor, paraded at the door. Two or three hundred people also attended at the early morning service. At Clonmel he occupied the court-house, and says he knew not when he preached to so well dressed and ill behaved a congregation. At Youghal the court-house was filled in the evening, and half full at five in the morning.

On May the 5th Wesley arrived at Cork, where he was the guest of Mr. Laffan;[7] and his reception was specially interesting when contrasted with the persecutions which the Methodists suffered here nearly forty years previously. The congregations were overflowing, including many of the rich and influential inhabitants, while the chief magistrate of the city, Sir Samuel Rowland, showed him marked attention. Wesley says: "I waited by appointment on the Mayor, an upright, sensible man, who is diligently employed from morning to night in doing all the good he can. He has already prevailed upon the Corporation to make it a fixed rule, that the two hundred a-year which was spent in entertainments, should for the future be employed relieving indigent freemen, with their wives and children. He has carefully regulated the House of Industry, and has instituted a Humane Society for the relief of persons seemingly drowned. When will our English mayors copy after the Mayor of Cork?" This change of public feeling affords a striking instance of the fulfilment of the assurance, "If a man's ways please the Lord, He will make even his enemies to be at peace with him."

At Bandon, where there had been some time previously a remarkable work of God, yet not without many backsliders, Wesley preached in the assembly room on "How shall I give thee up, Ephraim!" and God applied His word. There was a general melting among the people, and many purposed to return to the Lord. At five next morning the chapel was filled, when he again applied the Word directly to backsliders, and had strong hope that "the times of refreshing" would soon "come from the presence of the Lord." So large was the congregation in the evening, that the brave old man once more took his stand in the Main street, and testified to a listening multitude, "This is not your rest." During the service, he was rudely interrupted in a similar way to that in which Mr. Taylor had been, by a number of trumpeters, who sounded their bugles. Wesley stopped, waited until they had done, and then resumed, when they again sounded, but getting wearied of this perpetual blowing, they rested, and the servant of God, taking advantage of the

(7) *Wesley's Works*, XIII., p. 86.

intermission, was eagerly addressing an attentive audience, when up rode the Colonel, shouting to the trumpeters with the voice of a stentor, "Blow! blow! why don't you blow?"[8] At the close of this service the members of Society returned to the chapel, where the Lord's supper was administered to them, and God gave them a remarkable blessing.

Calling on one that was ill at Inishannon, word was brought to Wesley that the people flocked to the room in which the services were usually held, and it was soon well filled. So at once he proceeded thither, and proclaimed to them the glad tidings of salvation. At Kinsale the service was held in the court-house, and there was a large audience. How different, he says, from that he had in the bowling-green two years previously, which was one of the most indecent, ill-mannered congregations he had ever seen in Ireland! But this was as eminently well-behaved, and included the sovereign, Mr. Haddock Chudleigh, and many persons of influence. Amongst the soldiers then quartered in the town was a sergeant, who soon after, with his regiment, was removed to Barbadoes, and here he and his pious comrades united together in Christian fellowship and work, a room for their service being supplied by a local merchant friendly to the cause. Thus a hearty welcome and a prepared field were found by Dr. Coke and the missionaries, when they first landed on the island.[9]

At Kilfinnane Wesley preached in the court-house to large and attentive audiences, and then went on to Limerick, where he had as usual an affectionate reception, but found much coldness in the Society, owing to a misunderstanding that had continued for several months between the preachers and some of the leading officials. This he succeeded in removing, and each time he preached had more and more hope that God would revive His work in this city, particularly if the prayer meetings were restored. "These," said he, "are never without fruit." About three weeks later the junior preacher on the circuit, Thomas Seaward, was suddenly called to the home above. He had not completed his first year in the itinerancy, and was a young man of mental ability that promised fair to render him a special blessing to the Church and to the world.

At Kilchreest there were many at the service who were all attention except one young gentleman, but his sport was quickly spoiled, for before the sermon was half over he was as serious as his neighbours. At Ballinrobe the

(8) Bennett's *History of Bandon*, p. 445.

(9) Drew's *Life of Dr. Coke*, pp. 193-94.

congregation was large and influential, and at Castlebar the service was held in the new chapel. Here also misunderstandings had arisen in the Society, which hindered the work of God, and which with the Divine blessing Wesley succeeded in removing. At Sligo he preached in the new court-house to more numerous and attentive congregations than he had seen in the town for many years. At Manorhamilton, where he was announced to preach without his concurrence, a young man was present named Charles Buckardt whose mind was seriously impressed, and became a member of the Society, which exposed him to much persecution; but nothing daunted he persevered, and for upwards of sixty years, except during illness, was seldom known to be absent from class-meeting.[10]

Wesley now paid his first visit to Annadale, where, in the midst of his earnest labour and wearisome journeys, he "had a day of rest, only preaching morning and evening;" and then proceeded to Ballyconnell, where he had a large audience. Leaving Mr. Broadbent to preach at Ballyhaise, he hastened to Clones to be in time for the Church service, at which there was such a number of communicants as had never been seen in the church before. Here also he succeeded in reconciling some parties that had been estranged, and in removing some offences that had crept into the Society. At Aghalun, where a chapel had been built in the previous year, he found such a large congregation as he had not seen before in the kingdom. The tent or covered pulpit was placed at the base of a hill, on the side of which the vast multitude sat, row above row, while cries for mercy and tears of joy rose in all directions. At Lisbellaw, where he was the guest of Mr. James Copeland who had settled in the town about nine years previously,[11] he preached once in the open-air and again in the assembly room, and the people appeared to be prepared to receive the fulness of the blessings of the Gospel. Here also a godly Methodist mother dedicated her child to Christ by the hands of Wesley. The name of the boy, John Nelson, evidently attracted his attention, and led him to pray that God would make him a Methodist preacher, and the request was granted.[12]

At Enniskillen, "formerly a den of lions," Wesley preached in the market-house, the people assembled from all sides and were all attention, the Lord made bare His arm, and the mountains flowed at His presence. Many were

---

(10) *Primitive Wesleyan Methodist Magazine*, 1850, p. 318.

(11) *Irish Evangelist*, 1862, p. 2.

(12) *The Memory of our Fathers*, p. 36.

cut to the heart, and many rejoiced with joy unspeakable. At Sidaire also there was a very numerous audience. Here a lad named Wm. Keys, who had been converted during the recent revival in this neighbourhood, accompanied his mother to the service, and at its close the venerable evangelist laid his hands on the boy's head, and solemnly prayed that the blessing of the Triune Jehovah might rest upon him. Deeply impressed, the youth began to work for Christ, and eventually entered the itinerancy.[13]

At Omagh, it being market day, a great number of people assembled, who at first were innocently noisy, but soon became still as night. At Kirlish Lodge, Wesley was heartily welcomed by Mr. and Mrs. Boyle, with whose Christian spirit he was much impressed; and, although their house was ten miles from any town, he had a large congregation, and afterwards a comfortable love-feast. Mr. Boyle having spoken to the Rev. Dr. Wilson, the rector of Ardstraw, concerning a service in his church at Newtownstewart, and he having obtained the free and full consent of the Bishop, the Hon. F. A. Hervey, arrangements were accordingly made. When it was announced that Wesley would preach, it seemed as if all the people of the country round intended to go and hear. Meanwhile, however, one of the parishioners, a warm Seceder, took away the key, so the venerable evangelist preached in an adjoining orchard, and not in vain. Amongst those who were present was Miss Mary Drew, subsequently Mrs. Keys, who had previously been led to give her heart to God, through a sermon preached by Mr. Joseph Armstrong; but had not identified herself with the Methodists, owing to the ridicule to which it would expose her. The text was John 3:16, and while listening to the sermon she resolved at once to identify herself with the people of God at any risk; and from that time until the end of her protracted life continued a steady and consistent member of the Society.[14]

At Kilrail, as no house could contain the audience, Wesley went out into the open air, and afterwards administered the Lord's supper to about one hundred persons. At Strabane he had no intention of preaching until he heard that the town-hall was at his service, so he went to it without delay, and found an influential and attentive audience. He then proceeded to Londonderry, where the large chapel in Magazine street having been sold to pay the heavy debt that remained on it,[15] and the new building in Linen-hall street not being

---

(13) *Irish Evangelist*, 1863, p. 109.

(14) *Primitive Wesleyan Methodist Magazine*, 1856, pp. 186-91.

(15) *Irish Evangelist*, 1862, p. 218.

completed, he held the service in the town-hall, where large and interesting congregations assembled. He had no intention of preaching at Newtownlimavady, but while at breakfast the people assembled in such large numbers that he could not deny them a sermon. At Coleraine he preached in the barrack yard to people of whom he speaks as "good old soldiers," steady and affectionate, with whom one would willingly have remained a little longer.

At Ballymena, where the Society was very small and poor, but well established, the Presbyterian minister having kindly offered his meeting-house, Wesley willingly accepted it, and preached to a large congregation, on many of whom the Spirit descended as dew on the tender herb. At Antrim, also, the Presbyterian minister offered him the use of his large and commodious house.[16] Amongst those present was a Mrs. White, a pious woman who had collected all the people she could to hear the word preached, and brought her own daughter, a girl of eighteen years of age, who subsequently was converted and became a Methodist, and to the end of life had a lively recollection of the service.[17] At Belfast Wesley preached to numerous and seriously attentive congregations in the Linen-hall. At this period the Methodist services were usually held in the loft of a house, situated in a lane leading down to Smithfield, to reach which the members of the congregation had to ascend by a ladder.[18] But soon after he left the first chapel in this town was erected. It was in Fountain lane, at the rear of Donegal place, and was forty-six feet long, and twenty-two broad, with a gallery at the end, and could accommodate between three and four hundred people. The leading members at this period were well conducted, but not distinguished for either the ardour of their zeal or the extent of their usefulness.[19]

At Lisburn, where the Presbyterian meeting-house was lent to Wesley, the congregations were the largest he had seen since leaving England. Here about three months previously good old Mrs. Cumberland had died in peace. She might well have said with aged Simeon, "Lord, now lettest Thou Thy servant depart in peace, according to Thy word: for mine eyes have seen Thy salvation." During the last two years of her life she endured much physical

---

(16) Now occupied by the Unitarians.

(17) *Primitive Wesleyan Methodist Magazine*, 1849, p. 158.

(18) *Irish Christian Advocate*, 1883, p. 294.

(19) *Irish Evangelist*, 1868, p. 26.

suffering, together with considerable anxiety as to her religious experience. Sometimes she would say, with a flood of tears, "How it will end with me, God only knows: yet He often visits my soul with His sweet influences." A few weeks before death her bodily strength was greatly reduced; but her confidence in God so increased that all the clouds of unbelief, which had so long encompassed her soul, were completely dispelled. To some who were with her she said: "I have not the shadow of a doubt, but firmly believe all will be well with me. I am quite delivered from all things, and only wait for the welcome messenger of death." At another time, to an inquiry whether she found any doubts, she answered — "A doubt? O no; not even the shadow of one." Thus this good woman, with many doubts and fears, maintained her integrity to the last, and then God lifted up the light of His countenance upon her, and gave her a clear and blessed assurance of eternal and glorious felicity.

At Downpatrick the audience was larger than at Lisburn. At Rathfryland the Presbyterian minister offered the use of his new and spacious meeting-house, which was soon filled; and at Tanderagee the congregations were even more numerous. Here Wesley was as usual the guest of Dr. Leslie, but observing that the spiritual life of his host was not as strong as it had been, with characteristic fidelity and affection he wrote to him on the subject.[20] This letter was doubtless received in the spirit in which it was written, as the rector's house continued to be the welcome home of Wesley. At Charlemont he preached to a large congregation assembled from all the country round, it being the day of the quarterly meeting. Immediately after the close of the public service, as usual the love-feast was held; but as the chapel could not contain the half of the people, they obtained the use of the green in the fort, and admitted the members one by one through the wicket. Here they sat down on the grass, and many no doubt turned in thought to the multitude who of old, under similar circumstances, were fed by the Saviour. Amongst those present was a lad named Thomas Wilson, who had accompanied his mother from Derryscollop: and not only did the venerable preacher, his clear voice, both in speaking and singing, his method of marking time with his hand, and his almost angelic appearance, impress the mind of the boy; but also the word preached reached his heart, and thus he was led to take the first step in what proved to be a godly and useful career.[21]

---

(20) A copy of this letter appears in *Wesley's Works*, XII., p. 367, but by some mistake is dated 1775 instead of June 16, 1787. Vide *Wesleyan Methodist Magazine*, 1847, p. 332.   (21) *Primitive Wesleyan Methodist Magazine*, 1849, p. 29.

At Dungannon the Presbyterian minister had been requested to allow Mr. Wesley to preach in his meeting-house, but he declined. So the benches were removed from the preaching room, and it contained most of the congregation. Meanwhile the work of the Lord in this town had prospered so greatly through the labours of the preachers and leaders already named, with others, such as Richard Simmons, George Appleby and George Morrow, that it had been agreed to build a chapel, and after much effort the Society had the joy of seeing the house completed, and opened for public worship at the latter end of August by Messrs. Hugh Moore and G. Armstrong. Soon afterwards Messrs. Turner and Heather came to reside in the town, and thus the local influence of the Society was much strengthened, and two additional stopping places for the preachers secured.[22]

At Armagh, much to the astonishment of Mr. Wesley, the Seceders freely gave him the use of their meeting-house, as the chapel could not contain half the people who desired to hear. "Surely," he remarks, "there will be a harvest here also, by-and-by, although hitherto we have seen but little fruit." These anticipations were blessedly realized, as there have been reaped in this city many glorious harvests of saved souls. At Newry he again obtained the use of the large meeting-house, and such was the impression made on the vast congregation that the new chapel could not hold the people on the next morning at five o'clock, many having to stand outside. At Dundalk, which he now visited for the first time, and Drogheda, he expected tumults, but there were none, and the congregations were large and attentive. And at Swords, notorious "from time immemorial for all manner of wickedness," there was an audience who listened to the word with deep interest.

After this most gratifying journey Wesley returned to Dublin, where a short time previously the following incident occurred: Mr. Moore having been impressed with the feeling that much good could not be effected in the city while the preachers confined themselves to the chapels, resolved to try what could be done by preaching in the open air. Several of the principal friends strove to dissuade him, but he was not the man to be diverted from what he believed to be his duty. Accordingly one Sunday afternoon, accompanied by a number of members of the Society, he went to Lower Abbey street, where one of the largest chapels in the city now stands, and having mounted a chair, gave out a hymn. An immense multitude soon assembled, running from all

---

(22) *Primitive Wesleyan Methodist Magazine*, 1839, p. 213.

quarters, crying out — "What is the matter?" and surrounding him and his little flock. He soon saw that most of them were Romanists; during prayer several knelt down on the stones, and having concluded with the Lord's prayer, a woman shouted — "Where is the Hail Mary?" This produced a slight sensation, which soon subsided; and when he announced his text the people listened with eager attention until another woman, with uplifted hand, cried out — "Lord have mercy on us! Christ save us! And is it come to this? I know all about him; I knew his father and his mother. O, it is well his father is dead. What would he say to this?" and then began to relate particulars. The general impression soon obtained that the preacher was beside himself, and the congregation quickly divided, part of them listening to her and part to him. Some became boisterous and strove to get near to pull him down, but the little band of Methodists continued firm, until one fellow forced his way through them, and attempted to upset the chair; but this was held fast by Mrs. Moore and a young lady, probably Miss Acton, whom the rascal dare not touch, or he would have had the whole crowd on him. Mr. Moore attempted to continue his sermon, but attention was divided, and nearly lost. After some time hard clods of dirt were thrown in all directions, accompanied by a shower of rotten eggs. Nothing, however, was permitted to touch the preacher, and he at length concluded with an appeal to his congregation, which appeared to have some effect, as he retired unmolested. Meanwhile a drunken sailor jumped on the chair and began to sing, the multitude shouted, and when the song concluded he began to preach in his way. After he had thus amused himself and his auditors for a considerable time, on attempting to pass from the quay to his ship he slipped from the plank and was drowned. The services were continued in that neighbourhood with great success.[23]

But to return to Wesley. On examining the classes in the metropolis, and excluding one hundred and twelve members, he found one thousand one hundred and thirty-six remained. Here he had the pleasure of meeting John Howard, whom he pronounced "one of the greatest men in Europe;" adding: "Nothing but the mighty power of God could enable him to go through his difficult and dangerous employments." The great philanthropist was as much pleased with Wesley as Wesley was with him. "I was encouraged," said he to Alexander Knox, "to go on vigorously with my own designs. I saw in him how much a single man might achieve by zeal and perseverance; and I

(23) *Life of Rev. H. Moore*, pp. 86-87.

thought, why may not I do as much in my way as Mr. Wesley has done in his, if I am only assiduous and persevering; and I determined to pursue my work with more alacrity than ever."[24]

Wesley was also surprised with the sudden arrival of Dr. Coke from America, and desired all the preachers to meet him, to consider the state of the brethren in that continent. The Conference met on July the 6th, and closed on the 10th. Dr. Coke recounted what had befallen him in the West Indies and America, a recital which produced a general conviction that the time was come for a united effort for the establishment of missions in the isles which were so manifestly waiting for the Word of God. In the report which the doctor made of his foreign charge, he intimated that the membership of the new mission in the West Indies was two thousand nine hundred and fifty, and that in the States twenty-five thousand, the first-fruits of harvests of larger magnitude, as time has shown and will yet show.[25] The doctor was also greeted with details of the increased prosperity of religion in Ireland; the increase in the membership being nearly one thousand: open opposition had generally ceased, and the people were enabled to worship God under their own vine and fig tree, none making them afraid. No less than thirteen candidates were admitted on trial, which was an addition of twelve to the regular staff of preachers. Wesley says with regard to the Conference, there was no jarring string, but all from the beginning to the end was love and harmony.

The day following the conclusion of the Conference, Wesley, with Dr. Coke, Messrs. Rogers, Leech and several other preachers embarked for Parkgate. The voyage was attended with considerable peril, for the vessel struck on a rock. The captain, who had been in the cabin, leaped up, and running to the deck, when he saw how the ship lay, exclaimed: "Your lives may be saved, but I am undone." Yet no sailor swore, and no woman cried out. While the seamen endeavoured to preserve the ship, Wesley and his companions had recourse to prayer, that He who ruleth the winds and the seas would render their efforts successful. The prayer was graciously answered, as the vessel shot off the rock, and sailed on without any more damage than the breaking of a few planks. Thus was the Divine assurance fulfilled, "Call upon me in the day of trouble and I will deliver thee, and thou shalt glorify Me."

---

(24) Moore's *Life of Wesley*, II., p. 435.
(25) Etheridge's *Life of Dr. Coke*, pp. 226-27.

At the subsequent meeting of the British Conference it was resolved to send missionaries to the West Indies, while Dr. Coke undertook to aid the good work by soliciting subscriptions, and in this benevolent enterprise he persevered to the end of life.

Mr. Dinnen was appointed to Limerick, where he found a pleasing, friendly people, many of them truly devoted to God, and much good was done. The Rev. Jacques Ingram, who was married to a sister of the Rev. E. Smith, and his kind family received the preachers with much respect and affection. The country parts of the circuit were pleasant, and the work prospered there.[26]

Mr. Rogers was stationed in Cork, where he was gladly received by an affectionate people. Some unhappy jarring during the preceding year had considerably injured the good work, so that the Society was reduced from five hundred to three hundred and ninety-seven members; but peace was restored, and with it religious prosperity. The Lord graciously revived His work, and before the close of the year one hundred were added to the membership.[27]

CHAPTER 18

1788

THE work of the Lord continued to prosper greatly during the year 1788, more especially on the Charlemont and Cork circuits. Mr. Bates, who was stationed on the former, says, upon the closest investigation Mr. Hugh Moore and he had reason to believe that ninety-six were converted to God, also twenty-six backsliders in heart who had not left the Society and twenty-nine more who had gone into the world were restored to the flock of Christ's people. The whole increase amounted to about one hundred and eighty. Sixteen of the members were called to the home above, and they died in the full triumph of faith. Such a number of happy deaths proved a means in the hand of God of furthering the cause. In general the work was carried on with

---

(26) Crook's *Ireland and the Centenary of American Methodism*, p. 65.
(27) *Lives of Early Methodist Preachers*, IV., p. 322.

very little noise, though there were some meetings at which the people were constrained to cry aloud for mercy.[1]

On January the 24th Mrs. Rogers wrote to Mr. Wesley giving a most encouraging account of the Society in Cork, and anticipating as great a work of revival there as had taken place in Dublin. The Christmas morning services had proved a blessed season, many were convinced, and some converted. Many more were awakened and justified at the watch-night meeting, but the covenant service exceeded all. Fourteen souls were that day born of God, a number of backsliders were restored, and several believers perfected in love. During the succeeding three weeks between thirty and forty joined the Society, some of whom dated their religious awakening from the night of the covenant service. Several who knew and loved the Lord entered into solemn covenant with Him, and with each other never to rest until they experienced perfect love. A new preaching place, being the fifth, was opened in a convenient and populous part of the city, where at the first meeting a class of fourteen members was formed.[2]

As in the time of St. Paul, "not many mighty, not many noble" were "called;" yet there were some "honourable women:" so also, in the early days of Methodism in Ireland, the majority of the members were persons of humble origin and position; but there were a few of nobler blood and higher rank. Of these there was none who could trace a more illustrious ancestry than Mrs. Theodosia Blatchford, the daughter of Lady Mary Tighe, and granddaughter of John, first Earl of Darnley. She was thus a lineal descendant of the celebrated Earls of Clarendon, who took such a leading part in the stirring events of the nation in the seventeenth century. Mrs. Blatchford's claims to notice, however, do not rest on either her parentage or her social position, but on her saintly character, and life of exalted piety and Christian benevolence.

Miss Tighe was married in 1770 to the Rev. William Blatchford, a clergyman of extensive property, who, on account of his learning, was appointed to the charge of Marsh's Library, Dublin, in which position he rendered important and valuable service. About three years after his marriage a malignant fever carried off this excellent man, leaving his widow, with a son and daughter, to deplore his loss. This painful bereavement was no doubt sanctified to Mrs. Blatchford, and probably proved the means of her

---

(1) *Methodist Magazine*, Dublin, 1805, p. 242.
(2) *Experience of Mrs. H. A. Rogers*, pp. 141-43.

connection with Methodism and conversion to God.

Mr. Blatchford had two sisters, the elder of whom was married to Dr. Radcliffe, Judge of the Prerogative Court. The other, remaining single, resided with her sister and brother-in-law. She was much afflicted in body, but of an amiable spirit, and very sincere in her religious observances. Mrs. Blatchford was much attached to her, and frequently conversed with her on the subject of experimental religion. She listened, but was slow of heart to believe the privileges of the Gospel, especially that of the witness of the Spirit. Her affliction confined her to bed for a great length of time, and then Dr. Radcliffe used to read the service for the Visitation of the Sick out of the Book of Common Prayer every morning, previous to going to court. Though a very upright man, he did not like what was designated Methodism, which Mrs. Blatchford insisted her sister-in-law would enjoy before her death. One morning, as the doctor as usual read prayers for Miss Blatchford, and was about to repeat the Lord's Prayer, she said — "Stop, before you read that prayer, I wish to say a few words," and continued, while all the family, including Mrs. Blatchford, knelt around the bed — "Last night, as I was for hours unable to sleep, I lay contemplating my religious state. I prayed to God over it, and while thus engaged felt the power of God so present to my mind, enabling me in a manner I had never felt before, to claim Him as my Father who is in heaven, and I rejoice still in the holy assurance. Now, doctor, read for me that prayer." With much feeling he finished the service, and then immediately left the room. Mrs. Blatchford followed him, and said — "I told you she would die a Methodist; that is Methodism." He made no observation, but passed on to his professional duties. Miss Blatchford did not long survive, and died in the full assurance of faith.[3]

While thus the Lord was graciously carrying on His work in the north and the south, and in the midst of the spiritual prosperity with which Dublin was favoured, a serious division took place in the metropolitan Society, in which the Smyths were deeply involved. Nearly three years previously Mr. Wesley had written to his brother that Dr. Coke would have work enough with the Rev. E. Smyth, whom he doubted not needed a bridle,[4] but it was only now that these unpleasant anticipations were realized. During the course of the spring Dr. Coke arrived in the city, and found that many of the people were in the habit of attending Dissenting chapels on the Sabbath, and in order

(3) *Life of the Rev. H. Moore*, pp. 206-7.
(4) *Wesley's Works*, XII., p. 154.

to obviate this, it was arranged that on three Sundays out of four there should be service in Whitefriar street chapel in church hours, at which the liturgy should be read, and on the fourth Sunday the people should be recommended to attend St. Patrick's cathedral, and receive the Sacrament there. This gave great offence to the Rev. Edward Smyth, and, doubtless, through him, to his brother and some of the wealthy members of the Society, who objected to it, as tending to a separation from the Church. Most likely, however, the real reason was — at least so far as the Smyths were concerned — the fear of injury being done to the congregations at the Bethesda.

The case was referred to Mr. Wesley, who gave it as his judgment, that in the first instance the doctor was too warm; that he should have had more regard to so respectable a body of men as requested him not to carry out his proposal: and that there should be no more services in Whitefriar street chapel during church hours. But subsequently he allowed that while Dr. Coke was in the city, he might have service at eleven o'clock, and that on condition the brethren attended St. Patrick's or their own parish church one Sunday in four to receive the Lord's supper, Mr. Moore might read prayers the other three Sundays in the preaching-house.

Meanwhile, however, offence was given, and the Society lost some of its members. It is said that the number was upwards of one hundred, including a few of the most wealthy,[5] but according to Wesley it would appear that the number was only five or six altogether.[6] These seem to have been formed into a class referred to by Mr. Wesley as "Mr. Smyth's Society," which soon disappeared; while whatever loss, financially and socially, the Methodists may have sustained, numerically the gap was more than filled by additional members. A strong feeling, however, against the service still continued on the part of some of the leading officials of the Society, including Messrs. Henry Brooke, Arthur Keene, and Richard D'Olier.

John Miller, a German who had been a page to George II., but after his conversion entered the itinerancy, was, like most of his fellow countrymen, but unlike his brother preachers, fond of a smoke, and carried his pipe and tobacco in a tin case, which on one occasion at least proved of signal service. Travelling to Conference, with a considerable sum of money in his saddlebags, he was stopped by a powerful man, who caught hold of his bridle, saying — "Your money, I want your money." "I am a poor Methodist

---

(5) Tyerman's *Wesley*, III. p. 313.
(6) Ibid., p. 583.

preacher," said John. "I know who and what you are well enough," replied the robber; "but it is your money I want, and must have it." "But," said the itinerant, "what I have belongs to the Conference." "I care nothing for you or your Conference," answered the highwayman — "I want your money, so give it up instantly." A queer thought crossed the brain of John. "Well," said he, "if you must have it, and there is no other way, so be it; but," putting his hand into his breast pocket, drawing forth his tobacco case, and throwing back the lid with a sharp click, he added, "you must first take the contents of this." Seeing the motion, and hearing the noise, which sounded like the cocking of a pistol, the robber dropped the reins and fled, no doubt blessing his stars that he had escaped without a ball through his head, while the preacher put spurs to his horse, and also hastened on, rejoicing over deliverance from danger.[7]

The Conference met on July the 8th, under the presidency of Dr. Coke; all the preachers in the kingdom were present. The increase in the membership was nine hundred. Thirteen new candidates were received on trial, to whom two others were added during the course of the year. There were two deaths. John Mayly, worn-out in the service of his blessed Master, and John Burnett, "a very pious, devoted, and useful young man," from Dublin, who only travelled one year, and whose end was remarkably triumphant. William M'Cornock, sen., was left free to go to the West Indies, as he had long desired. Here he commenced a mission in Dominica, laboured with a zeal which plainly evinced that he had the interests of souls much at heart. Multitudes flocked to hear him preach, and many received the word with joy. Within a few months not less than one hundred and fifty persons were led to inquire what they must do to be saved. In the midst of these toils and triumphs, he was smitten with a fever, which proved fatal, and thus he was called to enter into the joy of his Lord.

At the close of the Conference Dr. Coke, accompanied by Mr. and Mrs. Henry Moore, Mr. and Mrs. Connolly, of Clones, and several preachers embarked for England, in order to be present at the British Conference, which was held in London. From these associates Mrs. Connolly, who had only been a short time married, was impressed with the necessity of conversion; during the sittings of the Conference, she made her home with Mr. Moore in the house adjoining City road chapel, and here after enjoying a season of

(7) *Memoir of the Rev. William Gurley*, pp. 53, 54.

prayer with the family, the Holy Spirit descended, and created her anew in Christ Jesus. She then became a Methodist, and continued heartily identified with the Society in Ireland and afterwards in America, during the remainder of her protracted life.[8]

At the Conference this year Mr. Roberts was appointed to labour with Mr. Rogers in Cork, where he had the satisfaction of living in the affections of the people, the Lord working by him in the awakening of sinners, and the edification of believers.[9] One of those converted at this period was a young man named Richard Dudley, who had joined with others in hooting and throwing stones at the venerable Wesley, during his previous visit to this city; but was now brought in penitence of spirit to the foot of the cross, and for more than half a century proved a consistent and useful leader of the Society.[10]

On a calm summer morning at about this time, two persons from Waterford visited the little town of Passage, which lies between the city and the sea. One of these was a young man of remarkably prepossessing appearance, whose heart the Lord had touched, and whose earnest desire that others should experience the love which welled up in his own soul had prompted him to go to the village uninvited and unknown. Mounting a chair, he sung a hymn in the market square, with no apparent listener but his one companion. Then closing his eyes, he poured forth his soul in earnest prayer: and on concluding saw on every side a dense crowd, while from open windows heads were projected, eager to catch every word. A discourse marked by great liberty of speech, with sound evangelical doctrine, made the time one long to be remembered. The preacher was Samuel Wood, who at the following Conference was received on trial, and whose theological attainments, sound judgment, and eminent ability in maturer years, amply justified his youthful promise.

Messrs. Rennick and A. Hamilton, sen., who were stationed on the Ballyshannon circuit, were the honoured instruments of introducing Methodism into Cashel. Previous to this period folly and sin abounded in the neighbourhood, the principles of the Reformation were nearly lost, and it was not unusual for Protestants to go to holy wells. Saturday nights were generally devoted to dancing and drinking, which continued until near day-

(8) *Heroines of Methodism*, pp. 124-25.

(9) *Life and remains of Rev. T. Roberts*, p. 35.

(10) *Primitive Wesleyan Methodist Magazine*, 1848, p. 234-35.

light: and the Sundays were employed in cock-fighting and gambling, which generally ended in quarrelling and fighting.[11] A Miss Ann Shanklin who resided here, went with her mother to a preaching service, and while Mr. Rennick proclaimed the truths of the Gospel, the Spirit of God applied the word so powerfully to her conscience that with difficulty she could restrain from crying aloud for mercy. After singing Mr. Rennick requested James Bell to pray. He was then a young convert, who had just emerged from darkness into the light of the glorious Gospel, and in 1791 entered the itinerancy. As Miss Shanklin had seen him a short time previously engaged in dancing, she was much surprised to hear him pray with liberty and power. "Is this man," thought she, "who was lately as worldly and wicked as myself, now possessed of the spirit of prayer? Surely this must be of God." And thus she was encouraged to hope for the Divine favour. For some time she continued to attend the Methodist services, her convictions deepened and at length God spoke to her in peace and blessing. Through the influence of her consistent life, and in answer to many prayers, her mother and brother, who had opposed and persecuted her, were led to decision for God, and their house was opened to receive the messengers of mercy. A marvellous moral change now took place in the neighbourhood.[12] Large numbers, and in some instances whole families were brought under the sanctifying power of religion, and the Divine assurance was graciously fulfilled, "Instead of the thorn shall come up the fir tree, and instead of the brier shall come up the myrtle tree; and it shall be to the Lord for a name, for an everlasting sign that shall not be cut off."

At Cortrasna there was at this time a gracious outpouring of the Holy Spirit, many were awakened and converted, so that in a few months the Society was more than doubled. Amongst those who partook of the blessings of this gracious visitation was a young man named John Robinson, who then entered upon his Christian course, which he maintained with uniform consistency for half a century. Shortly after his conversion he commenced in Newtownbutler a meeting for children on Sunday evenings at which he prayed, and heard the scholars read and repeat portions of Scripture.[13] This was the fourth Sunday school in Ireland of which there is any record. Mr. William Browne, who travelled in the Primitive Wesleyan Society for twenty-two years with acceptance and success, states that when about seven years

---

(11) *Primitive Wesleyan Methodist Magazine*, 1840, pp. 286-87.

(12) *Methodist Magazine*, Dublin, 1809, pp. 219-24.

(13) *Primitive Wesleyan Methodist Magazine*, 1839, p. 33.

old — that is, during this year — he "attended a blessed means for the improvement of the children then adopted in Newtownbutler. The superintendent commenced it with singing and prayer; he then gave each child a portion of Scripture to commit to memory for the ensuing Sabbath, after repeating which he asked a number of questions, and gave such advice as he thought suitable to the children's capacity." This Sunday school proved the means of leading Browne, as well as others, to seek the Lord; and thus at the very beginning of the movement in this country the seed sown brought forth fruit.[14]

Mr. John Black was appointed to the Enniskillen circuit. During his first round a mob assembled, consisting of some of those who ought to have been the most respectable Protestant inhabitants of the district, they violently seized the servant of God, tied a rope round his body, and dragged him several times through the nearest river. The cruel ruffians then cut off the ears of his horse, and threatened to do the same to himself. It is worthy of note that in the course of a comparatively short time every trace of these guilty parties and their descendants passed into oblivion.[15] "Verily, He is a God that judgeth in the earth."

In Omagh at this period Methodism had a feeble existence, the sphere of its operations was greatly limited, and its few adherents had no other influence than that derived from their piety. The only members of Society in the town were a few persons in humble circumstances, who were the objects of much scorn and contempt. Their leader, Richard Magee, was a man who strove to commend the Saviour to others. Sometimes the meetings were broken up through the violence of the mobs that surrounded the house where they met. On one occasion, as a preacher proclaimed the message of salvation in the street, a man standing at a distance lifted up a stone, and with a deliberate aim struck the champion of the cross. The villain then walked away in peace; but a good old gentleman, who was looking at the whole affair, turning to the crowd, said — "My name is not Sam Galbraith if that man dies in his senses." Few, however, seemed concerned one way or another; but not long after God laid His hand on the persecutor, he became a lunatic, and died in a state of dreadful insanity![16] Mr. Bates, who was stationed here, said that the aspect of the circuit was unpleasant and

(14) Ibid., 1851, p. 22.
(15) *Wesleyan Methodist Magazine*, 1853, p. 134.
(16) *Memoir of Mrs. Anne Graham*, pp. 23-6.

discouraging. He found very many who had little more than a name; yet he experienced the Divine presence in almost every place, which encouraged him to go forward. So he laboured on, and not in vain, for by the end of the year there was an increase of thirty members.[17]

Mr. Crook, after an absence of two years, was again appointed, with David Barrowclough, to Charlemont, from which a new circuit had been cut off, and their labours were much acknowledged of the Lord, many were turned from darkness to light, and the young converts engaged heartily in work for Christ, especially holding cottage prayer meetings, which attracted much attention.[18] Amongst those converted was a young man named David Woods, who lived in the neighbourhood of Moy, and had been a great profligate, much addicted to cock-fighting and such practices, and a great foe to the Methodists. His enmity carried him so far that he determined to face them on their own ground, in one of their class meetings and silence them. He went, but when he heard the leader asking each member concerning the state of his soul, and the replies, he trembled: and when the question was put to himself he told plainly his object in coming, but that such a fear had come over him that he could not understand. However he went again, but with a different intention, was greatly blessed, and became valiant for the truth. The young convert having an impression that he should work for Christ at Loughgall, could get no rest day or night thinking about it, and at length resolved to try and get some place near it for a service. On his way thither he met his uncle, an old companion in sin, who, addressing him said, "Ho! David, how are the cocks?" "Sir," replied the young Christian, "speak no more to me on that subject: I have served the devil long enough in that line, but have found a better Master." Waxing bolder through this avowal of his faith, he enquired — "Will you allow me to hold a meeting in your house next Sunday?" "You hold a meeting," said the uncle with a sneer. "Who taught you to preach? You may have the house, but I wont hear you." The time having been arranged, they parted, and the service was held, which led to similar meetings, in the house of Mr. Geo. Gainer, the congregations rapidly increased, and the Lord gave His blessing. Mr. Gilpin came to help, and a gracious awakening commenced. When a Society was formed, between forty and fifty persons were received on trial for membership: and Mr. Gainer's house became the stopping-place for the preachers, who were made a great

---

(17) *Methodist Magazine*, Dublin, 1805, pp. 243-44.
(18) *Primitive Wesleyan Methodist Magazine*, 1831, p. 258.

blessing to his family.[19]

George Morrow, one of the Methodists in Dungannon, got the conviction that he should go to the house of Mr. Thomas Shillington at Crew bridge, and try to raise a class there. He was received in the most cordial manner, and a Society was formed consisting of fifteen members. Mr. Shillington thus became a Methodist, and was led to the enjoyment of a large measure of those blessings which the Society has held forth so prominently as the believer's privilege.[20]

Towards the close of this year, a promising and devoted young preacher, named Hugh Pugh, was removed by death. His naturally frank, amiable and lovable disposition was elevated and sanctified by Divine grace. He was received on trial in 1787, and appointed to the Clones circuit, where his labours were much blessed; but excessive work laid the foundation of disease which compelled him to become a supernumerary, and return to his home on the Lisburn circuit, where the disease made rapid progress. As the end approached, his mother inquired if he realized that salvation which he had preached to others: and he replied — "Glory be to God, I do! Jesus is all in all!" and in holy triumph his ransomed spirit entered the Paradise of God.[21]

CHAPTER 19

1789

ABOUT the beginning of 1789 the following incident occurred, affording a striking example at once of God's care of His servants, and their fidelity and courage in His work. As one of the preachers journeyed he was met by three highwaymen, one of whom seized his horse by the bridle, a second presented a pistol to his breast, and the third attempted to pull him to the ground, swearing that he would have his money or his life. The servant of God, however, nothing daunted, looked at them steadfastly and inquired if they had prayed that morning. But they were not to be diverted from their wicked

(19) *Primitive Wesleyan Methodist Magazine*, 1823, pp. 335-40.

(20) Ibid., 1844, pp. 345-48.

(21) *Arminian Magazine*, 1789, pp. 635-38.

purpose by such a question, and without delay deprived him of his watch, took off the saddle bags, and pulled out a knife to cut them open, when the preacher told them to stop, that there was nothing in them but a few religious books to which they were welcome, and as to money, he had only twopence-halfpenny, which he gave them. He then said: "Now, shall I give you my coat? You are welcome to anything I have, only remember I am a servant of God, and am now engaged in His work. Let me pray with you before we part, and it may do you more good than anything I have to give." At this one of the robbers said they would keep nothing belonging to the man, for if they did, vengeance would pursue them; so the money and watch were returned, and the bags re-fastened to the saddle. The preacher thanked them, renewed his request that they would engage in prayer, knelt down on the road, and with much power pleaded with God on their behalf. Meantime, two of them made off; but the third remained to the close, and was much affected, so that there was reason to hope he resolved to become a new man![1]

This year Mr. Wesley, accompanied by Mr. Bradford, visited Ireland for the twenty-first and last time. After a stormy and protracted voyage he arrived in Dublin on Sunday morning, March the 29th: and, notwithstanding the illness from which he had suffered, went straight to the chapel, where he preached on the sickness and recovery of Hezekiah, with special reference to the illness of George III.; and afterwards administered the Lord's supper to about five hundred persons. At this sacramental service he was assisted by Mr. Myles, the junior preacher on the circuit. They had a very solemn meeting, the Lord crowning the ordinance with His presence, and separated, giving glory to God.

During this visit to the metropolis Mr. Wesley met with very great respect and attention from several persons of rank in Dublin and its vicinity, including the Earl of Moira. Mr. Myles says he never saw the venerable evangelist more honoured by those who were not members of the Society than at this time. They seemed to think it a blessing to have him under their roof: and such a sacred influence attended his words that it was no ordinary privilege to have the opportunity of listening to his conversation.[2]

He rejoiced much at the state of the Society, the congregations at five in the morning being much larger in proportion than those in City road chapel; Gravel walk house was filled as he had never seen it before; all seemed to

---

(1) *Lives of Early Methodist Preachers*, IV., pp. 323-24.
(2) *Wesleyan Methodist Magazine*, 1831, p. 298.

hear as for life; and in meeting the bands he found amongst them a greater number of those who were perfected in love than even in London itself.

Meantime Wesley had "letter upon letter" concerning the additional Sunday service, which had been introduced by Dr. Coke, and therefore wrote his views in full to "Certain persons in Dublin." In this letter he plainly states, he did not separate from the Church, and had no intention of doing so; that they had not done so who attended the Sunday noon services, for they had been present in the church and at the Sacrament there much more frequently than for two years previously; that there was no ground to fear that it would lead to any such separation; and that the strife was altogether on the part of the objectors, who themselves did not attend the services of the Establishment as frequently as they ought.[3]

How far Wesley succeeded in thus satisfying the minds of the objectors who continued in the Society and were sincere in their attachment to the Episcopal Church, is exceedingly doubtful. Evidently they could not see how having services in church hours was not, *ipso facto*, separating from the Establishment, no matter how frequently many of those who attended went also to church. Hence they appear to have persevered in their opposition to the innovation, until eventually a compromise was made, the hour of service being changed from eleven to two o'clock, when very large congregations attended.[4]

So far as the Smyths were concerned, who had separated from Methodism, and whose zeal for the Church was a mere pretence, the breach was not repaired, although Mr. Wesley was received by them with the utmost respect, and even preached three times in the Bethesda at the pressing invitation of Mr. Smyth. No sooner, however, had the venerable evangelist left the city than he was assailed in the public papers in the most bitter and scurrilous manner; the cry was raised "the Church is in danger," and the Archbishop and clergy were called upon to haste to the rescue: "for a Mr. Myles, a layman, had assisted Mr. Wesley in administering the Lord's supper, the greatest innovation that had occurred for fifty years!" This brought on a controversy which continued for three months, during which "every week, and almost every day," the devoted Wesley "was bespattered in the public papers, either by Mr. Smyth or by Mr. Mann, his curate."[5] This was certainly

---

(3) *Wesley's Works*, XIII., pp. 267-68.
(4) Smith's *History of Methodism in Ireland*, p. 71.
(5) Tyerman's *Life of Wesley*, III., p. 583.

an attempt to take a mote out of a brother's eye, by those whose own vision was obscured by a beam: for, however Wesley may have separated from the Church, they had done so much more. But these worthy ecclesiastics, who professed such zeal for the Establishment, did not see that they were the real separatists, in not only conducting service every Sabbath in church hours, but also in regularly administering the ordinances without either themselves or their chapel having the slightest recognition from the authorities. During this fracas Wesley sent at least one letter to the papers, in which he re-affirmed his life-long attachment to the Church, as unquestioned by the archbishops and bishops, and apparent in the course he had ever adopted, and replied to the objections which had been made to his conduct.[6] Such strife could not fail to cause profound sorrow to all who loved the prosperity of Zion. Many were in tears on account of it, and not a few terribly agitated, enquiring how this would end. Wesley replied with confidence — "in glory to God in the highest, peace on earth, and good-will among men," and so no doubt it did. People grew weary, and insisted that this violent and unmerited abuse should cease: and thus ended a controversy which brought lasting shame on those who originated it, and in the good providence of God brought forth the righteousness of His servant "as the light, and his judgment as the noon-day."

Meanwhile on April the 13th Wesley left the metropolis to make his last tour through the provinces. At Clonard, three or four times as many were present at the service as the building could contain, the power of God was remarkably present, and several were "pricked in the heart," including the master of the house. At Tyrrell's Pass, though the wind was piercingly cold, the multitude that had assembled obliged the evangelist to preach out of doors, after which he gave a plain account of the design of Methodism. At Mullingar the congregation in the court-house was small; but in Longford it was large and fervent. At Keenagh, also, where he was the guest of Mr. A. Kingston, the chapel could not contain the people.

At Athlone some of the leaders had, without reason, taken offence at Mr. Dinnen, the Assistant, who therefore cautioned one of them against imbibing the same prejudice, and warned him of the consequence. Misunderstanding this, he became very angry, others took part with him, and thus the Society was rent and torn. Wesley reasoned with the irate official, but in vain. "One might as well have talked to the north wind." So he gave him up to God,

---

(6) *Wesley's Works*, XIII., pp. 268-71.

and endeavoured to quench the flame among the people. On Sunday, as the hearers assembled in large numbers from the surrounding country, the chapel could not contain them; but the commanding officer having offered Wesley the use of any part of the barrack, he preached in the riding-house, a very spacious building, to a multitude of people. Some of the gentry especially, who had attended out of mere curiosity, were deeply impressed with the spirit and appearance of the venerable preacher, and declared that there seemed to be something superhuman about him.[7]

At Aughrim the service was held in the church, which was much more largely attended than when he was there before; many who had once been Romanists being present, who had attended church regularly after his previous visit. At Eyrecourt the church was well filled, and a large number of the hearers seemed to feel the word. At Birr, previously "one of the dullest places in Ireland," but now "one of the liveliest," the chapel and yard were full, and the time was one of special blessing. At Tullamore, in the beautiful new court-house, and at Brackagh Castle, the people listened with solemn and prayerful attention. At Portarlington "the congregation was exceedingly well dressed, but careless and ill-behaved." At Mountmellick the church was crowded with hearers, who were all attention; and at Maryborough the church, one of the most elegant he had seen in the kingdom, was thoroughly filled, although many of those present looked as if they had not been in a place of worship before. At Carlow, although the people were very civil, and many of them attentive, he did not think "the time of Carlow" had yet come. At Enniscorthy he preached in the place prepared for him, which he says "was large, but not very elegant;" however, God was there! At Wexford, where a chapel had been built during the preceding year, the service was held in the assembly room, and the congregation was large.

At Waterford evidently some difference of opinion had existed between him and Mr. Deaves, who probably was the lessee of the Wexford chapel, as to its settlement in accordance with the Deed Poll; but the first news he heard on his arrival was that Mr. Deaves was willing to settle the house in any way that Mr. Wesley desired. So with a relieved mind the venerable evangelist preached to a numerous congregation in the evening. The God of peace and love was in the midst, and His presence realized by the whole assembly. Next morning also there was a large congregation. Wesley met all

(7) *Irish Evangelist*, 1860, p. 82.

the Society, except eight or ten at breakfast on each of the two days he remained in the city, and closed his labours there by "strongly exhorting them all to rehearse no past grievances: and only to provoke one another to love and good works." At Cappoquin as he went up the street he was followed by a mob, hallooing and shouting with all their might, but a sentinel at the door of the barrack, in which the service was held, kept out the rabble, so there was a quiet congregation within.

At Cork, where he was the guest of Mr. Rogers,[8] the Lord had continued to bless His word to the salvation of many, especially among the soldiers; and it is probable more good would have been done, but for a few troublesome persons, who, under a pretence of standing up for the Church, hurt the minds of others. Notwithstanding every difficulty, the number of members had increased to six hundred and sixty, many of whom were much alive to God.[9] Wesley endeavoured to calm the feeling which had been excited among the people about separating from the Church, by preaching a sermon on Hebrews 5:4. In this discourse he showed the nature of the different offices in the Christian Church, ably vindicating the rights of lay preachers, and asserting that he did not knowingly vary from any rule of the Established Church, "unless in those few instances in which he judged there was an absolute necessity." This he considered was not separating from it, a course that he strongly deprecated.[10] Wesley administered the Lord's supper here to about four hundred and fifty communicants: and on the evening of the same day, says he preached with power to more than the house could contain, and afterwards to the Society, adding, "May God write it on their hearts! I am clear of their blood."

From Cork he went to Bandon, where he was the guest of Mr. T. Bennett. Here Messrs. J. Kerr and R. Bridge were stationed, who, having obtained the permission of the previous Conference, set about building a new chapel, the congregations having out-grown the old one on Kilbrogan hill. Ground was secured in the North Main street, opposite the present entrance to Kilbrogan church; and the erection was a square building, a little more than half the size of the present chapel, and two or three times as large as the old one. There were no class-rooms; but at the rear was the preacher's residence, which faced the river, with a garden in front. The opening service was con-

---

(8) *Wesley's Works*, XIII., p. 86.

(9) *Lives of Early Methodist Preachers*, IV., pp. 322-23.

(10) *Arminian Magazine*, 1790, p. 230.

ducted by Mr. Wesley on May 7th, when it was well filled, and he preached an impressive sermon from "To the Jew first and also to the Greek."[11] But he did not find the same spiritual life among the people as in Cork.

At Kinsale also a chapel was erected this year on the top of Compass hill, which served the Society there for about twenty-four years. At Kilfinnane[12] Wesley preached on "One thing is needful;" and next proceeded to Limerick, where he was the guest of the Rev. Mr. Ingram, and "wanted nothing the kingdom could afford." The chapel could not contain the congregation, and it seemed as if all were deeply sensible of the Divine presence. At Pallas the remains of the Palatines assembled from Ballingarrane, Courtmatrix, and Rathkeale; in each of which places a blessed revival had commenced, such as had not been known in this neighbourhood before. Large numbers were deeply convinced, many converted to God, and not a few perfected in love. Some of the Societies were doubled in their membership, and others increased six or even ten fold. At the service the people received the word gladly, and great was their rejoicing in the Lord.

At Kilchreest the congregation was so large that Wesley was obliged to preach out of doors, though it rained all the time. As he had not been well, this did him no good; but he continued his work until he came to Ballinrobe, when he had to give up, and let another conduct the service. Having had a day's rest, he went on to Castlebar, where he became much better and preached to a lively congregation. On meeting the Society he found it increased both in numbers and in grace. Here also he administered the Lord's supper, at which two of the Episcopal clergy were present and united. At Sligo, he was entertained in the barrack by Mr. Burgess, who invited a large party to meet him at dinner. During the repast the venerable minister suddenly laid down his knife and fork, clasped his hands, and looked up in the attitude of praise and prayer. Instantly every one was still and silent. He then gave out and sang, with great animation, the lines:—

> "And can we forget,
> In tasting our meat,
> The angelical food which ere long we shall eat;
> When enroll'd with the blest,
> In glory we rest,
> And for ever sit down at the heavenly feast?"

(11) *Irish Christian Advocate*, 1883, p. 317.
(12) Called in Wesley's Journal, Kilkenny, evidently an error.

A peculiar solemnity and hallowed feeling rested on all present. He preached in the evening, and says he never before saw such a congregation in the town, so numerous and serious, and again at five on the following morning. After breakfast his host and family bade a last farewell to their venerated friend, having the sad consciousness that they would see his face no more, and expecting "ne'er to look upon his like again."[13]

At Manorhamilton, where Wesley expected little good, he was surprised at the tokens of spiritual life; the power of God fell upon the congregation in a remarkable manner, so that scarcely anyone was unaffected. He then proceeded to Annadale, in associating with the genial host and hostess of which he soon forgot all the labours of the day. At Ballyconnell he was the guest of Mrs. Montgomery, whose son, Archibald, entered the itinerancy in 1794, and baptized her infant, who subsequently became a devoted and consistent member of the Society.[14] Here they had a comfortable meeting, and many found their desires after God increased. At Killashandra Wesley preached in a pleasant meadow to a numerous and attentive audience; and then went to Kilmore, where he was the guest of Mr. R. Creighton, and where a very large congregation assembled from all the country round. Having preached in the town-hall at Cavan, as he went through Ballyhaise the people collected, and would not be content until he came out of his chaise and spent some time with them in prayer. At this period the Smiths and Fergusons, of Drumliff, had lately joined the Society, and were very happy in God their Saviour.[15]

At Clones Wesley preached in the Danish fort to about four thousand people, who seemed ready to drink in every word. One of the hearers was William Ferguson, who in the following year entered the itinerancy, and became a most devoted, exemplary and useful preacher.[16] At Brookeborough, where the congregation was exceedingly large, the venerable evangelist was the guest of Mr. M'Carthy, of Abbey Lodge, whose son, then a lad of thirteen, passed to the home above in 1872, having been spared to live ninety-six years, and who all through life remembered distinctly, and took a special delight in speaking of the time when he sat at the feet and listened to the instruction of the venerable founder of Methodism.[17] Wesley says a more affectionate

(13) *Memoirs of the Rev. Joseph Burgess*, pp. 29-30.
(14) *Primitive Wesleyan Methodist Magazine*, 1845, pp. 234-36.
(15) *Lanktree's Narrative*, p. 8.
(16) *Life of the Rev. F. Tackaberry*, p. 187.

family he had not found in the kingdom. On the morning after the service, as they were talking together, one and another fell on their knees, and "most of them burst into tears and earnest cries, the like of which he had seldom heard, so that they scarcely knew how to part."

At Enniskillen Wesley preached in the market-house to an unwieldy multitude, and at Sidaire to the old steady congregation. At Kirlish Lodge there was a large audience, many of whom came from far. Thence he went to Moyle glebe, the residence of the Rev. Dr. Wilson, whose guest he was, and of whom he speaks as a man of uncommon learning, particularly in Oriental languages. In the evening a numerous congregation assembled in the castle yard, but as soon as Wesley began to preach the rain commenced, which led some of the hearers to leave: so he prayed aloud that God would stay the windows of heaven, and He did so, the people returned and were deeply impressed with this marked answer to prayer. Next morning the following characteristic incident occurred: Shortly after family worship, which had been conducted by the venerable evangelist, Dr. Wilson said to him: "My wife was so delighted with your prayer, that she has been looking for it in the Prayer-Book but cannot find it; I wish you could point it out to me." "My dear brother," said Wesley, "I cannot, because that prayer came down from heaven, and I sent it up there again."[18]

At Londonderry he found "a neat, convenient preaching-house just finished, a society increasing and well united, and the whole city prejudiced in its favour." Here he was the guest of Mr. Knox, who invited to his house a number of clergymen, including the Rev. J. Pitt Kennedy, a son of the gentleman with whom Wesley dined in 1765, and who was then Mayor of the city. During the course of dinner Mr. Wesley, addressing this minister, said that he had received from his father, twenty-four years previously, a most useful suggestion as to the best means of reconciling two parties at variance, which was by leading each to give full vent to everything which formed matter of mutual complaint, and then to take that moment for bringing them to mutual reconciliation; adding he had often followed that course, and seldom found it unsuccessful.[19] In regard to Mr. Wesley, Mr. Knox writes: "I was delighted to find his cheerfulness in no respect abated. It was too obvious that his bodily frame was sinking; but his spirit was as alert as ever;

(17) *Primitive Wesleyan Methodist Magazine*, 1872, p. 315.
(18) *Methodist Recorder*, 1879, p. 122.
(19) *Life of the Rev. H. Moore*, p. 300.

and he was little less the life of the company he happened to be in than he had been four-and-twenty years before, when I first knew him. Such unclouded sunshine of the breast, in the deepest winter of age, and on the felt verge of eternity, bespoke a mind whose recollections were as unsullied as its present sensations were serene."[20]

In passing through Newtownlimavady Wesley was informed that there was a congregation waiting for him: so he proceeded to the chapel, and found it filled with most attentive hearers, and the power of God was among them. At Coleraine the Society was just after his own heart, "in spirit, in carriage, and even in dress." The services were held in the large meeting house, which was well filled. But he was much concerned to find that the junior preacher, John Stephens, who had been received on trial at the preceding Conference, was far gone in consumption. This promising and devoted young man only survived a few days, and then died in the full triumph of faith.

At Ballymena and Antrim there were large congregations in the meeting houses. At Lisburn the evangelist preached in what he calls the new chapel, but in reality was the old one which had been enlarged and improved through the liberality of Mr. Johnson. It is described by Wesley as the largest and best finished preaching-house in the north of Ireland. Amongst those present at the service here was Mr. Thomas Collier,[21] who was then led to give his heart to God. He afterwards settled in Ballynacoy, where his house became a centre of religious light in what was then a very dark and benighted district of country.

In Belfast Wesley preached in the first Presbyterian meeting-house,[22] Rosemary street, which had been erected six years previously at a cost of £2,300; and he pronounces it "the most complete place of worship" he had ever seen, "being beautiful in the highest degree." It was so crowded that it was with no little difficulty he got in: and he had great liberty of speech in proclaiming here the glorious Gospel of the grace of God. One of those present was a young man, named Joseph Bradbury, who then received his first religious impressions, and soon after obtained the knowledge of salvation by the remission of sins. For nearly forty years he was a devoted, exemplary and faithful leader in the Society.[23]

(20) Tyerman's *Life of Wesley*, III., p. 577.

(21) Grandfather of the Revs. James and Robert Collier.

(22) Now occupied by the Unitarians.

(23) *Wesleyan Methodist Magazine*, 1829, p. 430.

At Newtownards Wesley preached in the Presbyterian meeting-house to a multitude of people, all of whom seemed much affected. At Portaferry also the meeting-house was placed at his disposal, and the large audience was most attentive. At Strangford the vicar invited him to the church, which was well filled, and the power of God was mightily present. At Downpatrick the evangelist preached to a numerous congregation in the grove, and afterwards met the Society, "now well established in grace, and still increasing both in numbers and in strength." At Tanderagee there was such a number present as he had not seen since coming into the country, and all listened with quiet and deep attention. At Killyman he was the guest of the Rev. C. Caulfield, and preached at the door of his house. At Dungannon the service was held in the castle-yard, which contained a large auditory. At Blackwatertown the word sank deep into many hearts, for the Lord was in the midst of the congregation. At Armagh there was once more a multitude of people in the avenue of Mr. M'Geough, who was then just tottering over the grave. Amongst those present upon whose minds deep and lasting impressions for good were made were John Waugh, who subsequently entered the itinerancy,[24] and a young man named Simon Reilly, who for half a century received the preachers, with much cordiality, in his house at Drummond.[25]

At Newry Wesley preached again in the Presbyterian meeting-house, which was well filled, and it proved a season of rich spiritual blessing. Having also proclaimed the glad tidings of salvation in the market-place, Dundalk, to a large and attentive congregation; at Drogheda, to a tolerably quiet auditory; and at Swords, he returned to Dublin. Here he preached, administered the Lord's supper, and visited the classes, which contained a little more than one thousand members, after he had excluded above one hundred. He then went to Rosanna, the residence of Mrs. Tighe, sister-in-law of Mrs. Blatchford, where he preached in the great hall to about one hundred of the most influential persons in the neighbourhood, most of whom seemed to feel as well as hear. At Wicklow he held the service in the court-house, and then returned to the metropolis.

The Conference met on July the 3rd, and concluded on the 7th. Ten candidates were admitted on trial. There was one death, in addition to the two already referred to — that of Francis Frazier, who entered the itinerancy in 1786. He is described as a good young man, and an acceptable preacher,

---

(24) Ibid., 1854, p. 384.
(25) Ibid., 1859, p. 96.

who died in great peace. The increase in membership during the year amounted to nearly one thousand eight hundred. It is rather amusing to read the following minute — "Except in extraordinary cases, every preacher is to go to bed before ten o'clock." This year the first pastoral Address was written. It was signed by Mr. Wesley, subsequently adopted verbatim by the British Conference, and consists of a statement of the increasing pressure that had come on the Contingent Fund, and an appeal for further assistance, urged on the ground of the increasing number and wealth of the Society. This Conference, which in the main consisted of Irishmen, as the great majority of the English brethren had retired from the country, included such honoured and familiar names as J. Crook, T. Barber, G. Brown, J. Kerr, M. Joyce, W. Griffith, J. M'Donald, M. Stewart, and many others. Of these brethren Wesley's final testimony is a high tribute to their sterling worth. He says — "I never had between forty and fifty such preachers together in Ireland before: all of them, we had reason to hope, alive to God, and earnestly devoted to His service. I never saw such a number of preachers before so unanimous in all points, particularly as to leaving the Church, which none of them had the least thought of. It is no wonder that there has been this year so large an increase of the Society." And again, "I found such a body of men as I hardly believed could have been found together in Ireland: men of so sound experience, so deep piety, and so strong understanding. I am convinced they are no way inferior to the English Conference, except it be in number"[26]

On the Conference Sunday, Wesley and his preachers, together with a large number of the members in the city, attended the service in St. Patrick's. "The Dean," says he, "preached a serious, useful sermon: and we had such a company of communicants as I suppose had scarce been seen there together for above a hundred years." The Friday following was observed as a day of fasting and prayer, chiefly for the increase of the work of God, and was concluded with a very solemn watchnight service.

On Sunday, July the 12th, Wesley preached his farewell sermon to a crowded and deeply affected congregation. At the conclusion he gave out the hymn beginning — "Come, let us join our friends above," commented on its sentiments, and pronounced it the sweetest hymn his brother ever wrote. Having administered the Lord's supper to several hundreds of the Society, he dined in the house of Mr. R. D'Olier, commended in prayer the family to the protection and blessing of the Almighty, and proceeded to the packet,

(26) *Wesley's Works*, IV., pp. 462-63.

accompanied by several members of the household and other friends, who were joined by a multitude at the quay. The scene here was most touching as Wesley bade adieu to Ireland for ever. Before going on board he gave out a hymn, and the crowd joined him in singing. He then knelt down, and asked God to bless them and their families, the Church, and especially Ireland. Shaking of hands followed, many wept, and not a few fell on the old man's neck and kissed him. He went on deck, the vessel moved, and then with his hands still lifted in prayer the winds of heaven wafted him from an island which he dearly loved, and the Irish Methodists "saw his face no more."[27]

Let us pause here and look at the noble work this honoured servant of God had been instrumental in accomplishing in Ireland. He visited this country, as has been stated, twenty-one times, embracing about five years and a half of his public life. Nor did he come unaided, men of kindred spirit accompanied him, and Ireland should never be unmindful of what she thus owes to English missionary zeal. At an early period several leaders in London expressed their regret that Wesley and his brother should expend so much time on this side of the channel, and send so many preachers here; but he responded with characteristic brevity — "Have patience and Ireland will repay you."

These words were prophetic, and had been blessedly and gloriously fulfilled long before he had ended his last visit to the country. Only a little more than half a century had elapsed since the introduction of Methodism, and notwithstanding fierce and persistent opposition, it had made amazing strides. Although Roman Catholics and Protestants, Episcopalians and Presbyterians alike opposed its progress, and endeavoured to crush its very existence, the proclamation of the Gospel had been made through almost the length and breadth of the land, and everywhere had been attended with signal success. The members of the Methodist Society multiplied, and its sphere of labour extended until its chapels numbered eighty-two, preachers sixty-five, and members upwards of fourteen thousand. From amongst the converts of Irish Methodism the Lord raised up a large staff of earnest devoted Christian workers, including not less than one hundred and thirty-seven who had entered the active work of the itinerancy. Some of these were princes in Israel, men who occupied a foremost place among the ministers of their day, such as William Thompson, Henry Moore, Adam Clarke and Walter Griffith.

The influence of Irish Methodism, however, extended far beyond the pale

(27) *Anecdotes of the Wesleys*, pp. 311-12.

of its membership. The Christian Churches of the land began to awake and shake themselves from the dust. When Wesley entered on his noble and self-denying mission he was regarded with suspicion, reproaches were heaped on him, and persecution followed him. But one of the high recompenses vouchsafed by the Divine Master was, that he was permitted to live to vindicate the purity of his motives, and to win the esteem of the more generous of his adversaries. On June the 26th, 1785, he writes: "I am become, I know not how, an honourable man. The scandal of the cross is ceased, and all the kingdom, rich and poor, Romanists and Protestants, behave with courtesy, nay, and seeming good-will! It seems as if I had well-nigh finished my course, and our blessed Lord was giving me an honourable discharge."[29] Many of the ministers and members of the Protestant Churches saw that through the influence of Methodism their membership was increased, their spiritual life deepened, and their ministerial ranks filled here and there with men of piety, zeal and Christian worth. Large numbers of all classes, who did not identify themselves with the Society, came under the quickening influence of the truth, as preached by the itinerants. Nor were the fruits of Irish Methodism confined to this country. The good seed was carried hence to France, Newfoundland, the West Indies, the Canadas, and the United States of America: and a glorious spiritual harvest was reaped, the extent of which eternity alone will reveal. Not to dwell upon the numerous and powerful influences for good which, unrecorded, and it may be unobserved, went forth from this country, it should be remembered that large numbers of the peasantry, who in humble homesteads had been brought to a saving knowledge of the truth, emigrated to distant lands, and proved a sanctifying leaven in the land of their adoption. Besides, there are countless unseen influences, the results of which can never be tabulated; for

> "Our many deeds, the thoughts that we have thought,
>   They go out from us thronging every hour;
>   And in them all is folded up a power
>   That on the earth doth move them to and fro;
>   And mighty are the marvels they have wrought
>   In hearts we know not, and may never know."

Fourteen hundred years ago Ireland was the great centre from which Divine light radiated through the western part of this continent. It was by means of Hibernian missionaries that two-thirds of Saxon England, the whole

---

(29) *Wesley's Works*, XIII., p. 65.

of Scotland, all Belgium, Switzerland, and the chief parts of Germany were turned from dumb idols to serve the living God. And so, in the last century, through God's blessing, Irish Methodism performed a similar work in the British Dominion and United States of America: and thus claims to stand in the same relation to the largest group of Churches in the New World, as the Irish Church occupied in the Old, when she was the Mother Church of Northern Europe.

> "When He first the work begun,
> Small and feeble was His day:
> Now the word doth swiftly run,
> Now it wins its widening way:
> More and more it spreads and grows,
> Ever mighty to prevail;
> Sin's strongholds it now o'erthrows,
> Shakes the trembling gates of hell."

This marks the end of the original Volume 1 of the 3 volume set.

CHAPTER 20

1789 (continued)

ABOUT the time of the Rev. J. Wesley's last visit to Ireland a most important movement commenced, which aimed at the conversion of the Roman Catholic population, by preaching to them in their own language. Although similar efforts had been put forth, attended with more or less success, they were unorganized, comparatively few in number, and exceedingly limited in their sphere of operation. A translation of the New Testament into Irish commenced by Bishop Walsh, and completed by William Daniel, was published in 1602. Twenty or thirty years subsequently, Bishop Bedell, being most desirous to provide the people with the whole Bible in their own tongue, engaged one of the best native scholars in the country to undertake the work, and so deeply was the good bishop interested in its execution, that at the age of sixty he commenced to learn the language himself, hoping to be able to render some assistance in the way of revision. He was not, however, permitted to proceed in this noble undertaking without disturbance. Romanists, of course, looked on it with aversion; but, strange to say, so also did some of his own brethren. Archbishop Laud, then in the zenith of his power, regarded it with disfavour, and prevailed on the Irish Viceroy to concur with him. The translator was subjected to annoyance and persecution, and the work when finished remained about half a century in manuscript.

The Lower House of Convocation, in 1703, passed a resolution desiring the appointment in every parish of an Irish-speaking minister, Trinity College made arrangements for teaching the language, and the Society for Promoting Christian Knowledge offered assistance. The practical results, however, of these promising proposals were exceedingly small, being confined to two or three parishes. The Rev. Nicholas Brown, rector of Rossorry in Fermanagh, and the Rev. Walter Atkins, rector of Middleton, read the liturgy and instructed the Romanists in their own language, with considerable success. The poor Catholics showed the greatest interest in hearing the services of the Church read in Irish, and when their priests endeavoured to dissuade them from attending by saying that these prayers were stolen from the Church of Rome, an old man shrewdly replied, "If so, they have stolen the best, as thieves generally do." The example of these two clergymen was followed by a few others; but as the Government discountenanced these efforts, and several bishops, in consequence, threw obstacles in the way, the good of immortal souls was sacrificed to a miserable and short-sighted policy.

In 1738, Dr. Samuel Madden, a devoted and influential philanthropist, warmly advocated the employment of a number of itinerant clergy to preach to the natives in Irish; and Bishop Berkeley not only supported the project, but intimated that, in the lack of ordained missionaries, persons less educated but conversant with Irish, and well instructed in the first principles of religion, should be sent among the people. These proposals, however, did not lead to any practical results; and nothing further was attempted by the Established Church during the last century.

Such an important means of usefulness was soon recognised and employed by the Methodists. Thomas Walsh, the first Irish Wesleyan missionary, was a perfect master of the language, fully alive to the power for good he thus possessed, and animated by a passion to save souls; he seized every available opportunity of proclaiming to his fellow-countrymen in their own tongue the Gospel of the grace of God, and with wonderful success. Hundreds of the Irish heard the word with joy, received it into their hearts, and brought forth fruit in lives consecrated to the service of Christ. But Walsh was alone in this work, had ample employment in the regular duties of the itinerancy, and his career though brilliant was brief.

The preaching of Wesley and his coadjutors was not without indirect benefit to the native population. In the counties where the Irish language was most spoken, Methodism won numerous triumphs, many of the upper and middle ranks of society embraced the truth, and in some cases these persons were familiar with Irish, and became faithful interpreters of the word preached to their neighbours, servants, and workpeople, who were thus brought to a saving knowledge of God. Frequently, when the preacher stopped at the house of one of these gentlemen, the schoolmaster and other Roman Catholics in the neighbourhood were invited, and the evenings spent in reading the Irish Bible, comparing it with the English version, and making such useful and practical observations as would be suggested. These efforts, however beneficial, could be brought into but limited operation, and were by no means commensurate with the moral necessities of the people.

During Dr. Coke's tour through Ireland in 1786, an incident occurred of little importance in itself yet deeply interesting as leading to very blessed and glorious results. When in Sligo, being impressed with the necessity of preaching to the Irish-speaking population in their own language, he asked Charles Graham if he could do so, and was told that he could not, having never attempted it, although he could speak in Irish very well. The doctor wondered very much at this, but Graham adroitly answered, by asking if he considered that every Christian who spoke English could preach in it. So the conversation ended; but the question did not rest there. The young disciple thought over the subject, made the attempt, and succeeded beyond his expectations. A vast concourse assembled, and God was present in power and blessing. The Romanists declared they never heard anything like it, and encouraged the evangelist to preach for them again, which he gladly did. Soon the priest took alarm, affirmed that the Methodist was a wolf in sheep's clothing, and forbade any of his flock to go near him. The Lord then opened another door at some distance, where all appeared hopeful for a time, and many heard the word of life in their own loved tongue. But here also persecution arose, for the Episcopal minister as well as the priest opposed this new way of working. Thus the Lord prepared His servant for a wider field and greater usefulness.

When Mr. Black came to the Sligo circuit, after the Conference of 1789, he told Graham that he had invited Bartley Campbell, "the Lough Derg Pilgrim," as he was called, to come and assist him in the work. This uncouth but devoted evangelist came in due course, but found to his great sorrow that Mr. Black had been suddenly called to the home above, having been drowned a few days before while bathing. However, Graham and Campbell determined to persevere in their contemplated work, and travelled through the country, preaching in Irish; multitudes flocked to hear, especially Romanists, and great numbers were converted.

Invitations were sent to the zealous evangelists to visit neighbouring circuits, and they responded to one from Mr. Barber of Longford, where they laboured with great success. After some time Campbell returned home, and Graham, at the earnest request of the Assistant, remained on the circuit until Conference, leaving his wife and farm to take care of themselves. Mrs. Graham wrote to him, thus, "Go, and labour away for God; I will abide by the stuff, and share the last penny to sustain you in all your expenses." "This," said he, "was as fresh oil to the wheel, and I bounded as a hart." On this circuit he had full scope for his talents, preaching daily in English and Irish, and with great acceptance and success.

As has been stated ten preachers were received on trial at the Conference this year. These included Samuel Wood of Waterford, and James Irwin of the county of Armagh, who had been called out during the previous twelve months, Thomas Ridgeway of Edenderry, Andrew Hamilton, jun. of Londonderry, James M'Quigg, and Thomas Worrell, each of whom subsequently was made exceedingly useful.

While thus the Lord blessed the labours of His servants, they were also cheered in witnessing the triumphant end of some of those who had been led to the Saviour. One of these, Jane Newland, claims special notice. She was an humble but devoted member of the Society in Dublin. In August, this excellent woman was seized with a nervous fever, from which she but partially recovered; a weakness remained, attended with a violent cough, and pain in her side, which terminated in death. At intervals during her illness she expressed herself thus: "I am now going into eternity. Zion has been all my care, my cry has ever been, 'Lord, prosper Zion.' I have often felt so much for its prosperity, that I thought my heart would break. O how have I mourned over the careless! I feel a hope that God will bless the Methodists more powerfully. I love them, they are near my heart. Come, let us languish for more of the love of Christ. Let us not be content till we bathe in that ocean,

— till we are lost and swallowed up in God. O the delightful days I now spend! The language of my heart is, 'Lord, let me hear, see, and feel nothing but Thee.' My soul is ravished with the thought that I shall shortly be with my dear Lord. He has been pleased to show me great things of late. I have been so led to view the glories of the invisible world, that I have often desired neither to see nor hear any person or thing around me. One day in particular I was apparently in a swoon, and felt as if the curtain was raised, and I was permitted to view my Beloved on the throne, and the elders, cherubim and seraphim, and all the company falling down before Him, and crying, 'The Lord God Omnipotent reigneth! Hallelujah!' I was quite overcome, and could say nothing but, 'O the glory! O the glory!' I feel my spirit united to those of the invisible world, and see the angels rejoicing to meet me. They shout the praises of the Redeemer, and I shall partake in the song which now overwhelms me. O glorious triumph! Who would not wish to die? Once I thought I could not leave my friends, they were so dear to me; but now I can with joy bid them all farewell. O Jesus, what hast Thou done for me! Glory, eternal glory to Thee, that ever I was born to taste such joys! O that all the world knew them!

> 'None is like Jeshurun's God,
> So great, so strong, so high.'

"O 'the unsearchable riches of Christ'! Help me to praise Him.

"I am now drawing very near to eternity, and the thought of dying delights my soul." At another time, seeing her mother standing by her side, she looked steadfastly at her; and, having grasped her hand, said: "I am going to leave you, but God will be your Friend. I feel no more at the thoughts of death, than at lying on this bed." She then sang:

> "Fearless of hell and ghastly death,
> I'll break through every foe;
> The wings of love and arms of faith
> Will bear me conqueror through;"

and immediately added: "I will shout 'Victory, victory!' when I get on the other side of Jordan." From this she seemed to gather new life, and cried out as in an ecstasy, "O glorious eternity! glorious eternity!" After a short sleep she repeated the lines:

> "Cease, fond nature, cease thy strife,
> And let me languish into life."

And then cried in a joyful tone: "I shall soon be at rest. O, it is a pleasing thought that I am so near home! I will tell them on the heavenly shore you are all hastening home." She paused, and then added: "Shout the Name I love — Sweet Jesus! Precious Jesus! O my loving Saviour, I had no idea of the great things Thou hast done for my soul." When some one spoke to her of the rest she would shortly enjoy, she calmly said:

> "I shall behold His face,
> I shall His power adore;
> And sing the wonders of His grace
> For evermore."

At length she became so weak that her voice failed her for some time; but, having recovered it, she said: "Who would not live to God in their health?" And then, with evident solicitude: "O, what delays His chariot-wheels?" Being asked whether she found Jesus precious, she replied, "Lovely, altogether lovely! Help me to praise Him." And added: "My tongue grows thick; that is delightful; everything which brings me nearer eternity increases my joy." She then cried with a strong voice, "The Lord God omnipotent reigneth! Sing to the Lord a joyful song. Let all the earth praise Him. 'Glory, blessing, and power, be to Him that sitteth upon the throne, and to the Lamb for ever and ever.'" On the morning of the day on which she died she said: "Come, Lord Jesus, and let me behold Thy glory. What are all my sufferings now I am come to a death-bed? My breath will not admit of time to talk of anything but Jesus." After having awoke from a short sleep, she said: "Whenever I fall into a slumber, I dream of Divine things. Just now I thought I was in a delightful pasture, conversing with one who said, 'You will finish your course this day.' This indeed is victory. I shall soon be wafted far above on the wings of angels." She asked what o'clock it was; and, having been told it was ten, replied with a degree of surprise, "What? ten, and not gone yet?" and then added, in a soft voice, "I am going to glory." Some one who came to see her repeated the words: "O the pain, the bliss of dying!" She answered: "The bliss, the bliss! The pain is nothing," — though at the time her sufferings were exquisite. Soon afterwards she desired to be turned in her bed, said, "I am now easy," and then, looking steadfastly at her mother, pressed her hand, and added, "I have fought the good fight." These were her last words; after which she lay quiet for a few minutes, and, without a struggle or groan, sweetly fell asleep in Jesus.

Turning our attention to other gospel triumphs. In the north the truth as taught by the Methodists had to contend not only with the doctrines of the

Romish Church, but with the rigid Calvinism of one set of Presbyterians, and the Unitarianism of another and highly influential body. There were some interesting converts from the latter. One of these was Thomas Brown, who was brought into great distress about his sins and saw no possible way of deliverance except that which he had been taught to despise as foolishness — that of faith in the Incarnate God as the propitiation. His distress increased more and more till "One day," said he, "I fell on my knees in an agony, and said 'O, Lord, if Jesus Christ is God, let me know it.' Quick as the lightning's flash, the Saviour was revealed to my inmost soul, and I cried aloud, 'My Lord and my God.'" No sooner was this young man made happy in the love of Christ than he began to feel for those whom he saw living regardless of their salvation, and remaining in that awful state of guilt and danger out of which he had been so blessedly delivered; and through the Divine blessing on his efforts many were awakened and turned to God.

Young Brown, having given indications of those superior ministerial talents, for which he was subsequently distinguished, was employed as a local preacher, and sent to the county of Donegal. Here, William Hamilton and he were the means of introducing Methodism into the town of Ballyshannon, under rather stormy auspices. A room in the barrack was secured for holding a service, and many assembled, including a number of rowdies, who blew out the candles, and then began to use their fists very freely. Brown fled out of the town for his life, but finding himself alone resolved to live or die with his brethren, and returning to the scene of conflict met the mob in hot pursuit of William Hamilton, and turned and pursued the preacher with them until they came to the road leading to the house where the servants of God were entertained. Here he found several of the members wounded and bleeding. Nothing daunted he published for another service on the following Sunday evening; but when the time came, no one would accompany him into Ballyshannon, as the rowdies had vowed vengeance against any of the Methodists who dared to enter the town. Brown, however, having disguised himself in the clothes of a stonemason, went, escaped their observation, and got a room in the house of John Hanley; the commanding officer sent a number of soldiers for the protection of the preacher, and the Freemasons also came to his help. Two or three times during the meeting the door was opened by spies sent to reconnoitre, who when they saw how the land lay, went away. Soon afterwards Brown formed a class, which became very large. He also went to many new places, sometimes wading through deep waters in order to preach to the people.[1]

At this time Mr. Burgess was quartered in Belturbet, where he had become a member of the Society ten years previously. The friends in the town had in the meantime erected a neat chapel, but had not been able to furnish it with a pulpit, so he supplied this lack. He was also encouraged by Mr. Joseph Armstrong, who had charge of the circuit, to speak in the name of the Lord. Accordingly he went in company with a friend to Enniskillen, where he preached his first sermon. After this he found his mind greatly relieved, and embraced all convenient opportunities of calling sinners to repentance. His preaching caused a great sensation in the barrack, and throughout the town. Many assembled to hear, and it pleased God to give him several seals to his ministry. Lieutenant Carrothers, who had been a regular attendant at church and the Lord's table, and on that account thought himself a very good Christian, was convinced of sin the first time he heard Mr. Burgess preach, and led to feel that he had only been saying "Lord, Lord," without doing the will of his Father in heaven. He became a member of the Society, was converted, and some years subsequently wrote to Mr. Burgess, saying, that his health was declining, but he had a good hope through grace of heaven; and, added he, "When I get there, next to my Saviour, I shall have to thank you, my dear Joseph, as the instrument of my salvation." His end was peace.

Soon after Mr. Burgess began to preach one of the quartermasters went to hear him, seemed much affected, and as he left exclaimed, "Did ever any one speak like that man? and the beauty of it is that when he describes a real Christian, he draws his own character." About the same time as one of the soldiers' wives, a thoughtless and turbulent woman, stood at her door, and saw him pass, she thought, "There is a man that is going to heaven; but where am I going?" Her slumbering conscience was instantly aroused, and answered, as with a voice of thunder, "to hell." This was not a transient conviction; she was brought under a deep sense of her sinfulness and danger, began to attend the means of grace, broke off her evil practices, and earnestly sought Divine mercy. She became a changed woman, and it is to be hoped continued steadfast in the way of righteousness.

Shortly before the regiment left Belturbet, Mr. Burgess was invited to Ballyhaise, where he was entertained by a man who did a good business as a blacksmith, and also had a small farm. He was the principal support of Methodism in the town, received the preachers regularly; and when the

(1) *Irish Evangelist*, 1873, p. 26.

quarterly meetings were held used to provide a plentiful dinner for those who attended, many of whom had to come a considerable distance. There was then in Ballyhaise, a young lady in a delicate state of health, and seriously concerned for the salvation of her soul. Having been much profited by hearing the Methodist preachers she wished to join the Society; but to this her husband, a local surgeon, was decidedly opposed. He had formed the opinion that the preachers were a set of ignorant enthusiasts, who went about to get a livelihood, and though he did not prohibit his wife from hearing them, he feared it would greatly lower his respectability as well as her own. When, however, informed that Mr. Burgess was coming, the thought arose that here certainly was a man who did not preach for temporal gain, whom therefore he would hear. He listened very attentively to the important truths, which were earnestly explained and enforced; and, at the close of the service, respectfully saluted the preacher and thanked him for the sermon. Not long afterwards Mr. Burgess received a letter from him stating that since he heard that discourse he had been seeking and had at length happily found redemption in the blood of Christ; and that he and his wife being of one heart and one mind had joined the Society, and were resolved through Divine grace to be wholly given up to the service of God. He subsequently became a very devoted man, zealously engaged in promoting the spiritual welfare of his fellow-creatures, and proved a great blessing to the neighbourhood.

But to pass from the county of Cavan to that of Armagh. Thomas Shillington, at this time a young man of twenty-two, resided at Aghagallon, and occasionally was present at the Wesleyan services till his father took a farm for him at Drumcree in the neighbourhood of Derryanvil, where he attended them regularly; and the preaching of the word was made a great blessing to him. The report soon reached his parents that he had joined the Methodists, and when they questioned him on the subject found he was only a hearer. His father said there was not much harm in that, provided he did not make a practice of it; but afterwards strongly objected to it, and used all possible means to prevent it. Through God's help, however, the young man stood firm, and united himself to the Society, with the hearty determination that this people should be his people, and their God his God — a step he never retraced or regretted. Six weeks after he had thus become a Methodist he was appointed to take charge of a class, and thus entered upon a course of extensive and great usefulness.

In the district of country in which Mr. Shillington resided, at Bluestone, in the parish of Seagoe, a Sunday school was opened during this year. A rock or immense stone formerly stood there, at a place where three roads met, and was dreadfully famous as the rendezvous of lawless bands, who posted on it their illegal and threatening notices. At length some murderers having been seized, tried, and convicted, were executed on this spot, and their remains, together with the bluestone, buried there. The place, however, has retained the name, and thus a memorial of what it once was. The founder of the school was Joseph Malcomson, who was spared for about a half a century to work for Christ, and rejoice in the abundant blessing which rested on his labours. Bluestone, from being a byword for all that is evil, thus became one of the most orderly and peaceable neighbourhoods in the county.

Another Sunday school, established at this period in Armagh, was at Derryscollop. An excellent leader named Thomas Taylor, came to reside in this most abandoned village. He was deeply impressed with the low moral tone of the rising generation; and the desire was awakened to try and stem the torrent of vice by religious instruction on the Sabbath, and in this he succeeded. He evinced great interest in the scholars, not only teaching them on Sunday, but also meeting in class during the week such of them as gave evidence of conviction of sin. One of those thus impressed was Thomas Wilson, who for more than half a century proved a faithful servant of God.[2]

At this period there resided at Willmount, near Lisburn, the Stewarts, — lineal descendants of the ancestors of the Earl of Galloway. Mr. Stewart was a gentleman of considerable influence and strict integrity; but an Arian, and much opposed to Evangelical religion. Some of the family, however, by witnessing the consistent Christian conduct and triumphant death of a servant maid, a member of the Methodist Society, were led to see the difference between the cold heartless morality preached by their own ministers, and the doctrines of grace taught in the sacred Scriptures. They were thus brought into connection with Methodism, invited the preachers to their house, and Mrs. Stewart and her nine daughters were savingly converted.[3]

In time the Rev. Thomas Higginson, an Evangelical clergyman was introduced to the family by the Methodists, and he brought the Rev. B. W. Mathias, — then curate of Drumgooland, — to the house. These clergymen came once a fortnight and conducted religious services, which were attended

_____

(2) *Primitive Wesleyan Methodist Magazine*, 1849, p 29.

(3) Three of the Misses Stewart subsequently were married to Evangelical clergymen:- the Revs. B W. Mathias, Blayney Mitchell, and Edward Hoare, curate of St. Mary's, Leicester.

by large numbers. Thus Mr. Stewart, who had consented to the visits of the servants of God merely to gratify his family, was awakened to a sense of his sinfulness and danger. The Spirit of God gradually dispersed the darkness of his spiritual night, and the Sun of Righteousness arose, shedding heavenly light into his soul, so that he was enabled to say, "My Lord, and my God." His faith was subsequently greatly strengthened by the happy death of one of his daughters, who rejoiced in the prospect of entering into the immediate presence of her God and Saviour. Shortly after this bereavement Mr. Stewart fell into declining health, and was observed to be much given to thought and prayer. On one occasion, believing his end was approaching, he called his family around him, and entreated them to devote themselves wholly to the Lord. "You know not;" said he, "how much I disliked and despised those whom I now know to be the people of God, and how much I was opposed to His Word, — now it is my delight." He then requested to have the twenty-third Psalm read, and when it was finished, repeated, "Yea, though I walk through the valley of the shadow of death, I will fear no evil: for Thou art with me." "Yes, dear Saviour, Thou art with me! Oh! it is like meeting a loved friend to lean on for support and protection, when surrounded by distress and danger." And in this spirit of firm faith and joyful hope he entered into rest.

Mr. Bates was this year reappointed, with Nebuchadnezzar Lee, to Omagh, a circuit, to the work of which he felt himself wholly unequal. Some persons advised him to write to Mr. Wesley requesting to be sent elsewhere; but considering the time required for a change, and the loss the cause might sustain by delay, he resolved to take up his cross in the name of the Lord, and set off to his appointed sphere. His position here proved exceedingly trying and discouraging. Left to himself, — his colleague having retired from the work, — in frail health, and the season one of unusual severity, with the accommodation so bad, that he was often obliged to sleep in damp beds or remain in wet clothes, yet he bravely struggled on, at times tempted to retire, but in view of the value of precious souls and the price paid for their redemption, compelled to do or die. The Lord so supported him that he was enabled to remain at his post until the end of the year; and he was cheered to find he had not laboured in vain or spent his strength for nought. Fatigue and exposure, however, had done their work, in sowing the seeds of disease which compelled him, at Conference, to become a supernumerary. He lingered a few years in much feebleness and pain, and then, full of hope and joy, fell asleep in the arms of his adorable Redeemer.

CHAPTER 21

1790

ON January 23rd, 1790, a young man named Matthew Lanktree, a native of Oldcastle, visited at Drumliff, in the county of Cavan, some friends, who had recently become Methodists, accompanied them on the following Sabbath morning to the chapel at Ballyhaise, and was much impressed with all he saw and heard. The preacher was Mr. James Irwin, the house was well filled, and the whole congregation appeared influenced by the spirit of devotion. They sang with melody, prayed with fervency, and heard the word with affectionate attention. All was simplicity and love; and young Lanktree was constrained to own that God was with this people of a truth. In the evening he attended a meeting, conducted by William Phair, a leader whose exhortations and prayers powerfully impressed his mind. On the following Lord's day he commenced meeting with these simple, earnest servants of God, and was brought into deep distress about his soul. The sinfulness of sin, the depravity of his nature, the hour of death, the day of judgment, eternity, and his utter helplessness, all passed before his mind in a most impressive manner, and led him to cry earnestly to Him who is able to save. At length, one Sabbath morning as Mr. Joseph Armstrong preached with great unction from "Jesus Christ, and Him crucified," the word came with power to the anxious seeker, and as he returned to Drumliff, God revealed Himself in mercy to his soul.

Having thus obtained a sense of sins forgiven, it became the earnest desire of the young convert that his kinsfolk and friends might be made partakers of the same glorious blessing; so he wrote immediately telling the great things the Lord had done for him. Mr. William Wilson was then stationed in Clones. He had been a teacher in a school near Corneary, in the county of Cavan, entered the itinerancy in 1788, and was a man of deep piety and thorough acquaintance with the Word of God. By a remarkable Providence, just at this time he felt his mind strongly drawn towards Oldcastle, and accordingly went there, and was in the house of the Lanktrees when Matthew's letter reached them. A service was at once arranged for, during which a profound impression was made on the minds of the people, and a general awakening took place. On returning to the neighbourhood, Mr. Wilson formed a society, consisting of about twenty persons, whom he placed under the care and guidance of young Lanktree. The good work greatly prospered, numerous conversions took place, new classes were formed, and so largely did the congregations increase in the parish church that the building was unable to accommodate the crowds that assembled Sabbath after Sabbath.[1] The most important additions to the Society were Mr. and Mrs. William Henry of Millbrook, who invited the preachers to their house, became active in promoting the cause of religion, and, until removed to the Church above, more than forty years subsequently, continued faithful to God and to Methodism. Through the influence of this worthy couple a flourishing Sunday school was formed in 1794, which proved the means of much and lasting good in the neighbourhood.[2]

The work of the Lord having so greatly prospered in Newtownbutler, that the large room of Mr. John Clarke proved too small for the congregations, the Society resolved to build a house. A piece of ground was given by John Adams, who had been for some years a member of the Society; valuable assistance was rendered by Andrew Thompson of Cornabrass, with his son-in-law, Robert Morrison — an acceptable local preacher — and the whole Society engaged heartily in the work, so that in a few months a commodious chapel was erected and dedicated to the service of God. This proved the means of much blessing to the town and neighbourhood, and the birthplace of many souls. John Clarke prospered in his business; during the course of a long life his character for integrity was unimpeachable, and having a good hope through grace of eternal life, his end was peace.

At this time there was led to decision for God a man named William Heazley, who is pronounced by Southey "the most extraordinary convert that ever was made." He resided in the county of Antrim, had been deaf and dumb from his birth, was a weaver, farm labourer, and barber — and passionately fond of horse-racing, cock-fighting, and similar brutal diversions. At length the Methodist itinerants visited the locality where he lived, and amongst the many awakened to serious concern was William, who gave evidence of the depth and sincerity of his repentance by an entire change of life, completely renouncing his former associates, and giving up all work on the Sabbath — his most remunerative day. When a society was formed, he rejoiced greatly on seeing his name enrolled with others, and became most zealous for the Master. On the Lord's day it was his custom to rise early in the morning, and watch for the coming of the leader, at sight of whom he immediately

(1) Lanktree's *Narrative*, pp. 11-13.
(2) *Primitive Methodist Magazine*, 1834, pp. 258-61, and 1837, pp. 441-47.

ran from house to house, apprising the members, and inviting them to the meeting; and during the class, if the leader happened to omit speaking to him, William appeared much distressed. The remainder of the day was spent in public worship, prayer-meetings, and association with the people of God.[3]

Up to this period no regular stopping-place for the preachers had been provided in Portadown, owing to the low state of the cause; but this year Mr. Thomas Bunting invited the servants of God to his house, in which was conducted by Mr. Steele, the first love-feast ever held in the town. Not long after this, the building of the first chapel was commenced, and to the small Society of that day it was an undertaking of no ordinary magnitude. Its promoters appear to have had views much in advance of their contemporaries, as the site selected was in a central and prominent position, very near where the Episcopal church now stands. But unexpected difficulties arose, by which not only was the project retarded, but the Society much weakened; and several years elapsed before the chapel was completed.

Mr. James Rogers now closed his three years' labours in Cork, where he had found three hundred and ninety members of Society, and left six hundred and sixty — a number probably unparalleled in that city. Mrs. Rogers says that she never before was happier in her soul, or enjoyed deeper communion with God than during her stay here. So much did the work prosper that a second chapel was rendered necessary, which was erected in Blackpool. During a visit of Dr. Coke, a Sunday school was established in Hammond's Marsh, which for many years stood at the head of the list in the reports of the Sunday School Society, and which still exists and flourishes.

The Conference met on July the 2nd, in Dublin, with Dr. Coke as president, and John Crook as secretary. Ten preachers were received on trial, including William Ferguson, Samuel Steele, Charles Graham, and William Smith. Although Graham was a married man, and forty years of age, these circumstances did not interfere with his acceptance, his case, as a preacher in Irish, not being considered an ordinary one. Smith had been in the army, where owing to his musical talents he was appointed bandmaster. His regiment having been quartered in Londonderry, the Society in that city showed their appreciation of his piety and worth by paying fifty pounds for his discharge, in order that he might be able to devote himself wholly to the work of the Lord; and never was that sum better expended. The Connexion thus obtained a minister, who for many years filled most important stations, and was exceedingly able and successful as a preacher.

(3) *Arminian Magazine*, 1794, pp. 438-41.

During the sittings of the Conference, a very blessed revival commenced in the metropolis. On Sunday evening, July 4th, as Dr. Coke preached in Whitefriar street chapel, the word was, accompanied with unusual and mighty power. At the close of the public service a love-feast was held, during which such a gracious influence was felt that it was considered wise to hold a revival prayer-meeting, which proved a second Pentecost. Many cried for mercy, others rejoiced aloud in their Saviour, the preachers and leaders prayed with the penitents and encouraged them to look to Jesus, and a number of boys especially were made so happy that they glorified their Redeemer with all their might. The services were continued night after night with similar success. Some of the conversions were of a remarkable character. One man, though surrounded with many, seemed as much alone with God as if he were in a desert. Another, who had been a Romanist, said, "A few days ago I was a curser and swearer, but to-night, glory be to God! He has not only enabled me to confess my sins, but has forgiven me, and I can praise Him." The work soon extended to Gravel walk chapel, where as Mr. Dinnen preached on the evening of July 11th, the sacred flame broke out, and spread from heart to heart until the whole congregation seemed on fire. A young woman who came to mock, when faithfully and lovingly reproved, burst into tears, and in less than an hour afterwards could say, she had found the Lord, who had filled her heart with love and peace. Many similar testimonies were borne by others.[4] One of those converted was Mr. James Freeman, son of the leader who took such an active part in the erection of this very chapel. This young man then joined the Society, and from that time until his death in 1832, was never once absent from class, except from illness.

Meanwhile the British Conference met on July 27th, and made several important changes in the stations of the Dublin Conference. A Building Committee for Ireland was appointed, consisting of Messrs. Blair, Clarke, Rutherford, and Mitchell. Joseph Burgess, having offered himself as a candidate for the itinerancy, was received on trial, and appointed to Liverpool, with permission to remain in Dublin for a month or two, to complete his arrangements for leaving the army. Here he preached frequently in Whitefriar street and Gravel walk chapels, and attracted crowded congregations. Thomas Worrell and James Lyons, senior, were sent as missionaries to the West Indies. The former was a very promising young man of considerable gifts, and eminent piety, who after an indefatigable and successful missionary career of a little more than twelve months passed in triumph to the home above.[5]

(4) Coke's *Account of the Revival in Dublin.*

Adam Clarke was appointed Assistant in Dublin, where he and his family were received with much cordiality. "The people," writes Mrs. Clarke to a friend, "appear affectionate and willing to do us good; if they could help it we should scarcely eat a meal at home. They esteem our company a privilege, and invite many friends on set days to meet us, especially to breakfast. These meetings in a particular manner I have found to be profitable for wisdom and instruction in the best things; they are also sociable beyond what I can express. A Dublin breakfast meeting I know you would delight in. I wish I could introduce you to one to-morrow morning."[6]

The metropolis, however, was not at this time in many respects a very desirable appointment. On arriving at the city, Mr. Clarke found that the Society was engaged in building a new residence, with which was connected a large room for the boys' free school. It was erected under the superintendence of Mr. Dederick Ayckbowm, aided by Messrs. William Andrews and Alexander Boyle, formerly of Kirlish Lodge, the stewards of the Society. The preacher and his family were to occupy the lower part and first floor, and the school was to extend over the whole of the second floor. Owing to the builder being an unprincipled man, the house was not made either according to the time or plan specified. Mr. Clarke and his family were, therefore, obliged to go into lodgings, which were far from comfortable; and then, owing to the inconvenience, to enter the new house before it was dry, which nearly cost them their lives, and compelled their return to England at the end of twelve months.

Soon after Mr. Clarke arrived in Dublin, he wrote to Mr. Wesley a long letter, stating that his colleague Mr. Rutherford had been laid aside by rheumatic fever, and that the results of the revival already referred to, had been destroyed by the extravagant irregularities of those who conducted the services during Mr. Rutherford's illness. These meetings were kept up till ten or eleven o'clock on Sunday nights, and sometimes till twelve or one; and it was no uncommon thing for a person in the midst of them to give an exhortation of half-an-hour or three-quarters. Mr. Clarke wished to correct these irregularities, and wrote for advice to Wesley,[7] who replied as follows:-

"You will have need of all the courage and prudence which God has given you. Very gently, and very steadily, you should proceed between the rocks on either hand. In the great revival at London, my first difficulty was to bring

(5) *Arminian Magazine*, 1792, p. 272.

(6) *Life of Mrs. Clarke*, p. 83.

(7) Tyerman's *Life and Times of Wesley*, iii., p. 623.

in temper those who opposed the work, and my next, to check and regulate the extravagances of those that promoted it. And this was far the hardest part of the work; for many of them would hear no check at all. But I followed one rule, though with all calmness: 'You must either bend or break.' Meantime, while you act exactly right, expect to be blamed by both sides. I will give you a few directions: (1) See that no prayer-meeting continues later than nine at night, particularly on Sunday. Let the house be emptied before the clock strikes nine. (2) Let there be no exhortation at any prayer-meeting. (3) Beware of jealousy, or judging one another. (4) Never think a man is an enemy to the work, because he reproves irregularities."[8]

Clarke acted upon Wesley's good advice, wrote him the result, and received the following reply:- "I am glad my letter had so good an effect. I dearly love our precious Society in Dublin, and cannot but be keenly sensible of anything that gives them disturbance. I am glad our leaders have adopted that excellent method of regularly changing their classes. Wherever this has been done, it has been a means of quickening both the leaders and the people. I wish this custom could be more extensively introduced. You did well to prevent all irregular and turbulent prayer-meetings, and at all hazards, to keep the meetings of the Society private. Poor Mr. Smyth[9] is now used just as he used me. He must either bend or break. Although you cannot solicit any of the Bethesda to join with us, yet neither can you refuse them when they offer their hand. You do well to offer all possible courtesy to Mr. William Smyth and his family. As long as the Society in Dublin continues upward of a thousand, you will have no reason to complain."[10]

Details have already been given with regard to the disputes in the Dublin Society concerning the Sunday noon service in Whitefriar street chapel, at which the liturgy was read. Much good might have been done if the rich members had not continued hostile to the arrangement. At length both sides had agreed, for the sake of peace, to request the British Conference to restore matters to their original state, by abolishing the service objected to. Mr. Clarke raised his voice against the innovation, before coming to the city, and at his recommendation the Conference yielded. This he subsequently regarded as the greatest ecclesiastical error he ever committed, and one which he deeply deplored. What he did was from fear that the service might lead to a separation from the Church, and the hope that the members might be induced

---

(8) Wesley's *Works*, xiii., p. 104.

(9) Rev. Edward Smyth.

(10) Tyerman's *Life and Times of Wesley*, iii., p. 624.

to attend the parish churches, and so all kinds of dissent be prevented. But many of them never had belonged to any church, and felt no religious attachment to any ministers but those who were the means of their salvation. When therefore they did not find among the Methodists religious services at the usual hours on the Lord's day, they often wandered heedlessly about, and became unhinged and distracted with strange doctrines. Of this Mr. Clarke was afterwards fully convinced, and saw the folly of endeavouring to force people to attend a ministry from which they never received any kind of spiritual advantage; and the danger of not trying carefully to cultivate the soil which with great difficulty and labour has been broken up and sown with the good seed of the kingdom.

While in the metropolis Mr. Clarke instituted the Strangers' Friend Society, for the purpose of relieving sick and distressed strangers, and the poor of every denomination, in their own dwellings; similar associations having been formed previously in London and Bristol. This Society has done a noble work for Christ, thousands having been rescued by it from the greatest misery, and not a few brought to a saving knowledge of God; and it still exists, a monument of the wisdom and benevolence of its illustrious founder.

On November the 26th Mr. Wesley wrote to Mr. Clarke as follows: "To retain the grace of God is much more than to gain it; hardly one in three does this. And this should be strongly and explicitly urged on all who have tasted of perfect love. If we can prove that any of our local preachers or leaders, either directly or indirectly speak against it, let him be a local preacher or leader no longer. I doubt whether he should continue in the Society; because he that could speak thus in our congregations, cannot be an honest man."[11]

But to turn from Dublin to the provinces, Charles Graham was appointed as a missionary to the county of Kerry, where there was at this time neither Society or congregation, and his reception was of the most discouraging kind. After a ride of nearly forty miles, he arrived at Castleisland, and was no sooner settled in the hotel than it was noised abroad that a false prophet had come to the town. Immediately the priest collected a mob, came to the inn, and insisted that the stranger should be turned out, which of course had to be done to please his reverence. Graham then started for Tralee, and when about half-way, called at a farm house, told his tale of ill-treatment, and was at once invited in. The host, who proved to be a stanch Protestant, sent out and collected a congregation for the missionary, and was himself deeply

(11) Wesley's *Works*, xiii., pp. 104-5.

affected under the preaching of the word. Next morning Mr. Groves bade the servant of God welcome to stay at his house as long and as frequently as he pleased. Thus Methodism at once obtained a footing in the county.

Cheered by this opening, Graham proceeded to Tralee, little knowing what awaited him there. He describes the town as notorious for folly and dissipation, and one in which he could not get a room for love or money; so he had no alternative but to deliver his message in the street, where he addressed "an unruly group of gapers," who raised such an uproar that he had to desist. But it was only to try again, with more success. Having taken his stand in the same place as before, the following plan was immediately adopted by two men to stone the servant of God to death. One of the wretched scoundrels took a position behind a wall, while the other stood near the preacher, to direct his companion. The signal was given, and the stone thrown, but missing the missionary, it struck the accomplice, who was carried off to the infirmary, seriously cut, and crying aloud for mercy. From this time forward the servant of God was allowed to preach in the town unmolested.

From Tralee Graham went to Milltown, on entering which he inquired of a lad, if he knew anyone in the town who read the Bible. "Oh, yes, I do, sir," responded the boy; "the clerk of the church." "Will you show me where he lives?" said the missionary, and the lad conducted him to the door of the man's house. When he came out, Graham said, "I understand that you read the Bible." "Oh! I do, sir," replied the clerk, "on the Sabbath, at church; but the Lord help me, I make a very bad use of it." "I am a preacher of the Gospel," said the missionary, "and would like to preach here." "Will you come in?" responded the other. This day salvation came to this man's house, and thenceforward it was the stopping place of the preachers. Being a holiday, the town was filled with country people, Graham took his stand on a block, opposite the market-house, and delivered his message faithfully, both in English and Irish, the latter being well understood. The word was "quick and powerful," the clerk was converted, and many deeply affected. The tidings of the service reached Sir William Godfrey, Bart., the lord of the soil, who at once sent a message to the missionary not to preach there again; but Graham had published that he would do so, and was of sterner stuff than to be intimidated by an order of that kind. Accordingly he preached, expecting every moment to be interrupted; the people assembled in large numbers, the power of God descended, and many received the message of salvation. Thus a foundation was laid for the cause in this town, which after a little time became the head of a circuit.

Thence Graham travelled round the country, and open doors presented themselves in all directions; societies also were formed that included several converted Roman Catholics. It was reported that the missionary had been a priest, but this only increased his audiences, many coming to hear from mere curiosity. The Catholic Bishop of Kerry took alarm, and charged his clergy to warn their people not to hear or go near the Methodist, that he was "a deceiver" and "a walking devil." One of the priests who had abused the missionary more fiercely than the rest, fell down stairs the same night in a drunken fit, and broke his neck. This alarmed the whole country, but apparently not the clergy; for another priest met Graham shortly after, and threatened to make him leave the county. The missionary said he would not leave for him or anybody else. On this the priest raised a cane to strike him, but was prevented by some bystanders, and a few days subsequently died raging mad. Such tragic circumstances could not fail to make a deep and general impression.

In another part of the county, the priest called out from the altar the names of sixteen persons who had gone to hear Graham preach, and insisted that each should go through bogs by night to a distant graveyard, barefooted and bareheaded, and bring back a human bone, and then appear, on the following Sabbath, in a sheet, bone in hand, before the congregation. Even some of the clergy of the Established Church opposed the preacher. But all did not avail. The common people still heard the servant of God gladly, for he made the way of salvation plain, and that in their own loved language. Even among the higher classes also there were some who saw his worth and hailed his visits with delight, and the Lord gave him many souls for his hire. The following instances may suffice.

The bursar on board a man-of-war, then in Dingle harbour, was a rigid Roman Catholic, although his wife was a Protestant. This lady heard Mr. Graham preach, and the word reached her heart, so that she penitently sought and found the pearl of great rice, and at once joined the Society recently formed in the town. This greatly exasperated her husband, who tried every means in his power to dissuade her from uniting with such a despised sect, until at length he resorted to violence, but in vain. On one occasion he followed her to the preaching place, bludgeon in hand, to watch for her coming out; but attracted by Graham's melodious and powerful voice, he entered the house, greatly to the terror of those present. He was then completely subdued, earnestly sought the mercy of God, and went home with his rejoicing wife a pardoned and happy man. At once he renounced Popery, joined the Society, and continued during the rest of life to adorn the doctrine of God his Saviour.

Another remarkable conversion was that of a bigoted devotee of Rome, named Roche, an abandoned drunkard, who came to one of the services to mock, but remained to pray. The word reached his heart; he sought and found mercy through Christ Jesus, and although much thwarted by his wife and bitterly persecuted by others, continued consistent and faithful, and finished his course with joy. Graham received during the year about two hundred members into the Society, besides many on trial. Most appropriately has he been designated, "the Apostle of Kerry."[12]

On September the 1st Mr. M'Gregor writes from Limerick to Mrs. Bennis, then in Waterford: "The Society here prospers; the select band meets regularly; but I can seldom be with them. I generally meet my class in my room, often in my bed. Blessed be God, for the love that subsists among us; they will not let me give them up until I am removed to my heavenly Father, which I expect will not be long. My sincere love to the Waterford preachers and people; remind them that this is a year of release and thanksgiving for their passage out of trouble; let us meet each other in spirit for the prosperity of the Gospel."[13]

In 1790, the Association of Friends of the Sick Poor was formed at Waterford. It originated at an evening social gathering of Methodists, in a conversation on the Christian duty of visiting the sick and those in prison, which ended in making a small collection. With this the brethren present called upon the prisoners in the jail on the following Sabbath, accompanying their pecuniary assistance with suitable religious counsel. The first experiment excited the hope that this labour of love might be made extensively and permanently beneficial. Among the members of the Society willing hearts and hands were found to co-operate in it, and a good working plan was drawn up by Mr. Robert Mackee, a leader and local preacher. The city was divided into districts, to each of which visitors were appointed, whose duty it was to inquire into, and personally inspect all cases of alleged sickness and infirmity; to give relief according to the exigency of each case, irrespective of religious distinctions; and to accompany the help afforded, whenever practicable, with suitable religious advice. An institution founded on such broad principles soon attracted public attention; funds were contributed by Christians of all denominations, and much good was accomplished. From this society

(12) *The Apostle of Kerry*, pp. 38-46.
(13) *Christian Correspondence*, p. 198.

originated the admirable Fever Hospital, the first institution of the kind, it is said, raised by voluntary contributions and on truly catholic principles, founded in the kingdom. In all times of distress the Association did most valuable service in guiding and assisting the distribution of public charity.

At this period a young man named Joseph Leech, who lived in Roscrea, was deeply impressed through the ministry of the Methodist preachers, began to meet in a class conducted by a good old leader called Row]and, and soon after obtained a sense of sins forgiven. From this time until his death, in 1860, the life of Mr. Leech was interwoven with the history of Methodism on the Roscrea circuit. The cause in the town was then very low, so much so that the members were compelled on the occasional visits of the preacher to contribute a few pence each to buy hay for his horse. Better days, however, dawned on the Society, which soon increased in numbers and wealth, until it rose to be one of the most influential in the kingdom. Mr. Leech became in succession leader, local preacher, and steward of the Society, and was for many years the pillar of Methodism in the town.

A short time before the Conference this year, Mr. Robert Boyd, whom Walter Griffith designates one of the holiest men he had known, died of a malignant fever. For many years he had been an honour to, and the principal financial support of the Society in Newry. He was engaged in business, possessed some property, and, having no children alive, after supplying the daily wants of himself and his wife, faithfully devoted every shilling that he made to the promotion of the cause of God, and the relief of persons in need. He was taken to his eternal reward when just past the prime of life, and in the midst of extensive usefulness. A short time previously he dreamed that he had a conversation with a son of his who had been dead several years, and who informed him, that before the end of the ensuing three weeks he also would be in the world of spirits. His friends endeavoured to divert his attention from this alarming communication; but he said that until the expiration of the time named he should feel himself on the borders of the eternal world. In the meantime his mind was calm, and exceedingly happy in God; nor did he remit his usual diligence in business, settling his temporal affairs with the composure of a man whose treasure was in heaven. Recollecting that he had to take up a bill in the course of a few days, he waited upon the man who held it, offered him payment, and when informed that it was not yet due, insisting on then paying the amount, adding that he might be dead when the proper time arrived. Soon afterwards, one night he retired to his room, without any symptoms of disease, and was seized by

the terrible malady, which proved fatal, a short time before the expiration of
the three weeks. Then the disease, of which her devoted husband had just
expired, seized Mrs. Boyd, and she followed him to another and better world.
They were lovely in life, and in death they were not long divided.[14]

When the congregation assembled, on the evening after Mr. Boyd's death,
and began to sing, they became so deeply affected as to be unable to proceed.
At that service there commenced such an outpouring of the Holy Spirit, as
the oldest members of the Society had never before witnessed. Mr. Griffith
preached the funeral sermons of Mr. and Mrs. Boyd, upon two successive
Sunday evenings, to attentive and crowded audiences. With holy fervour and
lively faith he pleaded with God for a rich baptism of His Spirit, and the
prayer was answered; though, in consequence of the preacher's removal to
another circuit, he was not an eye-witness of its blessed results. The
congregations increased, Divine power accompanied the word preached, and
a solemn awe prevailed at each service. Few nights passed without a prayer
meeting after preaching, chiefly for the penitents, whose cries could be heard
at a considerable distance from the chapel. Many of the careless and profane
gathered about the house, wondering what was the matter, but were not
admitted, lest they should disturb those who continued with one accord in
earnest prayer. Some pious persons, who were only acquainted with God's
ordinary method of working, began to reflect a little on what seemed to them
confusion; but having seen the blessed effects they were fully satisfied, and
heartily thanked God for thus working among the children of men.

September the 8th was a night much to be remembered; not only because
of those converted, but also because of the spirit of prayer poured out so
wonderfully that many went away under deep conviction. A man who loved
God with all his heart, said, as the people left, "Such of you, as have not
received the blessing now, will assuredly receive it to-morrow night;" and it
was so. Messrs. M'Donald and Grace, having been out of town on this
evening, on their return saw several persons just set at liberty, praising God
and full of joy, and others pleading for mercy; so they went to different parts
of the house, and prayed with the penitents, some of whom soon had their
sorrow turned into joy. Amongst others Mr. Grace found a man in deep
distress, who twenty years before had turned his back on the ways of God
and given himself up to drunkenness, and now while engaged in prayer, his
backslidings were healed. On seeing him rejoice in the Divine favour, his
wife, who had for some time walked in darkness, was informed of it. She

(14) *Wesleyan Methodist Magazine*, 1827, pp. 150-51.

then joined her husband, and they united in earnest prayer until the Lord restored unto her also the joys of His salvation.

Mr. M'Donald sent an account of the revival to Mr. Wesley, from whom he received the following reply: "You have great reason to praise God for His late glorious work at and near Newry, and I make no doubt but it will continue, yea, and increase, if the subjects of it continue to walk humbly and closely with God. Exhort all our brethren steadily to wait upon God in the appointed means of fasting and prayer; the former of which has been almost universally neglected by the Methodists, both in England and Ireland; but it is a true remark of Kempis: 'The more thou deniest thyself, the more thou wilt grow in grace.'"[15]

As the people of Newry prayed for and expected a gracious visitation at the December quarterly meeting, they were not disappointed. Amongst others, one who had been in Society for more than thirty years was enabled to rejoice in God his Saviour. A short time before the Lord visited him in mercy, one of the leaders said it was impressed on his mind that if they would all pray for that brother, the Lord would grant their request. They then united in earnest supplications until prayer was turned into praise. The watch-night was also a blessed season. During these two services twenty souls at least were converted.[16] Within about six months, the numbers in the Newry Society were more than trebled. For a time the Divine Spirit, "like mighty winds or torrents fierce," defied all opposition; the most profligate persons, who came to the chapel, literally fell down, and owned that God was with His people; and in the same religious assembly, Methodists and Episcopalians, Presbyterians and even Roman Catholics, joyfully proclaimed the great things which God had done for their souls. Very little, if any wildness appeared in this gracious work, which soon spread to several parts of the surrounding country. Amongst the many converted was Mr. Robert Walker, who for no less than three-score years, in Newry, in Dublin, and then in Athlone, witnessed a good confession, giving generously to support the cause of God, and labouring with much success as a leader and local preacher.[17]

---

(15) Wesley's *Works*, xiii., p. 119.

(16) *Arminian Magazine*, 1791, pp. 413-16.

(17) *Primitive Wesleyan Methodist Magazine*, 1850, p. 186.